NEITHER
BLACK
NOR
WHITE

NEITHER
BLACK
NOR
WHITE

Slavery and Race Relations in
Brazil and the United States

CARL N. DEGLER

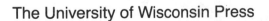

The University of Wisconsin Press

Published 1986

The University of Wisconsin Press
114 North Murray Street
Madison, Wisconsin 53715

First Wisconsin printing

Printed in the United States of America

Library of Congress Cataloging-in-Publication Data
Degler, Carl N.
    Neither Black nor white.
    Reprint. Originally published: New York : Macmillan,
1971.
    Includes index.
    1. Blacks—Brazil—History. 2. Slavery—Brazil—
History. 3. Brazil—Race relations. 4. Afro-Americans—
Social conditions. 5. Slavery—United States—History.
6. United States—Race relations. I. Title.
F2659.N4D42   1986   305.8'96081   86-4078
ISBN 0-299-10914-3 (pbk.)

*To Bernice, Bill, Erick, and Kirk Degler
—my "Brazilian" relatives in the United States*

Brazil is Hell for Negroes,
Purgatory for Whites, and
Paradise for Mulattoes.

—J. A. Antonil, *Cultura e Opulencia do Brasil* (1711)

CONTENTS

PREFACE

Like many other books, this one began as a minor inquiry; the most that was expected to appear in print was perhaps a short article in a scholarly journal. As a historian of the United States who had long been interested in slavery and black history, I intended merely to study the validity of the relationship between slavery and race relations that Frank Tannenbaum had advanced in his book *Slave and Citizen* in 1948. As I explain in some detail in the pages that follow, Tannenbaum had accounted for the absence of racial segregation and of the United States brand of racial hostility in Latin America by pointing to differences in the character of slavery in the two countries. In 1959, in writing about the historical origins of racial prejudice in the United States, I had rested my judgments on Tannenbaum's comparison. In short, like Tannenbaum, I had accepted the idea that slavery in the United States differed from that found in Latin America.

During the 1960s, as the issue of racial prejudice and the treatment of blacks in the United States became a national concern of great moment, historians of the United States paid increasing attention to the argument in Tannenbaum's book, often raising questions about its validity. Was a key to the problem of racial prejudice in the United States to be found in the Latin American experience? Or was there some reason to think, as a number of historians of Latin America contended, that the causal connection between slavery in the past and racial discrimination in the present, was less certain than Tannenbaum argued? And because the evidence available in the late 1960s was so ambiguous and inconclusive, if only because historical examples were unsystematically collected from a wide variety of national experiences with slavery, I decided to examine some of the relevant scholarly literature myself. But the more I looked into the history of slavery in areas of the New World outside of the United States, the more confusing and inconclusive the comparison became. Consequently, I decided to abandon the pursuit of selective evidence on the nature of slavery in Latin America as a whole and to study slavery intensively in a single South American nation. I chose Brazil because it was the only country in the New World that rivaled the United States in size and in the importance of slavery in its history.

Even after that decision had been made, though, a book was still far from my intentions. It is true that the decision necessitated my learning to read Portuguese and to work my way through a number of the many books that Brazilians and others had written on the history of Brazil. Even then my question remained relatively simple—to find out if slavery in Brazil differed substantially from that in the United States. Behind that question, though, lay a larger one—and in my mind, a more important one—namely, how does one account for the difference in race relations in Brazil and the United States? For, as the first chapter endeavors to make clear, the differences are indeed striking. Yet as I read more and more about Brazil, with whose history and culture I became intrigued, I found that my inquiry broadened. What had begun as a relatively circumscribed exploration of slavery in Brazil and the United States expanded to include contemporary race relations in the two countries. That expansion partly explains why almost a third of the following pages are given over to an examination of the similarities and differences in contemporary race relations in Brazil and the United States. Quite candidly, a further reason chapters III and IV are as full as they are is that I found the nuances of race relations in Brazil so complex and yet so simple, so different from and yet so similar to those in the United States that I wanted to set them down on paper, if only to clarify my own thoughts on the subject.

The book as a whole might be described as an attempt to understand the nature of black-white relations in the United States by projecting them against the background of another nation with at least some similarity in history but with apparently quite different contemporary results. As Marc Bloch, the great French historian, wrote many years ago, a comparison of the history of two different countries can suddenly make clear that certain historical developments or reactions were not necessarily in the nature of things. When we learn, for example, that Brazilians did not develop a full-blown racial defense of slavery such as was elaborated in the antebellum South of the United States, then we are forced to acknowledge that we cannot assume that such a defense was a natural consequence of a slave society. Hence, we must begin to look for an explanation of such a development. And that is what this book seeks to do: to explain historically the striking differences in the contemporary racial patterns of Brazil and the United States even though the history of both countries was similar in that slavery was important and only people of African ancestry were held as slaves.

Whether my conclusions or even my analyses along the way are convincing, the reader can judge. For those interested in pursuing further the comparison between the two countries, the footnotes will provide leads; for those who have no such interest, the footnotes can be ignored, though occasionally they offer some explanatory additions to the text. For this new printing, some scholarly studies that have appeared since 1971 are mentioned in the course of this preface.

Despite the footnotes, the audience for whom I have written is not my fellow historians, though I naturally hope they will find my conclusions of some interest. My primary audience is those Americans—professional historian and student, black and white, old and young—who recognize that it is still a central question of the twentieth century if the United States will be able to work out a biracial society in which blacks and whites will be able to live together in mutual respect and justice. That question is still open, not only because such a society has not been fully achieved in the United States, but also because it has not been achieved in any nation in which whites dominate. I say this even though in the United States much progress has been made over the last two decades in reducing and removing the social, legal, and political barriers to equality of opportunity for blacks. One of the inescapable conclusions to be drawn from an examination of Brazilian society is that equality between black and white is not a fact there either, however different race relations in Brazil may be from those in the United States. Needless to say, this book does not provide a final answer to the long-term question. Indeed, the evidence presented here can only make the achievement of full racial equality seem more difficult than many may anticipate. Some people may even conclude after reading this book that the goal of equality is illusory. That conclusion is certainly not my intention. The primary purpose of the book is to help Americans understand the possibilities for, as well as the difficulties of developing an egalitarian biracial society in place of one of white supremacy. I think the conclusions are realistic even if they are not optimistic. It is in that rather ambiguous spirit that the book is offered.

In this reissuance of the book, I have not attempted to update the text, even though much research has appeared in both the United States and Brazil on the nature of slavery and race relations in both countries. And the primary reason I have not is that, controversial as some aspects of the book have been, its essential argument has not been overturned or refuted by the new work. Indeed, some of the recent research has furnished additional support for the book's thesis; some, admittedly, has raised questions about parts of it. My purpose here is to suggest some of the lines the recent investigations of slavery and race relations in the two countries have followed. In that way, the reader may see how this book fits into the ongoing debate over slavery and race relations in Brazil and the United States. For though the history of slavery and race relations has not commanded the attention of scholars in the United States in the 1980s to the degree it did fifteen years ago when this book first appeared, the literature continues to appear. In Brazil, scholarly attention to race relations has become more insistent than it was then.

At the time of publication of *Neither Black Nor White*, only a few Brazilian scholars acknowledged the depressed and disadvantaged state of blacks and colored people in Brazil. Some of the work of those scholars was drawn upon in the original research for this book. For most Brazilians, however, the status of blacks was not of great interest, and even if it were, racial prejudice was thought to have little or nothing to do with it. After all, so the argument went, racial prejudice was virtually unknown in Brazil, so how could the low social and economic position of blacks be ascribed to racial discrimination? This view has come to be called the Brazilian "myth of racial democracy."

More recently, however, and especially in the last few years as Brazil began its cautious return to democratic government, the study of race relations has moved increasingly toward a frank recognition of the existence of racial prejudice. Some of this interest has been sparked by individual scholars, the work of some of whom will be discussed a little later in this preface. Equally important has been the emergence of a consciousness of color or race among Brazilian people of color, something that heretofore has been almost totally absent in Brazil. A landmark in this connection was the large mass meeting held in 1978 in Sao Paulo organized by the newly formed Movimento Negro Unificado Contra Discriminação Racial (Unified Black Movement Against Racial Discrimination). Significant, too, has been the growth of race awareness among university students, as shown in the Black Rio, Black Porto Alegre, and Black Salvador movements. Most striking of all for readers of this book was the seating of Abdias do Nascimento as one of the two Afro-Brazilians in the Federal Congress after the elections of 1982. Nascimento is a radical black advocate who had spent many years in the United States in the late 1960s and 1970s when the military regime that ruled Brazil did not countenance agitation on social questions and certainly not in regard to race. As the reader will discover, Nascimento has long been an outspoken advocate of the view that racial discrimination is widespread in Brazil.

The change in outlook reflected by these social and political developments has been increasingly evident in scholarly writings on the past and present social order in Brazil. By and large, these writings have been in accord with the position taken in this book in regard to slavery in Brazil and in the United States. For example, Robert Conrad, a leading United States authority on the history of Brazilian slavery, writes in a splendid compendium of sources on slavery in Brazil published in 1983 that he has "become convinced that the *physical conditions* endured by slaves in Brazil made life there considerably more precarious and uncomfortable—again in a physical sense—than it was for most slaves in the United States."[1] The harshness of Brazilian slavery has been stressed also in recent studies by Brazilian scholars, as, for example, in Oiliam Jose, *Racismo em Minas Gerais* (1981). At the same time, the still growing literature on slavery in the United States has increasingly portrayed slavery as allowing more "social space" for personal and social growth among blacks than Frank Tannenbaum's book seemed to admit. The books of Eugene Genovese, John Blassingame, George Rawick, and Herbert Gutman, to name only the most prominent examples, all emphasize the ability of slaves to carve out a life of their own, including forms of resistance, a sustaining religion, and enduring families, despite the limits which the undoubted power of masters placed upon them.[2]

The writings by Brazilians on modern race relations over the last five or six years, in line with some of the popular attitudes already mentioned, have increasingly emphasized the negative effects of racial prejudice on the status and future of people of color. One early sign of the shift in outlook was the translation of this book into Portuguese for a Brazilian edition in 1976. The recognition of race as a source of material disadvantages for blacks has been especially prominent in the work of Carlos A. Hasenbalg, particularly in his book *Discriminação e Desigualdades Raciais no Brasil* (Discrimination and Racial Inequalities in Brazil) (Rio de Janeiro, 1979). A similar point of view is taken in Lèlia Gonzalez and Carlos A. Hasenbalg, *Lugar do Negro* (Place of the Black) (Rio de Janeiro, 1981). This emphasis on racial as distinct from class discrimination as an explanation for the low position of people of color in Brazilian society is also spelled out from a variety of angles in the essays contained in Pierre-Michel Fontaine, ed., *Race, Class, and Power in Brazil* (to be published in early 1986).

At the same time that racial explanations have been receiving greater acceptance or recognition among Brazilian scholars, a

[1] Robert Edgar Conrad, ed., *Children of God's Fire: A Documentary History of Black Slavery in Brazil* (Princeton, 1983), p. xvi.

[2] Eugene D. Genovese, *Roll, Jordan, Roll* (New York, 1974); John Blassingame, *The Slave Community* (New York, 1972, 1979); George Rawick, *From Sundown to Sunup* (Westport, Conn., 1972); and Herbert Gutman, *The Black Family in Slavery and Freedom, 1750–1925* (New York, 1976).

comparable reversal of explanations for race relations in the United States has been in progress. Now that the structure of legal segregation has been dismantled in the American South, and the weight of legal and political authority in the United States as a whole is directed against the expression of racial discrimination, a number of American scholars have begun to emphasize the role of class or culture, and to downplay racial prejudice in accounting for economic deprivation among blacks. Economist Thomas Sowell, who also happens to be black, has been prominent in advancing this position. In several books, notably *Race and Economics* (1975) and *Civil Rights: Rhetoric or Reality* (1984), he contends that a free market can eliminate racial and ethnic discrimination if the market is truly free or uncontrolled and educational opportunities are reasonably equal for all groups. In short, in Sowell's view, racial prejudice is no longer a major cause for the economic disadvantages suffered in the United States by blacks. Indeed, in his book on civil rights he argues that affirmative action and other governmental devices for eliminating discrimination are detrimental rather than helpful in overcoming or eliminating the admittedly low economic status of American blacks.

Other recent students of race relations in the United States have not been as committed to the egalitarian force of the market as Thomas Sowell, but like him, they have tended to see racism as less of an explanation or cause for poverty and economic disadvantage among blacks than class or cultural causes. Stanley Lieberson, for example, in his comparative historical study of economic mobility among blacks and white immigrants, *A Piece of the Pie* (New York, 1980), concludes that though racism undoubtedly plays some role in accounting for the differences in the social mobility of blacks and white immigrants over the last century, it is neither a fundamental cause nor an enduring one. Much more influential, he contends, are history and culture. They, rather than racial prejudice, are the forces that encourage or limit the ability of social groups to seize available opportunities for economic advancement.

A similar conclusion is drawn by another sociologist, William Julius Wilson, in his book, significantly entitled *The Declining Significance of Race* (New York, 1978, 1980). Wilson's point is that the black population in the United States is today divided into two groups: those whose economic position may have been affected by racial discrimination in the past, but is no longer, and those whose low economic status today is largely a result of class disadvantages unrelated to their color or race. In short, he sees poverty and unemployment among blacks in American society as a matter of class, rather than racial discrimination. Like Sowell, Wilson, it is pertinent to note, is black.

Insofar as these trends in the scholarly literature in Brazil and in the United States reveal a tendency for an American emphasis on race to be rising in Brazil while a Brazilian emphasis upon class is coming to the fore in the United States, they are in accord with the suggestion made at the end of this book that in the future race relations and racial attitudes in the two countries were likely to converge. Relevant, too, in this connection is the recognition by Brazilian scholars that the Black Revolution of the 1960s and 1970s in the United States has deeply influenced, if not actually catalyzed the self-consciousness of people of color in Brazil. The American TV film "Roots," an American concept of the late 1960s and 1970s like "Soul," and practices like the "soul handshake" and the Afro hairstyle have been picked up by Brazilian people of color and used in behalf of their aspirations for recognition and equality, sometimes to the consternation of traditional white Brazilians, who tend to see awareness of racial identity as a sign of social divisiveness as well as a denial of the Brazilian myth of racial democracy.

Finally, a word about the title. It is both a pun and an attempt to sum up the central point of the book. A comparison of race relations and slavery in Brazil and the United States is not, as is sometimes said, a matter of polar opposites. Rather than being a matter of black and white, it is something in between. Similarly, the key to understanding the differences as well as the similarities in race relations in the two countries is someone between a black and a white—that is, a mulatto. In Brazil the mulatto is not a Negro, whereas in the United States he is. Out of this seemingly slight difference, as this book seeks to demonstrate, the divergence in race relations in the two countries grew. It is pertinent here to note that this point is still controversial. Some Brazilian scholars, for example, have not found as much evidence of difference in social mobility between blacks and mulattoes in Brazil as I have.[3] On the other hand, a Brazilian scholar like Hasenbalg has agreed with my suggestion that the Brazilian practice of socially distinguishing between *mulatos* and *negros* places significant limitations on the development of black leadership in Brazil as compared with the United States.[4]

Like any author, I have learned much in the course of writing this book. One of the ways I have learned is from the writings, the talk, and the advice of many other persons—too many, in fact, to enumerate here. To some, however, my debt is so great that I want to make specific acknowledgment, though I am of course solely responsible for any errors or inadequacies that readers may find in the book. One of the great pleasures one discovers in seeking to penetrate another scholarly field (in this case Brazilian history) is that one has the opportunity to make the acquaintance of men and women whom otherwise one would not have had the occasion to know professionally. As an interloper in the field of Brazilian studies, I have been the fortunate recipient of enormous help and encouragement from the professionals in that field. No one was earlier in offering that encouragement and assistance than my friend and former colleague at Vassar College, Charles C. Griffin, whose own interest in the comparative history of the United States and Latin America provided the congenial context in which my own explorations began. John Johnson, then of Stanford University, pointed out things for me to read when I had done nothing more than express an interest in Brazil. Stanley Stein of Princeton, and Lewis Hanke, formerly of the University of Massachusetts, provided not only encouragement and insights, but also opportunities for me to talk over my ideas with interested scholars. Herbert Hill of Dartmouth College, offered me a forum for my ideas when such opportunity was important in stimulating my thinking. Three young and knowing Brazilianists at the time, Robert Toplin, now of the University of North Carolina, Wilmington, Re-

[3] See Nelson do Valle Silva, "Updating the Cost of Not Being White in Brazil," in Pierre-Michel Fontaine, ed., *Race, Class, and Power in Brazil* (Center for Afro-American Studies, University of California, Los Angeles, forthcoming.)

[4] Carlos A. Hasenbalg, *Discriminação e Desigualdades Raciais no Brasil* (Rio de Janeiro, 1979), p. 237.

becca Bergstresser, then of Stanford University, and Stuart Schwartz of the University of Minnesota, were more than generous with leads and information that I would have lacked except for their interest and kindness. They have been more than eager to advance my beginner's understanding of Brazil and its history; I only wish that I had been able to absorb more of what they were eager to teach me. To Richard Graham of the University of Texas at Austin, another young Brazilianist then, I owe a special debt of gratitude. He took the time to read three of my chapters, and provided me with needed encouragement, informed advice, and constructive criticism. Because I did not always follow his advice, he cannot be held responsible for any errors that remain, but he certainly caused the removal of a number of them. Richard Morse, then of Yale University, Eugene Genovese of the University of Rochester, and Herbert Klein of Columbia University gave me the benefit of their critical reading of what is now chapter II of this book, when I presented it as a paper at a historical meeting. The chapter is now substantially altered as well as double in length; whether I repaired the weaknesses they discovered, they can determine, but I believe I profited from their criticism and for that I thank them. I want also to thank editor Robert Webb and the anonymous reader for the *American Historical Review* for their advice and criticism of my article on slavery in Brazil and the United States, which was published in that journal. Those comments helped me in rewriting that article for its appearance here as chapter II. I also want to express my appreciation to the Fulbright office in the United States and Brazil, which enabled me to visit Rio de Janeiro in 1967 and thereby become personally acquainted with a people of whom I have grown very fond. It was on that visit that I first met Mrs. Eulalia Lobo; for her interest in my comparative study, which provided insights and leaders for this book, I thank her. My appreciation is extended also to Mrs. Florence Chu of the Stanford University Library for her indefatigable work in securing strange and obscure books for me on interlibrary loan. If Mrs. Chu could not locate a book, then it could not be found in the United States. My thanks go also to Mrs. Beverly Oudijk for her expeditious and masterful typing of the manuscript, to my wife, Catherine Grady Degler, who somehow managed to take time from her own heavy load of work to read portions of the manuscript in the interest of clarity and directness of writing, and to the Institute of American History at Stanford University which met the costs of typing. I want also to express my appreciation to James J. Carroll, Jr., of The Macmillan Company, and Sheldon Meyer, of Oxford University Press, who, at an important stage in the development of this book, and quite independently of each other, showed an interest and tangible encouragement that were essential to its completion. For this new printing under the aegis of The University of Wisconsin Press, I want to thank Alice Van Deburg for suggesting an association and carrying it to completion.

Finally, the book is dedicated to my brother and his family, who, in their own lives and without even knowing it, were an inspiration.

January 1986   C.N.D.
Stanford

The Challenge of the Contrast

I

Simeon was the most ungrateful and perverse of men. But I say to you that if Simeon were not a slave, he would have been neither ungrateful nor perverse.

> —*A Vitimas Algozes* by
> Joaquim de Macedo, 1869.

"Good Gracious! Anybody hurt?" "No'm. Killed a nigger." "Well, it's lucky because sometimes people do get hurt. . . ."

> —*Adventures of Huckleberry
> Finn* by Mark Twain, 1884.

In Brazil the phrase *minha nega*, which means literally "my little Negro," is often used by a white man in speaking to his white wife or mistress. The phrase has connotations of warm affection and sympathy. To anyone familiar with race relations in the United States such a use of the word *Negro* is not only unknown but inconceivable.

The phrase *minha nega*, however, is only the beginning of the contrast between race relations in Brazil and the United States. But, before we examine the contrasts, at least two similarities are worth looking at because upon them rests the comparison of the United States and Brazil, which is the purpose of this book. The first is that in Brazil, as in the United States, black people account for a large part of the population. On the two continents of the New World no other country counts as large a number or as large a proportion of blacks in its population as does the United States or Brazil. (The small island countries of the Caribbean, of course, are not included in the comparison.) The second similarity is that in both countries Negroes were introduced and held as slaves for most of their history. Brazil and the United States were the two largest slave societies of modern times.

Contrast in History

Actually, Negroes have always constituted a larger proportion of the population in Brazil than they ever have in the United States. Indeed, until the 1880's, when large numbers of European immigrants began to enter the country, the majority of the Brazilian population was colored—that is, Negro or mulatto. During the colonial era, as far as can be estimated, most of the population of Brazil was both colored and slave. Even during the nineteenth century, visitors immediately were made aware of the preponderance of blacks. At Santos, Rio de Janeiro, and other ports it was not unusual for ships' passengers to be literally carried ashore through the shallow water and mud in the arms of black slaves. And, if that startling introduction were not enough to proclaim the importance of Africa in Brazil, the first walk through the crowded streets would. One English visitor to Rio de Janeiro in 1829 remarked that "my eye really was so familiarized to black visages that the occurrence of a white face in the streets of some parts of the town, struck me as a novelty." In the midst of talking about the number of free people in Brazil, Henry Koster, an English planter who spent many years in Brazil, inadvertently testified to the great number of colored people in the country. "In none of these districts which I saw, do I conceive that the slaves outnumbered the free people in a greater proportion than three to one." Also in the early years of the nineteenth century, another English visitor, Maria Graham, estimated that in the city of Recife, "not above one third are white; the rest are mulatto or Negro." [1]

In the United States, on the other hand, Negroes have never constituted more than 19 per cent of the population at any time (1790), and for the last one hundred years the proportion has been always around 10 per cent. Even in Mississippi, which has long been the state with the highest proportion of blacks, the ratio has never been above 60 per cent. Thus, Brazil in the nineteenth century was known as the country of blacks and mixed

[1] Figures on number of proportions of slaves and Negroes are given in Roberto Simonsen, "As Consequencias economicas da abolição," *Revista do Arquivo municipal de São Paulo*, XLVII (May, 1938), 261; Emilia Viotti da Costa, *Da Senzala à Colônia* (São Paulo, 1966), p. 227; Maria Graham, *Journal of a Voyage to Brazil and Residence There, during Part of Years 1821, 1822, 1823* (London, 1824), pp. 125, 193; R. Walsh, *Notices of Brazil in 1828 and 1829* (London, 1830), p. 465; Pedro Calmon, *História social do Brasil* (São Paulo, 1937), II, 229 quotes one traveler as saying, "It is rare to meet a white on the street; we tend to believe that we are in Africa, seeing on all sides black faces."; Henry Koster, *Travels in Brazil*, 2nd ed., 2 vols. (London, 1817), II, 302.

bloods, but the United States has always been dominated by whites and so perceived by outsiders.

Undoubtedly the most obvious measure of white dominance in the United States has been the institution of legal and customary segregation—that is, the separation of whites and blacks in the activities of daily life. Although historians have now made it clear that elaborate *legal*, as distinguished from *customary* segregation, is a relatively recent phenomenon in the history of the United States, dating principally from the late nineteenth century, the *practice* of excluding Negroes from theaters, hotels, parks, and segregating them on street cars, trains, and other major public institutions runs far back into the nation's history. As we shall see later, Brazilian colonial laws often discriminated against blacks, too, but the systematic separation of the races, whether legally or customarily, is a North American phenomenon. It has no analog in Brazil. Today Brazil lacks a tradition of formal separation of the races.

The difference in attitudes and practices toward blacks in Brazil is positive as well as negative. Not only are there no laws that stigmatize Negroes as inferior, but the history of Brazil offers many examples of Negroes or mulattoes who achieved relatively high status in church and state. Travelers from the United States, for example, were struck by the sight of Negroes in high positions in nineteenth century Brazil. "I have passed black ladies in silks and jewelry, with male slaves in livery behind them," wrote Thomas Ewbank in 1856. "Today one rode past in her carriage, accompanied by a liveried footman and a coachman. Several have white husbands. The first doctor of the province is a 'colored man'; so is the President of the Province." [2] The Brazilian acceptance of miscegenation always forcefully attracted the attention of North Americans.

Then, as now, Brazilians have been aware of the dramatic difference between their attitudes and practices and those of the United States. For example, Joaquim Nabuco, the great abolitionist of Brazil, made the contrast explicitly in a book published just before slavery ended there in 1888. In the United States, he observed, during slavery and after, a sharp and rigid line was

[2] Quoted in Gilberto Freyre, *New World in the Tropics. The Culture of Modern Brazil* (New York, 1959), p. 119.

drawn between the races with relatively little mixing. "In Brazil," he went on, "exactly the opposite took place. Slavery founded on the differences between the races never developed the color line and in this Brazil was infinitely wiser. The contacts between the races, from the first colonization of the *donatario*, up to today, has produced a mixed population . . . and the slaves who were granted a letter of manumission, also received induction into citizenship. Thus there were not among us perpetual social castes; there was not even any fixed division of classes. . . . This system of absolute equality certainly opened a better future to the Negro race than was suggested by his horizon in North America."[3]

Modern Brazilian commentators have echoed Nabuco's praise of the Brazilian solution to the problem of race, miscegenation. "The problem of racial assimilation and absorption among whites and blacks," Nelson de Senna wrote in 1938, "is a solved problem in Brazil, without conflict or hatred; it differs radically from the more serious North American Negro problem, where there still exists a racial block of twelve million 'coloured people'; the pure Negroes and their more direct descendants isolated and separated from the racial mass of whites, by an impenetrable barrier of prejudice." Perhaps the best known advocate of the view that Brazil has solved the problem of the races through miscegenation is the great Brazilian sociologist and social historian, Gilberto Freyre, who for many years has been proclaiming the racial democracy of his native land. Before Freyre began writing in the early 1930's, many Brazilian intellectuals were ashamed of the racially mixed character of their people, but Freyre, almost single-handedly, has turned them around.[4]

The absence of the caste line or the acceptance of miscegenation is only the most obvious difference between race relations in Brazil and the United States. In the United States, for example, the role of the Negro in the making of the nation is only now being recognized. Ten years ago Negro History Week was little

[3] Joaquim Nabuco, *O Abolicionismo* in *Obras completas,* 14 vols. (São Paulo, 1944–49), pp. 149–51.

[4] Nelson de Senna, *Africanos no Brasil* (Belo Horizonte, Brazil, 1938) p. 48. Perhaps Freyre's best known and most influential work is *Casa Grande e Senzala,* which has been translated as *The Masters and the Slaves,* trans. Samuel Putnam (New York, 1946).

more than a casual concession to a few self-conscious Negroes; not many whites participated in it and fewer still learned much about the place of the Negro in United States history. In most history courses in high schools and colleges in the United States, the Negro figured primarily as an anonymous slave. Neither the achievement nor the problems confronted by Negroes in American society were touched upon in most classes or in most textbooks in United States history. Generally, the Negro entered the nation's history primarily as a problem, not as a contributor to the making of the society. How many students of American history ten years ago ever learned, for example, that Negroes fought in the Revolution—on both sides—or that Negroes were cowboys on the Great Plains? Today, of course, the interest in black history is high and even survey courses in United States history include material on the role of the black man in the nation's history. Moreover, there now are courses in black history in high schools as well as in colleges.

Brazilians, on the other hand, have known and recognized for a long time that blacks have been a part of their history. Early in the nineteenth century, for example, Karl F. P. Martius, in his prize-winning essay, "How the History of Brazil Should be Written," set the pattern that has been followed ever since. The essay emphasized the diversity of the nation's origins. The historian of Brazil, Martius advised, "must not consider Brazil's unique fusion of different elements as unfavorable, but rather see them as a fortunate and important union. The history of Brazil will always be primarily a history of a branch of the Portuguese. However, if Brazilian history is to be complete and to deserve the name of history, it can never exclude the roles played by the Ethiopian and Indian races." [5] Many Brazilian historians add that the African influence is second only to the Portuguese, and a few even place the African first! Even children's histories of Brazil discuss, as a matter of course, the role of the Negro in the making of the nation, and scholarly studies develop the point at some length. So many are the contributions of the Negro to the creation of Brazilian society, one historian of slavery has written, that it is impossible to enumerate them. "They run from the culinary art

[5] The von Martius quotation can be found in Lewis Hanke ed., *History of Latin American Civilization*, 2 vols. (Boston, 1967) I, p. 510.

to the manner of making love and of suffering. We owe more to the Negro than to the Portuguese, as a race and even as a civilization. Without him, the white colonist would not have conquered the land, as happened in the Orient, where the activity was transitory and achieved by the power of arms and force." [6]

Not surprisingly, therefore, knowledge of Brazilian Negro history is widespread among Brazilians, as North American black history has not been in the United States. All literate Brazilians, for example, know of Palmares, the great slave hideaway or *quilombo* of the seventeenth century. Some Brazilian historians significantly refer to it and the struggle to destroy it as "The Black Troy." Until the publication of William Styron's novel, *The Confessions of Nat Turner,* probably few white North Americans knew of the Turner uprising in Virginia in 1831. In Brazil, even during the nineteenth century, in the midst of a going slave society, foreign travelers quickly learned of Palmares and its heroic leader, Zumbi, who allegedly and romantically plunged to his death from a promontory rather than be captured by the white soldiers who destroyed the *quilombo* of Palmares. Quite different was the reaction in the antebellum United States to slave resistance. The Turner revolt, for example, precipitated an anxious debate in the Virginia legislature over the dangers of retaining slavery in the state; ten years earlier, the discovery of Denmark Vesey's plot in Charleston, South Carolina resulted in near panic among the whites and the passage of laws to restrict the activities of free Negroes still further because Vesey, the alleged leader of the plot, had been a free Negro.

Brazilians, in fact, have been including Negroes in their written history at least since the seventeenth century. Albuquerque Coello's seventeenth century history of the Dutch invasion and occupation of Pernambuco in the first half of the century made much of Henrique Dias, a Negro captain of Negro troops who fought on the side of the Portuguese. Indeed, throughout the colonial period Negro troops were known as "Henriques" in remembrance of Dias' prowess as fighter and leader. "If Henrique Dias had been known to English or French writers," writes literary historian Raymond Sayers, "he might easily have served

[6] João Dornas Filho, A *Escravidão no Brasil* (Rio de Janeiro, 1939), p. 211.

as the original of the Noble Negro, a figure that became important in eighteenth century literature. Dias was brave, resourceful, intelligent, and self-respecting, as we learn both from Coello's account and Dias' own letters—he is probably the first Negro writer in Brazilian history." [7]

Contrast in Cultural Response

The Negro appears frequently and significantly in all kinds of Brazilian literature, especially in the nineteenth century. Indeed, whole books and doctoral dissertations have been written about the Negro in Brazilian literature; a few examples will point up in yet another way the differences between the United States and Brazil in relating to black people. With perhaps one exception, which will be discussed later, Brazilian writers have been overwhelmingly sympathetic toward the Negro, especially as a slave. Thus J. J. Norberto de Souza e Silva published fragments of a long narrative poem in 1850 in which he told the story of the Negro state of Palmares. In one of the fragments a Negro slave complains of his lot, saying that he is treated no better than a beast. "The slave has no wife nor child/Race of servants, we are like cattle./We reproduce in order to provide slaves." In his anger he runs away to become the leader of Palmares,[8] for he is the great Zumbi himself. This long poem might be contrasted with William J. Grayson's "Hireling and the Slave," which the Charleston poet published in 1856 in defense of slavery and its alleged idyllic character as compared with the miserable life of the northern white workingman. Grayson, incidentally, was no fire-eater or extremist; he supported the Union in the nullification crisis of 1832, for instance.

Poetry was only one form of Brazilian literature in which sympathy for the slave was displayed. In 1860 José de Alencar's play *Mae* (Mother) was produced for the first time. The central figure in the play is a Negro woman, Joana, who poses as the slave of her son in order to conceal his origin as the offspring of a slave and a white man. The son is a medical student who thinks

[7] Raymond S. Sayers, *The Negro in Brazilian Literature* (New York, 1956), p. 38.

[8] Ibid., p. 92. The translation is mine.

he is white and who is actually being supported by the earnings of his slave–mother as a washerwoman and ironer. Although Joana does everything she can to help her son, including giving herself sexually to a money lender, her identity comes out, much to the horror of her son and his friends. She commits suicide with the words "my son" on her lips. Joana is presented fully, as well as sympathetically; above all, she is clearly the model of the self-sacrificing mother regardless of her status or her race. It also is not without significance, as Sayers points out, that Alencar, who was white, later said he modeled Joana after his own mother, an aristocratic lady from the northern province of Ceará.[9] Can one imagine a white North American in the age of slavery saying he modeled a Negro character after his aristocratic mother?

Among nineteenth century novels that treat of the Negro and the race questions in Brazil, perhaps the best known is Aluízio Azevedo's *O Mulato*, which, though first published in 1881, is still widely read in Brazil. The principal figure in the novel is a mulatto, a young man named Raymundo, who is the offspring of a slave woman and a white planter in Maranhão, in northern Brazil. Unaware of his origins, Raymundo receives a first-rate education at the University of Coimbra in Portugal. When the novel opens he is returning to his birthplace in Maranhão to close out his affairs, in preparation for his permanent settling in Rio de Janeiro. When he asks for the hand of his white cousin in marriage, however, his ancestry is revealed to him and he is prevented from marrying the girl. When Raymundo first learns of his Negro slave origins he suddenly understands "the coldness of certain families with whom he visited; the abruptly interrupted conversation at the moment he came near; the reticence of those with whom he spoke about his past; the reserve and caution of those who, in his presence, discussed questions of race and of blood."[10] As in *Mae*, the mulatto is not only the central figure, but the superior person. In fact, the villain in *O Mulato* is a

<hr>

[9] Ibid., pp. 148–49. Sayers points out on pp. 153–54 that there were other plays with the same theme of boys' having their mothers as slaves without their knowing the relationship. In *Os Cancros sociais* (The Social Cancer) by Maria Ribeiro, the mother is so attractive that she is thought by the son's wife to be a sexual threat!

[10] Aluízio Azevedo, *O Mulato*, 13th ed. (Rio de Janeiro, 1951), pp. 252–53.

white man and a canon of the church, to boot. It is the canon who frustrates Raymundo's elopement and finally arranges for the mulatto's assassination by another suitor. In short, despite the evidence of prejudice against mulattoes and Negroes in novels and plays like *O Mulato* and *Mae*, the clear and unmistakable thrust of the depiction is one of sympathy with people of color.

As these summaries of plots make evident, the depiction of the Negro in individual pieces of Brazilian literature is often idealized and even sentimental. Yet over the whole range of writing it emerges as eminently realistic. The Negro is not always the hero or simply a black version of a white man, as he frequently is in the novels of Harriet Beecher Stowe, for example. José de Patrocinio, for instance, who was a mulatto and one of the best-known abolitionist agitators in Brazil, wrote a minor novel in which a principal figure is a female African witch doctor, who hates whites and seeks to harm them in any way possible. A similar figure, this time male, occurs in a trilogy published in 1869 by Joaquim de Macedo, a white writer. On the other hand, Alencar includes in *Mae*, along with the strong figure of Joana, the mother, another Negro, Vicente, who is clearly a comic figure, not unlike the childish type that used to appear frequently on the stage and in movies in the United States.[11] Still another story tells of a mulatto slave who is freed after thirty-seven years and becomes an overseer, in which job he goes to work whipping slaves with pleasure. Furthermore, as a slave dealer he is depicted as being as heartless as any white. Yet even these stories, novels, or poems that show the depravity, silliness, or meanness of the Negro generally do so as part of the author's hostility toward slavery. In Brazilian literature slavery is generally deplored, and one way in which the evils of slavery are depicted is to show its deleterious effects upon the slave.

Virtually unique, therefore, is Julio Ribeiro's *A Carne* (Flesh) (1888), a novel that breathes real hatred for the Negro and consistently depicts him as evil.[12] Probably this novel comes the closest of any in all of Brazilian literature to Thomas Dixon's *The Leopard's Spots* (1902) and *The Clansman* (1905), the second of which was made into the well-known movie "The Birth of a Na-

---

[11] Sayers, *Negro in Brazilian Literature*, pp. 196, 173, 150, 187.
[12] Ibid., pp. 188–89, 221–22.

tion." The denigrating portrayal of the Negro in Dixon's novels was not unusual in the United States. Generally in the literature of the United States written by whites in the nineteenth and early twentieth centuries, the Negro is ignored; when he is not, he is usually either sentimentalized into a white man (or woman) as in *Uncle Tom's Cabin* or viciously denigrated as in Dixon's novels.

The accommodating Negro also figures in Brazilian literature; not all are Zumbis or Henrique Diases, by any means. For example, the giant black, slave or free, who puts his physical strength at the service of a white man, even for the purpose of killing blacks, is well represented in Brazilian poetry.[13] The black hired killer appears as recently as 1942 in Jorge Amado's classic novel *A Terra sem Fin,* which has been translated as *The Violent Land.* The faithful slave also appears in Brazilian novels; in one such work a white character says of a slave, "Happy is he who has a friend like that slave." Even Souza e Silva's long poem on Palmares includes Negroes who preferred to be slaves of the whites rather than members of the *quilimbo.* One of them is killed for freeing the white daughter of his old master, after she has been raped by her captors.[14]

José de Alencar's play *O Demonio Familiar* (Household Demon) (1857) portrays a house slave, Pedro, who is irresponsible, prankish, and trivial, and for whom Alencar invented a special and ludicrous form of speech to point up his lack of education. Pedro, Sayers concludes, lives "only to realize his private desire of making the family rich enough to set up a coach so that he may be the coachman." Although Pedro is clearly what Stanley Elkins has called in the United States a "Sambo," the important fact is that in *O Demonio Familiar* the institution of slavery, not race, is blamed for making him so. When Pedro is being freed, his master says, "Take this: it is your letter of freedom; it will be your punishment from this day forward because your transgressions will now fall only on yourself; because morality and the law will take severe account of your actions. As a free person you will feel the necessity of honest work and will appreciate those noble sentiments which today you do not comprehend." [15]

13 Ibid., p. 111.
14 Ibid., p. 169; 92.
15 Ibid., p. 147. My translation.

Perhaps the most famous example of the faithful retainer and the one that comes closest to Harriet Beecher Stowe's Uncle Tom is *Pai João* (literally Father John). He appears in Arthur Azevedo's play *O Dote* (The Dowry), published twenty years after the abolition of slavery in Brazil. Pai João speaks an inferior and confused Portuguese as befits a native African, but his faithfulness to whites is unquestioned. There is also a Pai João in Brazilian folklore, whom Arthur Ramos compares to Uncle Remus. "Pai João is symbolical," Ramos writes, "an ancient Negro from the cane fields, well on to a hundred years in age, a shuffling figure of mumbling speech and soft eyes. . . . He was the good slave, content with his lot, living in the glow and warmth of a past rich in legend and tradition." [16]

In the literature of Brazil, in short, the person of color appears not only frequently and importantly, but also in all garbs and stations. He is the faithful as well as the rebellious slave; he is the irresponsible *moleque* and the highly educated urban sophisticate; the person of color appears also as the carnal beast and the self-sacrificing mother.

Such a wide range simply cannot be duplicated in North American literature. The portrayal of the slave Jim as a human being in *Huckleberry Finn* is unusual in nineteenth century writing, for few novels, aside from abolitionist fiction, bothered to include the Negro as an important figure, much less depict him as a human being with depth and character. In the literature as in the society of the nineteenth century United States the Negro was largely invisible. Even in abolitionist novels, the slaves who are heroes of the stories are often quadroons or octoroons—that is, Negroes who are almost white—apparently on the ground that white readers would find the enslavement or torture of white flesh more compelling than black. Abolitionists were fascinated by the nearly white slave girl, whose beautiful body was presumably at the disposal of the slaveholder's lust. (The sexually repressed culture of English, Protestant North America precluded the explicit presentation of the consequences of that lust that the freer and Latin culture of Brazil permitted. But the sexual implications underlying abolition were evident in the antislavery

---

[16] Ibid., p. 160; Arthur Ramos, *The Negro in Brazil*, trans. Richard Pattee (Washington, 1939), p. 135.

literature of both countries. In those writings much was made, for example, of the availability of slave women to male slave-holders, but one has the feeling that behind the expressions of horror lurked a tinge of envy.)

It is not until the twentieth century that the literature of the United States exhibited the realism and diversity of characterization of the Negro that was evident in nineteenth century Brazilian poetry, drama, and novels. Sterling Brown, for example, in his study of the Negro in the literature of the United States, singles out T. S. Stribling's *Birthright* (1922) as a landmark because, despite its continuation of some of the old stereotypes of the Negro, it at least recognized that not all Negroes are happy-go-lucky. Nor is it accidental that a similar breakthrough occurred in drama at about the same time. The first production of Eugene O'Neill's *Emperor Jones* took place only two years before, and in 1925 Du Bose Hayward wrote his play *Porgy*. In O'Neill's masterpiece, for the first time a truly memorable Negro figure strode manfully upon the American stage, whereas in *Porgy*, the Negro became a tragic hero for the first time in major drama.[17]

The difference in the place of the Negro and the mulatto in Brazilian culture as compared with that in the United States is even more marked when one examines the participation of people of color in the high culture of the two societies. Negro writers are certainly not unknown in the nineteenth century in the United States, but they clearly do not figure among the major writers. The first significant Negro novelist is probably Charles W. Chesnutt, but his first works appeared only at the very end of the 1890's. Prior to the Negro renaissance of the 1920's there simply is not any Negro novelist, with the possible exception of Chesnutt, whose work has lasted or who is today recognized as a distinguished craftsman. Much the same judgment is warranted for other forms of artistic achievement.

The fact is that, prior to the twentieth century, the weight of slavery, prejudice, and discrimination lay so heavily upon the black population in the United States that there was only a narrow base from which a genius could spring. The vast preponderance of Negroes were simply untutored and narrowly

---

[17] Sterling Brown, *The Negro in American Fiction* (New York, 1969, originally published in 1937), pp. 115, 124, 118.

restricted in their opportunities to express themselves. Those who did manage to write or paint or compose, like Phyllis Wheatley, Benjamin Banneker, or Paul Laurence Dunbar were not only strikingly exceptional, but unsupported. Their achievements were remarkable in the light of the obstacles they hurdled, but those same achievements could not be compared to the work of the geniuses of the society in general.

How different was the situation in Brazil! Probably the greatest writer of Brazil, Joaquim Machado de Assis, was a mulatto. His novels are still being translated, for his economical style, wry humor, and penchant for psychological analysis make his work highly attractive to modern readers though his writing was done in the last half of the nineteenth century. It is highly likely that if he had not written in that "sepulchre of literature"—Portuguese —and had not lived in a backward South American country, he would today be recognized as the giant of world literature that he truly is. Another nineteenth century Brazilian litterateur, Tobias Bareto, was also a mulatto. José do Patrocinio, the son of a priest and a Negro vegetable woman, became not only one of the most articulate and best known of the abolitionists at the end of the nineteenth century, but was a novelist of some accomplishment as well. In his achievements and his talents, Patrocinio reminds North Americans of Frederick Douglass, the escaped slave who became a leader, orator, and newspaper editor in the abolitionist cause in the United States.

Such analogies are rare. In the United States, for instance, there was no one comparable to André Rebouças, perhaps the most distinguished engineer under the Empire in Brazil, who was a mulatto. Today in Brazil all literate people know of Rebouças, but few white people in the United States know of Benjamin Banneker, a black contemporary of Thomas Jefferson, who worked on the planning of the city of Washington and who could be compared with Rebouças in field, though not in achievement. The history of the United States, moreover, contains no Negro at all comparable to Antonio Lisboa—"Aleijadinho" (the little cripple) —perhaps the greatest sculptor of Brazil, who lived at the end of the eighteenth century. Aleijadinho was the son of a Portuguese man and a black slave woman; his nickname was given to him when he was in his forties and his hands began to crumble because of leprosy; yet some of his best work was done late in life, after he was crippled. Several churches of Minas Gerais still exhibit his work in their exterior design and interior decoration. Perhaps his most famous work, however, is the "Twelve Prophets" at the church of Nosso Senhor de Mattosinhos. Even when a United States Negro gained world renown in the arts during the nineteenth century, as did Ira Aldridge, the actor, his success came only in Europe. Aldridge, who was one of the great interpreters of Shakespeare on the European stage, earned both fame and fortune in Europe (he lived in a mansion in London), though he had been born and reared in the United States. Despite his achievements how many Americans today know his name as all literate Brazilians know Aleijadinho's?

Contrast Acknowledged

To make such comparisons of individuals of color in Brazil and the United States is to point up what was well recognized in the nineteenth century. White North Americans freely acknowledged that they found it difficult if not impossible to accord equal status to blacks, even when free, whereas the whites of Brazil and other countries south of the Rio Grande did not. In Mexico "and in Central America, and in the vast regions still further south," the *United States Magazine and Democratic Review* observed in 1844, "the negro is already a freeman—socially as well as politically, the equal of the white. Nine-tenths of the population there is made up of the colored races; the Generals, the Congressmen, the Presidents are men of mixed blood.

"Let the emancipated negro find himself on the borders of Mexico and the States beyond," the magazine continued, "and his fate is no longer doubtful or gloomy. He is near the land of his fellows, where equal rights and equal hopes await him and his offspring." [18] As can be gleaned from this quotation, the writer is arguing for the annexation of Texas, an issue that does not directly concern us here. The article and viewpoint, however, are relevant for what they reveal about attitudes toward Negroes on

[18] "The Re-Annexation of Texas: in its Influence on the Duration of Slavery," *United States Magazine and Democratic Review*, XV (July, 1844), 14.

the part of white North Americans and on the part of Latin Americans at that time.

The justification for the annexation of Texas that is implied in the quotation was originally propounded by Senator Robert J. Walker of Mississippi earlier in that same year. Walker argued that the annexation of Texas would help to solve the problem of slavery and race, which was then agitating the country on the eve of the presidential election. Walker contended that slavery would eventually become unprofitable in the Southeast as it had in the border and northern states earlier. As a result, planters would migrate with their slaves to the Southwest, eventually ending up in Texas, the newest state. But even there, in time, the soil would become depleted and slavery rendered unprofitable. Under such circumstances, he went on, the planters would be willing to free their slaves, who would then drift over the border to Mexico and the regions to the south. In that way both slavery and the race question would be solved for white North Americans, for not only would slavery end, but the Negro would also leave, thus answering the two principal demands of the antislavery whites. One could even argue, Walker pointed out, that the solution would benefit Negroes, for they would end up in areas where they enjoyed civil and political rights unlikely to be gained in the United States. That kind of migration seemed preferable to the colonization schemes that sought to send free Negroes to Africa, where the culture was actually unfamiliar to the majority of United States slaves, who had been born in the New World. As George Bancroft, the Jacksonian politician and later historian said in accepting the Democratic nomination for governor of Massachusetts in 1844, the acquisition of Texas would provide Negroes with an avenue "to pass to social and political equality in the central regions of America, where the prejudices of race do not exist." [19]

The merit of, or motivation behind Walker's proposal does not concern us here. The point is that in the nineteenth century, North Americans recognized not only their own prejudice against colored persons, but also the relative lack of such prejudice in the countries of Latin America.

[19] Frederick Merk, "A Safety Valve Thesis and Texan Annexation," *Mississippi Valley Historical Review*, XLIX (December, 1962), 413–36.

Even today North Americans who travel to Brazil are invariably struck by the absence of segregation and the consequent mingling of the races on the streets and in public places (and apparently in private places, too, when the wide and varied spectrum of colors among the population is taken into account). In 1965, for example, *Ebony* magazine published a two-part essay on miscegenation in Brazil in which the conclusion was, "Amalgamation may not be the complete answer to the racial problem, but so far it is the best. Should a serious problem of racial discrimination develop in Brazil [note the use of the future conditional] they have the framework of a solution, the temperament to cope with matters racial and a law to prosecute those who violate the Brazilian concept of justice for all." [20] Some Brazilian students of race relations report that in the cultural environment of Brazil even the most hard-shell Southern segregationist from the United States loses his prejudices. Professor René Ribeiro quotes a Protestant informant who told him, "The American missionaries [Baptist] who have worked among us since 1881, all came from the Southern United States, where prejudice against persons of color and the race problem work together in a very emphatic way. . . . Among us, however, they never took a step in the direction of acting as their compatriots there . . . . They receive, eat, live, and act shoulder to shoulder with men or persons of cólor; some of them have been members of churches whose pastors are men of color." When North Americans do display their prejudice, white Brazilians gently, but tellingly reprove them, as in the case of a Protestant Brazilian girl who was criticized for becoming engaged to a mulatto. The girl replied, "I asked God for a Protestant boy, honest and worthy, but I forgot to ask for the color." [21]

In short, no matter where one looks—at the culture, in the streets and meeting places, or in history—the contrast rises before one. In Brazil, as in other places in Latin America, the prejudice of race, which nineteenth century North Americans readily admitted, is apparently absent. In this contrast lie the problem and the challenge. How does one explain this difference, which has developed despite the fact that the Negro entered both North and South America as an involuntary immigrant, as a slave? Is

[20] Era Bell Thompson, "Does Amalgamation Work in Brazil?" *Ebony*, XX (September, 1965), 42.
[21] René Ribeiro, *Religião e Relações raciais* (n.p., n.d.), pp. 225–27.

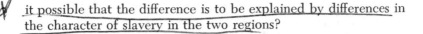
it possible that the difference is to be explained by differences in the character of slavery in the two regions?

An Explanation Advanced

Just that answer to the problem was cogently and powerfully presented in a little book published in 1947 by Frank Tannenbaum, a well-known authority on the history of Latin America.[22] His *Slave and Citizen* accounted for the differences in the position of the Negro in North and South America by pointing to the different forms of slavery in the two places. Tannenbaum did not direct his attention to Brazil particularly, but included all of Latin America in making the comparison with the United States. But he often drew upon Brazilian examples for his argument.

Essentially, Tannenbaum argued that in the Spanish and Portuguese colonies, Negro slaves were viewed as only temporarily degraded, that slavery was a social or historical accident, so to speak, which could have happened to anyone, not only Negroes. Even under slavery, in short, Tannenbaum contended, Negroes were conceived of as human beings, who just happened to be slaves. In North America, on the other hand, Negroes as slaves were treated and conceived of as something less than human. One measure of this difference in the nature of slavery, Tannenbaum went on, was the differing attitudes toward manumission. In Latin America manumission was easy and open, and both state and church by laws and practices encouraged it. Moreover, both state and church sought to protect or preserve the Negro's humanity as a slave against the power of the master, thereby preventing the Negro from being viewed as a thing, as he was in the United States. The slave family, Tannenbaum argued, was protected by state and church in Latin America, whereas in the United States the family of the slave was at the mercy of the whim and economic interest of the slaveholder. Thus, Tannenbaum's argument ran, after emancipation in Latin America, the Negro could assume a place as a free and equal citizen of society, whereas in the United States the long association between an inhuman form of slavery and race kept the Negro, even after

[22] Frank Tannenbaum, *Slave and Citizen* (New York, 1947).

emancipation, in a degraded position. In sum, Tannenbaum explained the differences in the present patterns in race relations in Latin America and the United States as the result of a quite different kind of slavery in the two areas.

Tannenbaum's work became the foundation for a much more influential book, written ten years later by Stanley Elkins.[23] His *Slavery* took for granted Tannenbaum's assertion of the difference in the two slave systems, arguing that slavery in the United States was the consequence of unrestrained capitalism in its exploitation and degradation of Negro slaves. He contrasted this picture with the situation in Latin America, where the institutions of church and state helped to prevent the reduction of blacks to commodities or things. Elkins' book concerned itself with several other aspects of United States slavery, but his acceptance and elaboration of the Tannenbaum contrast between the institution of slavery in Latin America and in the United States justifies coupling it with Tannenbaum's point of view.

In the years since Tannenbaum and Elkins published their books, the merits of their argument have been debated at great length by historians, anthropologists, and sociologists. Even public officials have been influenced by Elkins' formulation of the argument. For example, Daniel Patrick Moynihan, as we shall see in more detail later, accepted the Tannenbaum–Elkins position in his famous report on the Negro family. Not all scholars, however, have accepted the sharp differentiation between the two systems which Tannenbaum and Elkins drew. Arnold Sio and David Brion Davis,[24] for instance, have separately emphasized the essential similarities between slavery in the United States and in Latin America. Neither Sio nor Davis, it needs to be said, have sought to relate their conclusions on the nature of slavery in

[23] Stanley M. Elkins, *Slavery, a Problem in American Institutional and Intellectual Life* (Chicago, 1959). The second edition (1968) is identical with the first except for an added appendix.

[24] Arnold Sio, "Interpretations of Slavery: the Slave Status in the Americas," *Comparative Studies in Society and History,* VII (April, 1965), 289–308; David Brion Davis, *The Problem of Slavery in Western Culture* (Ithaca, N.Y., 1966), Chapters 8 and 9. Herbert Klein, *Slavery in the Americas* (Chicago, 1967) has not been mentioned in the text even though it is an attempt to support Tannenbaum's interpretation because it is concerned with Cuba and Virginia, and therefore does not directly involve comparison between the United States and Brazil.

North and South America to contemporary race relations in the two places. By more than implication, however, both Davis and Sio call into question Tannenbaum's accounting for the difference in race relations by reference to the differences in the institutions of slavery. Moreover, Sio and Davis, like Tannenbaum and Elkins, have compared the United States experience with that of all of Latin America. At the very least, such a comparison is unwieldy, for it involves the cultures of some twenty-five or more societies. Under such circumstances comparison becomes difficult. The amount of data alone is overwhelming and the task of trying to gain even a cursory knowledge of two dozen cultures is virtually unending. The result is a tendency to select from all the societies those facts that seem to support a conclusion, without really examining any society in detail.

Considering the problems facing any examination of slavery and race relations in the New World, this book draws a comparison only between the United States and Brazil. The selection is dictated simply by the recognized difficulties of trying to encompass all of some two dozen countries into which Negroes were introduced as slaves. It is also justified by the important fact, already alluded to, that Brazil and the United States were the two largest slave societies in the New World. Moreover, only in Cuba and Brazil did slavery continue longer than in the United States; and Brazil was the last country in the Western world to end slavery (1888). Finally, today Brazil and the United States contain more people of African descent than any other countries outside of Africa. Thus it is the assumption of this book that a rather close and detailed comparison of slavery and race relations in these two societies will tell us a good deal about the origins and nature of the tantalizing differences that we have noted in this chapter.

Tannenbaum and Elkins, in calling attention to the differences in race relations in the United States and Latin America, emphasized the causal role of slavery. Therefore, let us begin our investigations with an examination of slavery in Brazil and the United States.

Slavery Compared

II

In 1771 the viceroy ordered the degradation of
an Amerindian chief, who, "disregarded the signal
honours which he had received from the Crown,
had sunk so low as to marry a Negress, staining
his blood with this alliance."
> —Quoted in Charles Boxer,
> Race Relations in the
> Portuguese Colonial Empire.

September 17, 1630. Hugh Davis to be soundly
whipped before an assembly of Negroes and others
for abusing himself to the dishonor of God and
shame of Christians, by defiling his body in lying
with a Negro; which fault he is to acknowledge
next Sabbath day.
> —"Minutes of the Judicial Pro-
> ceedings of the Governor and
> Council of Virginia," Hening's
> Statutes of Virginia.

Until Frank Tannenbaum published his book *Slave and Citizen*
it was generally thought that slavery, at least as legally defined,
was much the same wherever it occurred, whether in ancient
Rome and Greece, in medieval Europe, or in North and South
America. And certainly in most times and places two common
elements clearly differentiated slavery from other kinds of legally
defined labor systems. The status of a slave lasted through his
lifetime and was inheritable. In the seventeenth century, for
example, indentured servitude was common, especially in the
English colonies of North America, and though many elements
of that status were similar to those of slavery, the term of service
was limited, usually from four to seven years, and the status was
not inheritable; a child born to a servant was free. One further
element common to all systems of slavery, modern and ancient,
was that the status was inherited from the mother. Thus the
offspring of a slave woman and a free man was a slave whether
in Brazil, the United States, or ancient Rome. Modern slavery,
however, differed from the ancient form in one important way.
It was imposed upon colored people only. In Brazil, as in the
United States, white people were never slaves, though Indians
were held as slaves in both places during the colonial period. To
the implications of this fact we shall return later.

Frank Tannenbaum contended that despite these admitted similarities between the modern slave systems of North and South America, there were important differences between them. In Tannenbaum's view, the law of slavery in Latin America and the attitudes of the Roman Catholic Church toward the slave differed significantly from the laws and the religious practices in English North America. It was the differences in slavery, according to Tannenbaum, that explained the differences in the race relations of today. Because of the emphasis that Tannenbaum placed upon the role of the state and the church in differentiating the systems of slavery, the practices of slavery in the two places need to be examined in some detail. In that way we will be able to determine the ways in which the two systems of slavery in fact differed. From that we can then judge the role of the state and the church in bringing about those differences. Thus we will be in a position to evaluate Tannenbaum's broader contention that differences in the two systems of slavery account for the differences in modern race relations in the two countries.

Who Protects the Slave's Humanity?

In comparing slavery in Brazil and the United States, let us first look at the ways in which they were alike. (Although slavery has a long history in both Brazil and the United States, the basis of the comparison here will be slavery at its maturity in both places —that is, during the nineteenth century, if only because the evidence for making such comparisons is most abundant during that period.) Both Tannenbaum and Stanley Elkins stress the different conception of the slave in the eyes of the law in the United States and in Latin America. Tannenbaum, for example, contrasts the legal definition of a slave as a chattel in the United States with the more ambiguous definition in Latin America. "In fact," Tannenbaum wrote, *"the element of human personality was not lost in the transition to slavery from Africa to the Spanish or Portuguese dominions.* He [the Negro] remained a person even while he was a slave. . . . He was never considered a mere chattel, never defined as unanimated property, and never under the law treated as such. His master never enjoyed the powers of life and death over his body, even though abuses existed and cruelties were performed." [1]

Yet a comparison of Brazilian and United States law reveals striking similarities in the legal definition of a slave. Although by the nineteenth century the text of the law in the southern states of the United States defined a slave as chattel property, the judicial interpretations of that legal concept were not those that Tannenbaum assumed. The law always recognized that a slave was both a human being and a piece of property. The very fact, for instance, that slaves were legally responsible for any crime they committed immediately suggests that their status as chattel property was different from that of any other piece of property, even of an animate variety. The courts of the Southern states were quite explicit in their recognition of the humanity of the slave. "A slave is not in the condition of a horse or an ox," declared a Tennessee court in 1846. "His liberty is restrained, it is true, and his owner controls his actions and claims his services. But he is made after the image of the Creator. He has mental capacities, and an immortal principle in his nature that constitutes him equal to his owner but for the accidental position in which fortune has placed him. The owner has acquired conventional rights to him, but the laws under which he is held as a slave have not and cannot extinguish his high-born nature nor deprive him of many rights which are inherent in man." In 1818 a court in Mississippi went so far as to observe that "Slavery is condemned by reason

---

[1] Frank Tannenbaum, *Slave and Citizen* (New York, 1947), pp. 97–98. Emphasis in original. See also p. 103. For a comparison with medieval slavery of a particular kind see Iris Origo, "The Domestic Enemy: The Eastern Slaves in Tuscany in the Fourteenth and Fifteenth Centuries," *Speculum*, XXX (July, 1955), 321–66. I am indebted to Professor Benjamin Kohl of Vassar College for calling this reference to my attention. The definitive general work on medieval slavery in France and the Iberian peninsula is Charles Verlinden, *L'Esclavage dans L'Europe medievale.* Tome Premier. Peninsula Iberique—France (Brugge, 1955). The standard work on Roman slave law is W. W. Buckland, *The Roman Law of Slavery* (Cambridge, England, 1908). For more recent scholarship and references see William L. Westermann, *The Slave System of Greek and Roman Antiquity* (Philadelphia, 1955); Carl N. Degler, "Starr on Slavery," *Journal of Economic History*, XIX (June, 1959), 271–77; Moses I. Finley, ed., *Slavery in Classical Antiquity: Views and Controversy* (Cambridge, 1960).

and the laws of nature. It . . . can only exist through municipal regulations, and in matters of doubt, . . . courts must lean 'in favorem vitae et liberatis.' " [2]

A few years later, in 1821, the Mississippi court elaborated upon the status of a slave in deciding whether the homicide of a slave by a white man was murder. "In some respects, slaves may be considered as chattels, but in others they are regarded as men," the court noted. "The law views them as capable of committing crimes. This can only be upon the principle that they are men and rational beings. The Roman law has been much relied on by the counsel of the defendant [the white man]. That law was confined to the Roman empire giving the power of life and death over captives in war, as slaves, but it no more extended here, than the similar power given to parents over the lives of their children. . . . It has been determined in Virginia, that slaves are persons. In the Constitution of the United States slaves are expressly designated as 'persons.' In this state, the Legislature have [sic] considered slaves as reasonable and accountable beings and it would be a stigma upon the character of the state, and a reproach to the administration of justice, if the life of a slave could be taken with impunity, or if he could be murdered in cold blood, without subjecting the offender to the highest penalty known to the criminal jurisprudence of the country. Has the slave no rights because he is deprived of his freedom? He is still a human being, and possesses all those rights, of which he is not deprived by the positive provisions of the law, but in vain shall we look for any law passed by the enlightened and philanthropic legislature of this state, giving even the master, much less to a stranger, power over the life of a slave. Such a statute would be worthy [sic] the age of Draco or Caligula, and would be condemned by the unanimous voice of the people of this state, where, even cruelty to slaves, much less the taking away of life, meets with universal reprobation. By the provisions of our law, a slave may commit murder, and be punished with death; why then is it not murder to kill a slave? Can a mere chattel commit murder, and be subjected to punishment? . . . The right of the master

---

[2] Ford v. Ford (Tennessee, 1846) 7 Humphreys 95; Harry et al. v. Decker and Hopkins (Mississippi, 1818), 1 Walker 36.

exists not by the force of the law of nature or of nations, but by virtue only of the positive law of the State. . . . The taking away the life [sic] of a reasonable creature, under the king's peace, with malice aforethought, express or implied, is murder at common law. Is not the slave a reasonable creature, is he not a human being, and the meaning of this phrase *reasonable creature* is a human being, for the killing of a lunatic, an idiot, or even a child unborn, is murder, as much as the killing of a philosopher, and has not the slave as much reason as a lunatic, an idiot, or an unborn child?" [3]

Later in the antebellum years judicial cases in other states also testified to the courts' insistence upon the human character of the slave. Three cases in North Carolina in which slaves were accused of killing white men offered another kind of evidence. In the last of the three, State v. Caesar (1849) the appeals court refused to accept the murder conviction of a slave who had killed a white man who was brutally beating another slave. Because the slave who was being beaten was unresisting, the court pointed out, Caesar, the defendant slave, "must either run away and leave him at the mercy of two drunken ruffians, to suffer, he knew not how much, from their fury, and disappointed lust—the hour of the night forbade the hope of aid from white men—or he must yield to a generous impulse and come to the rescue. He used force enough to release his associate and they made their escape, without a *repetition* of the *blow*. Does this shew he has the heart of a murderer? On the contrary, are we not forced, in spite of stern policy, to admire, even in a slave, the generosity, which incurs danger to save a friend? The law requires a slave to tame down his feelings to suit his lowly condition, but it would be savage, to allow him, under no circumstances, to yield to a generous impulse." And as late as 1861 an Alabama court concluded that "slaves are human beings, and are endowed with intellect, conscience, and will. . . . Because they are rational human beings, they are capable of committing crimes; and, in references to acts which are crimes, are regarded as persons. Because they are slaves, they are necessarily, and, so long as they

[3] State v. Isaac Jones (Mississippi, 1821) 1 Walker 84–85. The court ordered that the white slayer of the Negro slave be executed.

remain slaves, incurably, incapable of performing civil acts, and, in reference to all such, they are things, not persons." [4]

The statement from the Alabama court is close in phraseology as well as meaning to that set forth in Brazilian slave law by its principal authority, Perdigão Malheiro. "In regard to the penal code," Perdigão wrote, "the slave, as subject of the offense or agent of it, is not a *thing*, he is a *person* . . . he is a human entity." Hence he is held personally responsible for crimes. But when he is an "object or sufferer of a crime" the matter is different. The slave is not indemnified for such injuries, though the master may be. "In the latter case the question is one of *property*, but in the other it is one of *personality*." In another place Perdigão Malheiro speaks of the slave as "only an *instrument of labor*, a *machine*." All rights were denied slaves, "all the sentiments, even those of the family. They were reduced to the condition of a *thing*."

Moreover, as he makes clear, the position of the slave in a Brazilian court was not much different from that of the slave in the United States. No slave in Brazil could enter a complaint himself; it had to be done by his master or by the public authority. Nor could a slave make an accusation against his master. In fact, a slave could not give sworn testimony at all, only information. Perdigão Malheiro points out that in only three circumstances did a slave have standing in court: (1) in regard to spiritual matters, such as marriage; (2) in regard to his own liberty; and (3) in matters of obvious public concern.[5] In the United States, too, slaves had the right to go to court to establish their freedom; 670 suits for freedom by slaves have been reported by Helen Catterall in her monumental compendium of cases concerning slavery. Incidentally, over half of those who took their

[4] State v. Caesar (North Carolina, 1849) 9 Iredell 391. The court ordered a new trial for Caesar on the charge of felonious killing. The other two cases, well known in the history of slavery, are State v. Will (North Carolina, 1834) 1 Devereaux and Battle 121 and State v. Jarrott (North Carolina, 1840) 1 Iredell 76. The quotation from the Alabama court is from Creswell's Executor v. Walker, 37 Alabama Reports 236 (1861).

[5] Agostinho Marquis Perdigão Malheiro, *A Escravidão no Brasil Ensaio Historico-Juridico-Social*, 2 vols. (São Paulo, 1944), I, pp. 39–40, 34–35, 67. See also Dr. Agostinho Marques Perdigão Malheiro, *A Escravidão no Brasil Ensaio Historico-Juridico-Social* (Rio de Janeiro, 1866), Part 3, pp. 14–15 for the statement on the slave's being a thing.

cases to the appeal courts—the only ones that Catterall reports—won their freedom.[6] On the other hand, in the United States, slave marriages enjoyed no legal basis.

If the law in both Brazil and the United States defined the slave as at once a human being and a thing and limited his rights in court, there was also little difference in the way in which the law protected the slave's humanity. Tannenbaum, for example, has emphasized that in Latin America the law prohibited punishments and other kinds of treatment that would degrade or dehumanize the slave.[7] Yet all the slave states of the United States in the nineteenth century enacted laws against the mistreatment or killing of slaves by masters. Kenneth Stampp, in his general study of southern slavery, which certainly offers no apology for slavery, summarizes the legal situation as follows: "The law required that masters be humane to their slaves, furnish them adequate food and clothing, and provide care for them during sickness and old age. In short, the state endowed masters with obligations as well as rights and assumed some responsibility for the welfare of the bondsmen." [8]

Because both societies had laws seeking to protect the humanity of the slave against his master's power to exploit, the important question is whether the state's law or the church's authority interceded between the master and the slave, in behalf of the latter. Generally historians of slavery in the United States have not put much weight upon the influence of the law, believing generally that the master on his isolated plantation was beyond the reach of the law. There are very few cases, for example, of cruel masters being summoned to court for violation of these laws. As the already cited Mississippi case of 1821 shows, occasionally masters were executed or otherwise punished for killing a slave and a cruel master did suffer the condemnation of his neighbors, if nothing else. All in all, however, the sanctions against mistreatment or even a high crime like murder of a slave were less rigorously applied than those against similar crimes against a white person in the United States. Informal controls over harsh or sadistic masters were probably more effective than

[6] See Marion J. Russell, "American Slave Discontent in Records of the High Courts," *Journal of Negro History*, XXXI (October, 1946), 411–34.

[7] Tannenbaum, *Slave and Citizen*, p. 93.

[8] Kenneth M. Stampp, *The Peculiar Institution* (New York, 1956), p. 192.

modern commentators often recognize, but in the United States the law's protection of the slave's humanity is not impressive on the basis of the record.[9]

A similar gap between law and practice seems to have prevailed in Brazil, too, where the power of the state or the church to affect the conditions of life of the slave was perhaps even more limited than in the more thickly settled and more highly organized United States. As Henry Koster, an English planter who lived for many years in Brazil, pointed out in the early nineteenth century, the Brazilian government was a weak reed on which to lean for anything, much less for control over the members of the slaveholding class. He tells, for example, of an instance in which one of his own slaves injured the slave of another man, but adds that nothing was done about the matter. The owner of the injured slave, Koster pointed out, might have pressed charges, if he was so minded, "but the law of itself seldom does anything. Even in the cases of murder the prosecutor . . . has it at his option to bring the trial forward or not; if he can be bribed or otherwise persuaded to give up the accusation, the matter drops to the ground." Occasionally, Koster writes, a cruel master was fined for maltreating his slaves, "but I have never heard of punishment having been carried farther than this trifling matter of correction." [10]

Later in the century another foreigner, the German painter John Rugendas, put the matter even more directly. Although there are laws in Brazil limiting the use of the whip and fixing the number of lashes that may be imposed at one time, he wrote in 1835, "these laws have no force and probably may be unknown to the majority of the slaves and masters; on the other hand, the authorities are so removed that in actuality the punishment of the slave for a true or imaginary infraction or the bad treatment

[9] Ibid., pp. 221–24.

[10] Henry Koster, *Travels in Brazil*, 2nd ed. (London, 1817), I, pp. 375–76; II, p. 237. A French traveler in Brazil in the 1860's conceded that in the big cities like Rio de Janeiro a slave might occasionally be able to make a complaint to the police of bad treatment, but away from the cities, he contended, the story was quite different. There, the Frenchman wrote, the power of the master is like that of a "feudal baron, who exercises the highest and lowest justice in his dominion." There are no appeals from his sentences. "No guarantee is conceded to the slave." Charles Expilly, *Mulheres e Costume do Brasil*, trans. Gastão Penalva (São Paulo, 1935), p. 361.

resulting from the caprice and the cruelty of the master only encounters limits in the fear of losing the slave by death, by flight, or as a consequence of public opinion. But these considerations are never sufficient to impede the evil and it is inescapable that examples of cruelty are not lacking, which result in the mutilation and death of slaves." And even when the slave does know his rights, Rugendas pointed out, "it is much more difficult to uphold" the complaint than to make it. The masters "have at their disposal a thousand ways of retarding or of even rejecting the complaint, without counting the possibility of taking revenge on the bold act of a slave, of subjecting him to every kind of trouble and intimidation." A Pernambuco newspaper in 1856 reported that a slave who complained to an official about his punishment by whipping was ordered to receive "a double dose," which the paper found to be "an excellent way to handle such complaints." [11] Only toward the end of slavery in Brazil, when the abolitionists brought cases of mistreatment to court, did the laws in behalf of the slave actually protect him.

Sometimes it is said that an important distinction between the slave practices of Latin America and those of the United States is that in the former the Roman Catholic church protected the slave's humanity. Both Tannenbaum and Elkins, for example, emphasize the role of the Catholic church in providing the Negro slave in South America with a higher "moral" position than that afforded by the dominant Protestant churches in the United States.[12] It is not always clear what *higher moral position* means in this context. If it means that the church in Brazil accepted Negro slaves as members, then it has to be said that the Protestant churches of the United States did, too. From the beginning of slavery in the United States, slaves were members of churches. In the eighteenth and nineteenth centuries the Methodist, Bap-

[11] João Mauricio Rugendas, *Viagem pitoresca atraves do Brasil*, 3rd ed., trans. Sergio Milliet (São Paulo, 1941), pp. 185, 189; Gilberto Freyre, *The Mansions and the Shanties*, trans. Harriet de Onis (New York, 1963), p. 266.

[12] Tannenbaum, *Slave and Citizen*, pp. 62–64, 98; Stanley M. Elkins, *Slavery, A Problem in American Institutional and Intellectual Life* (Chicago, 1959), pp. 73, 76–77. For a penetrating critique of Elkins' whole approach to comparative slavery, which also distinguishes between Elkins' faults and Tannenbaum's virtues, see Eugene D. Genovese, "Rebelliousness and Docility in the Negro Slave: A Critique of the Elkins Thesis," *Civil War History*, XIII (December, 1967), 293–314.

tist, and Presbyterian churches, particularly, dispatched rather extensive missions to the slaves in the southern states. In the nineteenth century some Baptist churches even ordained slave members as preachers. In one Episcopal diocese in Louisiana the black members actually outnumbered the whites. Slaves in the Protestant congregations were relegated to the balcony or to special sections within the white churches, but there was never any question that a slave could be accepted as a Christian in the United States. Indeed, early in the eighteenth century it was widely believed, though unfounded in law, that to convert a slave to Christianity would automatically free him. Catholic doctrine never threatened the security of slave property in that way.[13] Again, as with the impact of the laws, the important question in regard to the church is the degree of protection that the acceptance of the slave by the church afforded him in the two countries.

If Tannenbaum's assertion that the church in Latin America maintained a higher moral position for the slave than in the United States means that the Roman Catholic church intervened between master and slave in behalf of the latter, then it needs to be said that in Brazil, at least, the church's interest in and power to protect the slave's humanity was as limited as that of the state. For one thing, few plantations had priests on the premises; most of them saw a priest only once a year, when he came to legalize unions and to baptize. During the nineteenth century there simply were not sufficient priests in the country for them to be able to affect the daily life of the slave on the plantation, even if they had the interest to do so. And even where a priest was resident on a plantation, it seems doubtful that his will could withstand the master, on whom the priest depended so heavily. More important, there is abundant evidence

[13] Orville W. Taylor, *Negro Slavery in Arkansas* (Durham, 1958), p. 180; Joe Gray Taylor, *Negro Slavery in Louisiana* (Baton Rouge, 1963), pp. 141–46; Stampp, *Peculiar Institution*, pp. 371–77; Charles Sackett Sydnor, *Slavery in Mississippi* (New York, 1933), pp. 55, 59; Chase C. Mooney, *Slavery in Tennessee* (Bloomington, 1957), pp. 96–97; James Benson Sellers, *Slavery in Alabama* (University of Alabama, 1950), pp. 317–22; Donald G. Mathews, *Slavery and Methodism* (Princeton, 1965), *passim;* for English colonial beliefs on the effect of conversion upon slaves see Marcus W. Jernegan, "Slavery and Conversion in the American Colonies," *American Historical Review,* XXI (April, 1916), 504–27.

that officially the church showed little interest in interfering with the institution of slavery, even in regard to matters that might seem to fall under the heading of moral behavior. Thus it was not until 1885 that the Archbishop of Bahia—the chief churchman in Brazil—ruled that no master could prevent a slave from marrying or sell him away from his spouse. Yet even at that late date—slavery was finally abolished in Brazil in 1888 —a slave could marry against his master's will only if the slave could demonstrate that he knew Christian doctrine—that is, the Lord's Prayer, the Ave Maria, the Creed, the Commandments, understood the obligations of holy matrimony, and was clear in his intention to remain married for life—a formidable set of requirements for an untutored slave! Furthermore, as in the United States, religion was used by the church in Brazil as a way to support slavery, not to weaken it. One priest told a group of planters, "Confession is the antidote to insurrection, because the confessor makes the slave see that his master is in the place of his father to whom he owes love, respect, and obedience." [14]

Certainly abolitionists in Brazil did not consider the church sympathetic to their cause. In 1887, on the eve of abolition, the Brazilian abolitionist Anselmo Fonseca wrote a long book castigating the Brazilian Catholic clergy for its lack of interest in the cause of abolition. With heavy-handed irony Fonseca observed that in 1871, when antislavery statesmen fought for the law of the free womb for slave mothers, the church was silent. At that time, Fonseca sarcastically noted, slavery "still had much vitality. . . . It was dangerous to take it on frontally." He recalled, too, that in 1873–74, when the church sought to combat Freemasonry in Brazil, two of its bishops went to prison rather than accede to the power of the Emperor himself. "Why did not the Bishops . . . show the solidarity and courage and the energy" against slavery in 1871 "with which in 1873–74 they combatted masonry and the government?" he asked. Some modern historians such as Tannenbaum have drawn a contrast between the alleged Catholic concern for the slave and Protestant indifference. It is worth noting, however, that a contemporary abolitionist, Fonseca, contrasted the massive indifference to the plight of the slave on

[14] Emília Viotti da Costa, *Da Senzala à Colônia* (São Paulo, 1966), pp. 250, 271, 249.

the part of the Brazilian Catholic clergy with the activities of a Protestant clergyman like William Ellery Channing in behalf of the slave in the United States.[15]

Although the Catholic church in Brazil did not interpose itself between slave and master in protection of the former, it did permit slaves to join lay charitable brotherhoods, or *irmandades*. These brotherhoods had no counterpart in Protestant North America. They constituted, therefore, one of the few concrete ways in which it made a difference to the slave whether the society in which he was held was Catholic or Protestant. The brotherhoods, it is true, were generally segregated by color as well as by class, but sometimes the brotherhood would help to buy the freedom of a slave, for both slave and free men were in the same chapter. Moreover, the brotherhoods provided a life beyond or outside of slavery for its members. In colonial Bahia, there were thirty-one brotherhoods, of which six were for Negroes and five for mulattoes. In fact, however, the field of operation of the brotherhoods was rather limited because they were located in the cities and would have had little effect upon the plantation slaves. Yet they do constitute at least a passive ameliorative effect of the Church upon the lot of the slave.[16]

One of the most often cited ways in which slavery in Latin America, and in Brazil in particular, is supposed to have been more protective of the slave's humanity is that marriages between slaves were recognized by the Catholic church. Church or religious marriages between slaves in the United States also qualified as sacramental acts, though masters, it was understood, were not bound to honor such unions. Given the weakness of the Brazilian church's control over slave masters, it is not to be expected that marriages of slaves in Brazil were any more enduring or protected from disruption through sale than in the United States.

[15] Luis Anselmo Fonseca, *A Escravidão, O Clero e O Abolicionismo* (Bahia, 1887), pp. 1–27, 440–41. The references to William E. Channing are on pp. 12–15.

[16] On the lay brotherhoods see Manoel S. Cardozo, "The Lay Brotherhoods of Colonial Bahia," *Catholic Historical Review*, XXXIII (April, 1947), 12–30. "Such was the profusion of these coloured brotherhoods [in Bahia city] that any person of colour, a slave or a freed man, African or Brazilian, could find a brotherhood to suit his condition," writes A. J. R. Russell-Wood, *Fidalgos and Philanthropists, The Santa Casa da Misericordia of Bahia, 1550–1755* (Berkeley, 1968), pp. 142–43.

Indeed, one Brazilian commentator in the middle of the nineteenth century said in so many words that masters could sell their slaves separately even when married, and certainly married slaves were sold apart.[17]

In any event, in Brazil only a small proportion of slaves were in fact married by the church. Early in the nineteenth century the Brazilian reformer José Bonifacio asked that masters be legally compelled to permit slaves to marry freely and to require that at least two-thirds of a master's slaves be married. Yet, forty years later, travelers still reported that only a small proportion of Negroes were married and "rarely were [marriages] confirmed by a religious act." One traveler in 1841, for example, found only ten slaves married out of 2,500 on the Isle of Santa Catherina in southern Brazil. In northeastern Brazil, in Rio Grande do Norte province, a local document listed only about 5 per cent of the 13,000 slaves in the province in 1874 as married or widowed, though 30 per cent of free persons were wedded. In the census of 1872, the province of Ceará reported that 1,070 male slaves were married or widowed out of almost 15,000 then in the province. Of the 660,000 slaves in all of Brazil in 1875, who were of marriageable age, only about one out of six was recorded as married or widowed.[18]

The lack of protection from either state or church for the slave family in the United States is well recognized. Tannenbaum has summarized it succinctly and accurately. "Under the law of most of the Southern states there was no regard for the Negro family, no question of the right of the owner to sell his slaves separately, and no limitation upon separating husband and wife, or child from its mother." [19] Yet, for most of the nineteenth century, the same generalization would fit the situation in Brazil. Prior to 1869, for example, there was no protection under the law for the slave family in Brazil. But, as was the case in the United States, a

[17] F. A. Brandão, A Escravatura no Brasil (Bruxelles, 1865), p. 29; W. D. Christie, Notes on Brazilian Questions (London, 1865), p. 76.

[18] Viotti da Costa, Da Senzala, p. 268; Fernando Henrique Cardoso and Octavio Ianni, Côr e mobilidade social em Florianopolis (São Paulo, 1960), pp. 128–29; Robert Edgar Conrad, "The Struggle for the Abolition of the Brazilian Slave Trade: 1808–1853." Ph.D. dissertation, Columbia University, 1967, 55–56; Raimundo Girão, A Abolição no Ceará (Fortaleza, Brazil, 1956), p. 48.

[19] Tannenbaum, Slave and Citizen, p. 77.

vigorous internal slave trade broke up many families, whether the unions had been solemnized by the church or not. The internal slave trade in Brazil was especially active after 1850, when the foreign slave trade was closed and the growth of the coffee producing regions of southern Brazil drew hundreds of thousands of slaves from the old sugar regions of the northeast. One modern authority has cited 30,000 as the number of slaves that were annually brought from the north to São Paulo state between 1850 to 1870.[20]

But the internal slave trade is not the only reason for believing that slave families in Brazil suffered disruption, at least prior to 1869. Indeed, to take an extreme example, one of the great Brazilian abolitionists, Luis Gama, was sold into slavery by his own white father. Stanley Stein, in his study of a coffee county west of Rio de Janeiro, writes that in the 1870's one planter was known to have sold his mulatto offspring to a passing slave trader. Furthermore, a law passed in 1876, prohibiting the sale of one's own children, suggests that such practices on the part of white fathers was not unknown even at that late date.[21]

If fathers sold their own children, it is not likely that they scrupled to sell other men's. But there is other evidence to show that slave families, insofar as they existed, were disrupted in nineteenth century Brazil. One important and broad category of evidence is the complaints of antislavery reformers who, at the opening of the nineteenth century and as late as the 1860's, were calling for laws to prevent the breakup of the slave family. Even men who were not opposed to slavery noticed the evil. "It is a horror, gentlemen," João Mauricio Wanderley told the Senate in 1854, "to see children ripped from their mothers, husbands separated from wives, parents from children! Go to Law Street . . . and be outraged and touched by the spectacle of such sufferings. And this happens at the Court of the Empire! I am not given much to sentimentalism, but I confess that I am disturbed; it horrifies me when I consider all the consequences of this barbarous, inhuman traffic, and I will say even more barbarous, more

[20] Pedro Calmon, *História social do Brasil* (São Paulo, 1937), II, p. 151.

[21] Richard M. Morse, *From Community to Metropolis. A Biography of São Paulo, Brazil* (Gainesville, Fla., 1958), p. 146; Stanley J. Stein, *Vassouras. A Brazilian Coffee County 1850–1900* (Cambridge, Mass., 1957), p. 159; Magnus Mörner, *Race Mixture in the History of Latin America* (Boston, 1967), p. 117.

inhuman than the traffic from the coast of Africa." Later, as Baron Cotegipe and prime minister, Wanderley would oppose abolition. As late as 1866 Perdigão Malheiro was still pleading that the law find means to prevent the separation of married slave couples and children of less than seven years. If the slave family was to exist at all, he contended, such minimal legal protections were indispensable. In another place he spoke of the slave family as being destroyed by slavery.[22]

Despite the long agitation for legal prohibitions on separation of husband and wives or of children and parents who were slaves, no such law was enacted until 1869. *Most* slave states in the United States, as Tannenbaum correctly pointed out, never enacted such laws at all. A few did, however, and those that did passed them long before 1869. A Louisiana law of 1829, for example, prohibited the sale of children under ten and apparently it was adhered to by slave traders. The laws of Alabama and Georgia forbade the breaking up of *inherited* slave families, but did not place the same restrictions upon the sale of other slaves.[23] Although most planters in the United States tried to avoid breaking up slave families in practice, regardless of the law, as in Brazil, many in fact were disrupted.[24]

Manumission: How Easy, How Common?

Perhaps the most frequently stressed difference between Latin American and United States slavery is the amount of manumission. Generally it is said that in Latin America manumission was

---

[22] Arthur Ramos, *The Negro in Brazil*, trans. Richard Pattee (Washington, 1939), pp. 58–59; Maurilio de Gouveia, *História da Escravidão* (Rio de Janeiro, 1955), p. 134; Perdigão Malheiro, *A Escravidão*, II, pp. 223, 229.

[23] Viotti da Costa, *Da Senzala*, p. 385. The law of 1869 prohibited the sale of children under fifteen, but in 1871 the Law of the Free Womb lowered the age to twelve. Joe Taylor, *Slavery in Louisiana*, pp. 40–41. The Louisiana law imposed a fine of $1,000 to $2,000 for selling children separate from a living mother. Taylor found several cases of traders who were both fined and jailed for disobeying the law though sales documents he consulted showed that most traders apparently obeyed the requirement.

[24] Stampp, *Peculiar Institution*, pp. 239–41, 252, acknowledges the effort of planters to avoid breaking up of families; see also Edward W. Phifer, "Slavery in Microcosm: Burke County, North Carolina," *Journal of Southern History*, XXVIII (May, 1962), 48.

both more common and easier than in the United States. Yet, even in this area of comparison the contrast is less sharp than is often said; manumission in Brazil was not without restriction and in the United States it was not absolutely denied. Moreover, the purchase of freedom by the slave himself, so much emphasized in discussions on the nature of Brazilian slavery, was far from rare in the United States. Sumner Matison, for example, found several hundred examples of self-purchase. James Hugo Johnston, searching the governors' papers in Virginia, came across at least ninety-one instances of free Negroes who had purchased their own freedom, a number of them being assisted in the accumulation of money by whites. Luther Jackson, studying self-purchase in three cities of Virginia, uncovered twenty examples even at the height of the sectional tensions of the 1850's and despite a law requiring removal of manumitted slaves out of the state. Kenneth Stampp cites instances, too, of slaves buying their own time, and on occasion, one buying his freedom by installments.[25]

On the Brazilian side of the comparison it needs to be said that prior to 1871, despite tradition and the assertions of some historians, there was no law requiring a master to permit a slave to buy his freedom, though many undoubtedly did. One American historian of Brazil made a search for such a law, but found none prior to 1871, when emancipationists insisted upon it, a fact that in itself suggests the practice of self-purchase was not as firmly protected as often is alleged.[26] It is true, nevertheless, that Brazilian law contained none of the limitations on manumission that prevailed in the southern United States, especially after 1830. All of the southern states, for instance, threw obstacles in the path of the master who sought to free his slave, not the least of which was the requirement that all newly freed slaves must leave the state. Under Brazilian law, on the other hand, emancipation was

[25] Sumner E. Matison, "Manumission by Purchase," *Journal of Negro History*, XXXIII (April, 1948), 165; James Hugo Johnston, *Race Relations in Virginia and Miscegenation in the South, 1776–1860* (Amherst, Mass., 1970), p. 8; Luther P. Jackson, "Manumission in Certain Virginia Cities," *Journal of Negro History*, XV (July, 1930), 306; Stampp, *Peculiar Institution*, p. 96.

[26] Mary Wilhemine Williams, "The Treatment of Negro Slaves in the Brazilian Empire: a Comparison with the United States of America," *Journal of Negro History*, XV (July, 1930), 331.

legal in almost any form, whether by letter, by will, or by simple but explicit statement at baptism.[27] The law in Brazil, however, did contain a curious qualification to its otherwise openhanded attitude toward emancipation. It provided that freedom might be revoked by the master for ingratitude on the part of the freedman, even if that ingratitude was expressed only orally and outside of the presence of the former master! Perdigão Malheiro, who reports this provision of the law, doubted that it was still valid in 1866. But in 1871 this power to revoke freedom was explicitly withdrawn by an antislavery law, suggesting that the old provision was not such a dead letter that opponents of slavery wanted it to remain on the statute books.[28]

The provision also raises a question as to whether the law in Brazil was in fact helping to preserve the Negro's moral personality under slavery, as has sometimes been argued. At the very least such a provision encouraged masters to think of their Negroes as minors or wards rather than as persons on an equal footing with themselves. At worst, the provision perpetuated in the Negro that sense of subordination and inferiority derived from the degraded status of slavery. To the extent that such a sense of subordination was inculcated in blacks it would tend to nullify whatever sense of independence and hopeful expectations that the generally easy and open opportunities for manumission might have encouraged in Negro slaves.

Some commentators on slavery in the United States and Latin America assert that the slave's right to hold property in South America, as contrasted with the lack of such a right in the United

[27] Perdigão Malheiro, *A Escravidão*, I, p. 95 sets forth the ways in which manumission may be obtained in Brazil; ibid., II, pp. 94–95 makes evident that the thrust of the law was toward liberty.

[28] Ibid., I, pp. 167–68; Gouveia, *História da Escravidão*, p. 396. The Code Noir of Louisiana, which also had liberal provisions for manumission, contained the following restrictions: "We command all manumitted slaves to show the profoundest respect to their former masters, to their widows and children, and any injury or insult offered by said manumitted slaves to their former master, their widow or children, shall be punished with more severity than if it had been offered by any other person." Quoted in Joe Taylor, *Slavery in Louisiana*, p. 16. A similar provision was a part of the medieval law of slavery of Portugal; see Manuel Heleno, *Os Escravos em Portugal* (Lisboa, 1933), I, p. 166: "In case of ingratitude, the patron had the possibility of annulling the manumission."

States, made it easier for him to buy his freedom in Brazil than in the United States. Actually, the law in Brazil did not permit slaves to possess property—or a peculium—until near the end of the slave era. For as Perdigão Malheiro wrote in his treatise on slave law in 1866, "among us, no law guarantees to the slave his peculium." However, he goes on, most masters permitted slaves to keep whatever property they gathered, letting them use it as they saw fit.[29] Generally, the same situation in law and in practice prevailed in the United States. Slaves' property was neither recognized nor protected by law in any of the southern states, but in practice most slave owners permitted their slaves to keep whatever property they earned from work on their own time. It was a cruel as well as a rare master in the United States, as in Brazil, who deliberately, if legally, confiscated earnings that his slave may have accumulated. Occasionally in the United States, on the other hand, the courts would throw a protective arm around the peculium, as in a South Carolina case in 1792. The court held that a slave was capable of possessing property separate from that of his master. On the basis of that decision, fifty years later the South Carolina high court concluded that though the earlier case "goes further than I desire to go . . . it is ample authority to prove that by the law of this state a slave might acquire *personal property.*"[30]

Finally, in trying to put into perspective the argument that manumission was much easier in Brazil than in the United States, a remark of Joaquim Nabuco, the great Brazilian abolitionist, is appropriate. Writing in 1881, Nabuco noted that between 1873 and that date some 87,000 slaves had been privately manumitted in the country. Although admitting that such a number testified to the generosity of some Brazilians, Nabuco pointed out that most of the manumissions, even at that late date in the history

[29] Perdigão Malheiro, *A Escravidão*, I, p. 60.
[30] Helen T. Catterall, ed., *Judicial Cases Concerning Slavery and the Negro*, 5 vols., (Washington, 1926), II, p. 267; Carmille v. Carmille (South Carolina, 1842), 2 McMullan 646. At another place on the same page the judge expanded his statement to read, "Looking back over our legislation, and our decided cases, and the usage of our people, I think that we are well sustained in saying *that a slave may acquire and hold in possession personal property, (not prohibited to him or her by Act of the Legislature) with the consent of the master or mistress, and that such property is in law to be regarded as the property of the owner of the slave.*" Emphasis in original.

of slavery, were mostly by small, urban holders, not by large planters. With some irony, he pointed out that in the province of Rio de Janeiro over the previous ten years, death "freed" 51,269 slaves whereas masters freed only 12,849 in a province that counted 333,000 slaves.[31]

Yet, after making all these qualifications to the usually optimistic picture of the opportunities for manumission in Brazil, the balance must still come down on the side that sees that country as more liberal in this regard than the United States. In this aspect of slavery lies one of the principal differences between the two systems. The chief reason for drawing that conclusion is the considerably higher proportion of free Negroes in nineteenth century Brazil than in the United States. Although there is some reason to believe that the disparity may not have been as great in the colonial period, the paucity of even reasonably accurate figures prior to 1800 compels us to confine the comparison to the nineteenth century. According to the traditional estimates, in 1817–18 the number of slaves in Brazil was about three times that of free Negroes and mulattoes. This ratio may be compared with that in the United States in 1860, when the number of free Negroes reached its maximum under slavery. At that date there were eight times as many slaves as free Negroes in the whole of the United States and sixteen times as many slaves as free blacks if the comparison is made in the slave states alone. After abolition in the United States, the number of free Negroes in Brazil grew enormously. Thus in 1872 the number of free Negroes and colored was more than double the number of slaves![32] Here is certainly a striking difference between the two slave societies. How might one account for it?

Two explanations are worth looking at. One of these is that Brazilian masters freed the sick and the old in order to relieve themselves of responsibility and financial loss. Frequent denunciations in newspapers and laws seeking to stop such practices

---

[31] Joaquim Nabuco, *O Abolicionismo* in *Obras completas,* 14 vols. (São Paulo, 1944–49), p. 209. The French traveler Ribeyrolles noted that manumission was "rarer on the plantation than in the city and almost always" involved the skilled workers and domestics. Charles Ribeyrolles, *Brasil pitoresco,* 2 vols. (São Paulo, n.d.), II, p. 38.

[32] Perdigão Malheiro, *A Escravidão* (1866), Part 3, pp. 13–14; Raymond S. Sayers, *The Negro in Brazilian Literature* (New York, 1956), p. 7.

leave no doubt that some masters were indeed freeing their infirm, aged, and incurably sick slaves.[33] Yet it is difficult to believe that such practices, even as widespread and common as the sources lead us to believe them to be, could have been the principal source of the relatively large free colored population. Infirm, aged, or sick slaves simply would not have been numerous enough themselves or have been able to produce offspring in sufficient numbers to account for the great number of free Negroes and mulattoes in the society.

A more persuasive explanation is derived from the different processes of settlement and economic development in the two countries.[34] As we have noticed already, Negroes and mulattoes made up a majority of the population of Brazil prior to the last quarter of the nineteenth century. Whether as slaves or as free men, Negroes and mulattoes had a place in a society that was only sparsely populated and in a slave economy that concentrated upon staple production. The free blacks and mulattoes were needed to raise cattle, grow food, to serve as shopkeepers, craftsmen, peddlers, boatmen, and for a thousand other tasks. They filled the innumerable petty jobs, the interstitial work of the economy, that the constraints of slavery would not permit the slave to perform and that white men were insufficient or unwilling to man.

Furthermore, the booms and busts so characteristic of the colonial economy in Brazil provided incentives for manumission during the busts and jobs for freed slaves during the booms. Thus when the sugar economy of the northeast, where many slaves were concentrated, declined at the end of the seventeenth century, many planters escaped the burden of excessive slaves by freeing them or letting them support themselves as *negros dos ganhos*, or self-hired slaves. The discovery of gold and diamonds in Minas Gerais in the early eighteenth century (the second boom and bust cycle) opened a new frontier, which in turn created a

[33] Viotti Costa, *Da Senzala*, pp. 262–63; Stein, *Vassouras*, p. 79n.; see also the report of the British Minister to Brazil, August, 1852, quoting the effort of the President of Bahia Province to have the practice stopped by law, reprinted in Christie, *Notes on Brazilian Questions*, pp. 218–19.

[34] Marvin Harris, *Patterns of Race in the Americas* (New York, 1964), pp. 84–89; see also Edison Carneiro, *Ladinos e Crioulas* (Rio de Janeiro, 1964), pp. 11–12, 20–25.

new demand not only for slaves to work as miners, but also for cooks, shopkeepers, muleteers, and skilled and unskilled workers. Free and slave Negroes and mulattoes could and did fill these jobs. In the mining towns hired Negro slaves were exploited as never before, Edison Carneiro points out, leaving the Negro "more autonomous, more independent of the master, more responsible, personally, for his labor and for his behavior." A lucky find of gold or diamonds might also give a slave a chance to buy his freedom. Then, when the mines were largely worked out, masters of slaves once again escaped the burden of excess labor by freeing their slaves or letting them support themselves. In short, in colonial Brazil the master sometimes had good reason to free his slaves—to be rid of their expense in bad times—while the undermanned society and economy had a place and a need for the former slave.[35]

In the United States the economic and demographic patterns worked in the opposite direction. It is true that many plantations in the South also concentrated their slave labor on staple production and imported food and other supplies rather than growing or fashioning themselves. But the food and the supplies were produced by a large number of nonslaveholding whites in the South itself and in the Old Northwest. From the beginning of settlement in the South, much less in the United States as a whole, there had always been more than enough white men to perform all the tasks of the society *except* that of plantation worker. In a society with much empty land, few white men could be found to work for others. By the end of the eighteenth century white indentured servitude was fast dying out and the tobacco and rice plantations of the southern colonies had come to depend upon the labor of black slaves. In the nineteenth century perhaps three-fourths of the cotton grown in the South came from plantations on which black slaves supplied the labor. Indeed, it seems clear now that without black slaves the great Cotton Kingdom of the South simply could not have developed as rapidly as it did. Off the plantations, however, unlike the situation in Brazil, white

[35] Nelson de Senna, *Africanos no Brasil* (Belo Horizonte, Brazil, 1938), p. 62; Carneiro, *Ladinos e Crioulas*, pp. 20–25; Octavio Ianni, *As Metamorfoses do Escravo* (São Paulo, 1962), p. 175; Caio Prado, Junior, *História Economica do Brasil*, 10th ed. (n.p., n.d.) p. 45 suggests that cattle raising in the back country of the Northeast required free men rather than slaves.

labor was more than ample for the needs and expansion of the economy. Indeed, throughout the antebellum years, as for years afterward, the South actually exported white people to the rest of the nation.

In the nineteenth century Cotton Kingdom there was little need or compelling economic reason for emancipation, for generally the economy prospered. The boom and bust pattern of Brazil did not occur in the cotton South. The only time that the slave economy of the United States came close to the boom and bust cycle was just after the Revolutionary War. At that time indigo production in South Carolina was failing rapidly because of the withdrawals of the British subsidy and tobacco markets were depressed by the loss of British markets and by the competition from other tobacco producing areas in the New World. Furthermore, the English demand for cotton had not yet brought the Cotton Kingdom into being. Not surprisingly, during this period of transition, before cotton gave slavery a new lease on life, several thousand slaves were manumitted in Virginia and slavery was abolished in all the states north of the Mason and Dixon line. At the time many men, both north and south of the line, honestly believed that slavery would be abolished throughout the nation within a short time. In fact, of course, abolition made no more progress for another three quarters of a century, but that story is not our concern here. The point is that for a brief period in the United States a decline in a staple product had affected masters' willingness to emancipate in much the same way as a comparable economic situation had affected Brazilian masters.

Shifts in the late eighteenth century economy of the United States may have provided a brief and inadequate inducement to emancipation, but at no time did the United States economy provide a place for those who might be manumitted. Slaves in the United States supplied a unique, yet important kind of labor, as we have seen; one that was in high demand in a society in which land was plentiful but hired labor expensive. All other forms of labor, however, were easily and quickly taken care of by the large free white population, which was steadily increased by an ever growing white immigration from Europe. In Brazil, on the other hand, the small size of the white population and relatively small amount of free white immigration (at least until the European immigration in the last quarter of the nineteenth century) meant that Negroes and mulattoes served as settlers, in the broadest sense of the word, as well as slaves.

We shall have occasion to return to the question of manumission before the end of this chapter, for behind the explanation just offered lies another meaning for this crucial difference between the two slave systems. And that meaning will require a broader cultural explanation than can be essayed at this point. For the moment, however, let us return to other differences between the slave systems of Brazil and the United States.

Rebellions and Runaways

Comparisons between Brazilian and United States slavery commonly emphasize the greater rebelliousness of slaves in Brazil. Certainly historians of the United States have often commented upon the relatively few slave rebellions in the long history of slavery. Herbert Aptheker in *American Negro Slave Revolts*, it is true, identified some 250 revolts. But when it is recognized that he defined a revolt as any act of collective resistance involving ten or more slaves and that the period of time he covered was more than a century and the area was about the size of western Europe, the number ceases to be impressive. When it is further recognized that Aptheker accepted rumors of revolts and unverified reports in reaching his total, it becomes clear that large numbers of revolts by slaves were indeed not frequent in United States history. When one has counted the revolt at Stono, South Carolina, in 1739, that at New Orleans in 1811, and the Nat Turner upheaval at Southampton, Virginia, in 1831, the principal revolts have been listed. Others often cited, such as those led by Gabriel Prosser (1800) and Denmark Vesey (1822), never even came to a head; they remained conspiracies. Throughout the whole of the Civil War no major slave revolt took place, it is worth recalling, though controls at that time were, perforce, probably the weakest in the history of slavery.

Few and far between as the rebellions may have been in the United States, the contrast with Brazil is not as sharp as the usual comparisons often assert. The most often cited measure of the greater rebelliousness of Brazilian slaves, for example, is the great slave hideaway or *quilombo* of Palmares, situated deep in the backcountry of northeastern Brazil and counting 20,000 inhabitants at its height. For almost the whole length of the seventeenth century Palmares fought off the repeated assaults of governmental and other troops before it was destroyed in 1698. Many other *quilombos,* less spectacularly enduring or less well known than Palmares are equally well documented.[36]

It is questionable, however, whether such collective runaways, no matter how long-lived or however large in scale, ought to be classed as slave rebellions. Generally, the *quilombo* neither attempted to overthrow the slave system nor made war on it. *Quilombolos* clashed with white society only when the whites sought to bring back the runaways or, as in the case of Palmares, acted to remove what the whites perceived as a threat to the unity of Brazilian society. The rulers of Palmares, on the other hand, would have been quite content to have remained aloof as an African state, separated by the forest from white society, if the government and whites in general had let them alone. Edison Carneiro, a leading Brazilian student of *quilombos* and of Palmares in particular, contends that the hideaways were always the attacked and never the attackers. "It appears certain," he writes, "that the type of agriculture and the hunting and fishing developed by the Negroes in the larger, more populous and more enduring *quilombos* pricked the cupidity of the neighboring villages, desirous of adding a little more to their lands, and of the back country people, ambitious for riches and power. It was well known that the lands of Palmares were the best in all the captaincy of Pernambuco—the war of words for its possession was not less nor more gentle than the war against Zumbi [the

[36] The best and most recent study of Palmares in English is R. K. Kent, "Palmares: An African State in Brazil," *Journal of African History,* VI, No. 2 (1965), 161–75. Kent emphasizes the African character of Palmares more than most commentators. See also Clovis Moura, *Rebelioes da Senzala (Quilombos, Insurreiçoes, Guerrilhas)* (São Paulo, 1959), pp. 72–79; Russell-Wood, *Fidalgos and Philanthropists,* p. 141 refers to a *quilombo* in Minas Gerais in 1747 that numbered a thousand persons; Maria Stella de Novaes, *A Escravidão e a abolição no Espirito Santo* (Vitoria, Brazil, 1963), pp. 85–88 reports on several *quilombos,* as does Carneiro, *Ladinos e Crioulas,* p. 27.

black leader of Palmares]." One of the major eighteenth century *quilombos* of Mato Grosso was discovered accidentally by gold seekers and destroyed in an effort to seize its wealth.[37]

In short, if the criterion is armed uprisings against slave holders, like that which took place under Nat Turner, then the total number of rebellions in Brazil is considerably smaller when the *quilombos* are not included. For as Carneiro has pointed out, "The most used resource by black slaves in Brazil for purposes of escape . . . was without doubt that of fleeing to the forest, from which resulted the *quilombo*." [38] In Brazil, as in the United States, the commonest expression of slave unrest was the runaway, not the insurrectionist.

Confusing *quilombos* with revolts is not the only reason for questioning the Brazilian slave's traditional reputation for rebelliousness. Foreign travelers during the nineteenth century and historians of Brazil since have also done so. Henry Koster, the English planter living in Brazil, for example, wrote in the early nineteenth century that "Pernambuco has never experienced any serious revolt among the slaves," though the province at that time probably contained a majority of slaves. Later in the century the German artist John Rugendas reported that "revolts of the blacks . . . have been rare in Brazil and never have had great importance," although he had been told of Palmares. Modern historians of the coffee country point out that neither slave revolts nor *quilombos* were on anything but a small scale. One recent study, for example, speaks of revolts "as rare in the coffee regions." Another student of slavery found little opportunity for, or evidence of slave revolts in the southern province of Rio Grande do Sul, though he also depicted slavery as particularly harsh in that region. In the northern province of Ceará "fugitives were not common and rebellions very rare," concludes one historian of slavery in that province. Octavio Eduardo reports that "no series of revolts occurred in Maranhão [province] as they

---

37 Ibid., pp. 31–32, 77–83.

38 For Negroes in the South during the Civil War see James H. Brewer, *The Confederate Negro* (Durham, N.C., 1969), and Bell Wiley, *Southern Negroes, 1861–1865* (New Haven, Conn., 1938). Carneiro, *Ladinos e Crioulas*, p. 26 notes that running away was the most common form of slave resistance in Brazil.

[*sic*] did in Bahia, although the revolt of the Balaios from 1838–41" attracted runaway slaves to its cause.[39]

Even those modern historical works that emphasize the rebelliousness of Brazilian slaves raise doubts in the reader's mind. Certain Brazilian historians of the Negro, like their counterparts in the United States, apparently feel called upon to defend the Negro against charges of docility while in slavery.[40] "What is intended in this book," writes Luiz Luna in his recent *O Negro na Luta Contra a Escravidão* (The Negro in the Struggle Against Slavery), "is that the mass of captive Negroes did not remain in slavery with their arms crossed. The Negroes resisted in every way that they could." Later he writes, "The Negro, contrary to what is customarily said, never submitted peacefully to slavery. In general he reacted by any means he could. When he did, the reaction—individual or collective—was violent."[41] Such comments suggest that the author protests too much; one begins to suspect that the reputation for docility was not only widely held, but not entirely wrong. Unfortunately, writers like Luiz Luna and historians of a similar persuasion in the United States have mistakenly equated a dearth of slave rebellions with the acceptance of slavery by Negroes. To admit that slave rebellions were few or even unimportant is not to indict Negroes for docility or racial suitability for slavery or any equally absurd charge to which rebelliousness is supposed to be the proper answer. Slave rebellions were extremely difficult as well as dangerous to plan and carry out at any time or place, regardless of the race of the slaves. Slave revolts were not common in antiquity, either. And when the slaves were readily identifiable as were Negroes, planning and organizing was even more difficult. Moreover, the difficulty stemmed not only from the fact that the preponderance

[39] Koster, *Travels in Brazil*, II, p. 258; Rugendas, *Viagem pitoresco*, p. 204; Roger Bastide, ed., *Relações raciais entre negroes e brancos em São Paulo* (São Paulo, 1955), p. 199; Viotti da Costa, *Da Senzala*, pp. 315, 300–301; Fernando Henrique Cardoso, *Capitalismo e Escravidão no Brasil meridional* (São Paulo, 1962), pp. 159–60; Girão, *A Abolição no Ceará*, p. 42; Octavio da Costa Eduardo, *The Negro in Northern Brazil* (New York, 1948), p. 18.

[40] See, for example, Moura, *Rebeliões da Senzala;* Aderbal Jurema, *Insureições negras no Brasil* (Recife, 1935); Luiz Luna, *O Negro na Luta Contra a Escravidão* (Rio de Janeiro, 1968).

[41] Ibid., pp. 13, 65.

of power was in the hands of the masters, but also from the psychological handicap that slavery imposed upon those raised under the system. Most slaves could not help but see slavery as a part of the natural order of the world. Once the difficulties, if not the dangers to the slaves, stemming from rebellion are appreciated, then there is no need to inflate relatively minor clashes between masters and slaves into rebellions, as is too often done, or to insist upon continuous violence when sporadic outbreaks were all that could be expected.

Yet even when these qualifications are taken into consideration, it is still accurate to see slave rebellions as more numerous in Brazil than in the United States. Among the good reasons for arriving at that conclusion are the series of bloody rebellions in and around the city of Bahia between 1807 and 1835, which have no analog in the history of United States slavery. We shall return to these remarkable uprisings a little later for they are worth examination in their own right as well as for the light they shed on the reasons why there were more rebellions in Brazil than in the United States.

The revolts in Brazil were not only somewhat more numerous, but were generally also larger in size. A mid-nineteenth century revolt in the province of Rio de Janeiro, for example, mobilized three hundred slaves and required federal troops to suppress it. In 1820 at least two revolts, involving several hundred slaves each, were reported in the province of Minas Gerais.[42] On the other hand, of the three uprisings in the United States that have already been mentioned as the largest, only the one that occurred outside of New Orleans engaged more than a hundred slaves.

Similarly, *quilombos* or maroons in the United States were considerably fewer and smaller in size than those in Brazil.[43] As far as the *quilombos* are concerned, probably the best explanation for the difference is simply the climate. Winter in most of the United States is much too harsh for a *quilombo* to survive for long; almost all of Brazil, on the other hand, lies in the tropics, which requires less substantial shelter and provides easier access to food for runaways than the changing seasons of the United

[42] Stein, *Vassouras*, p. 145; Viotti da Costa, *Da Senzala*, p. 304.

[43] The principal study of *quilombos* or maroons in the United States is Herbert Aptheker, "Maroons Within the Present Limits of the United States," *Journal of Negro History*, XXIV (April, 1939), 167–84.

States. Furthermore, even the frontier areas of the United States were too well settled and accordingly too well policed, especially after the seventeenth century, to provide safety for maroons for any length of time. The only example of a United States maroon's approaching the size and endurance of Palmares was the one that history calls the Second Seminole War. During that struggle in the 1830's runaway blacks and Indians held out against the United States Army for seven years.[44] Significantly, the hideaway was located in the warmest part of the United States—Florida—and in an area then only thinly settled by whites.

The International Slave Trade As Cause

The conclusion that on balance, revolts and *quilombos* were of greater frequency and size in Brazil than in the United States serves to introduce another difference between the two slave societies. That is the greater dependence of the Brazilians upon the African slave trade. There is good reason to believe, as we shall see, that the greater number of revolts and *quilombos* in Brazil is directly related to the continuation of the slave trade.

Although the slave trade from Africa to Brazil was supposedly ended in 1831 by treaty with Great Britain, the importation of slaves continued at high annual levels for at least another twenty years. Over 300,000 slaves, for example, entered Brazil from Africa between 1842 and 1851 alone.[45] On the other hand, the importation of large numbers of slaves into the United States ceased in 1808, when the federal government prohibited the further importation of slaves. In fact, the importation of large numbers of slaves had slowed down considerably even before that date. Prior to 1800 each one of the slave states had itself prohibited importation at one time or another. Only in South Carolina was the slave trade open at the time it was closed for

[44] For a discussion on the *quilombo* among the Seminoles, see Kenneth W. Porter, "Negroes and the Seminole War, 1835–1842," *Journal of Southern History*, XXX (November, 1964), 427–40.

[45] Maurício Goulart, *Escravidão africana no Brasil*, 2nd ed. (São Paulo, 1950), pp. 249–63; the total figure for slaves is given in Stein, *Vassouras*, p. 294. Christie, *Notes on Brazilian Questions*, pp. 69–70 insists that when he was writing, in 1865, slaves numbered three millions; the lack of a national census makes it impossible to arrive at a more precise or definite figure.

good by the federal government in 1808. It is therefore quite accurate to see the United States as ceasing to depend upon foreign importations even before the nineteenth century opened.

That Brazil kept open the slave trade while the United States closed it accounts for a number of differences in the nature of slavery in the two places. The larger size and number of *quilombos* in Brazil as compared with those in the United States was in part, at least, a consequence of the large number of African-born slaves in Brazil. As Raymond Kent has shown, the great *quilombo* of Palmares is most accurately seen as a reproduction of an African state, suggesting that it was African-born slaves who founded this greatest of Brazilian slave hideaways. Edison Carneiro has concluded that African-born slaves generally provided a nucleus for the formation of *quilombos*. "The type of social organization created by the *quilombolas*," he has written, "was so close to the type of organization then dominant in the African states that even if there were no other reasons, one could say with confidence that the Negroes responsible for it were in large part recently arrived from Africa, and not creole Negroes, born and raised in Brazil." The Brazilian-born slaves, he goes on, used other means of expressing their discontent with slavery. Because they were familiar with the Portuguese language, for example, the creole slaves were more likely to run away to the cities where they could pass themselves off as free blacks. A French scholar who has studied the maroons of the French Caribbean colonies also has emphasized the influence of Africans in sparking and implementing the slave hideaways in that area of the New World.[46]

[46] Kent, "Palmares," *Journal of African History* (1965) emphasizes the African origins of the great *quilombo* of the seventeenth century. "The quilombo of the Palmares was a Negro State similar to the many which existed in Africa in the seventeenth century" is the comment in Edison Carneiro, *O Quilombo dos Palmares*, 3rd ed. (Rio de Janeiro, 1966), p. 4; Carneiro, *Ladinos e Crioulas*, pp. 26, 29, 335 also emphasizes the role of the African-born slaves in the *quilombos* and among runaways in general. Yvan Debbasch, "Le Marronage. Essai sur la desertion de l'esclave antillais," 1re Partie, *L'Annee Sociologique*, Troisieme Serie (1961), pp. 5–9 also calls attention to the significant role of Africans in the revolts and runaways in the Caribbean islands. He tends to think that contemporaries placed more emphasis upon the African-born sources of runaways than was in fact the case. See also Roger Bastide, *Les Ameriques Noires. Les Civilizations africaines dans le nouveau monde* (Paris, 1967), pp. 51–57.

Newly imported Africans also seem to have played a part in bringing about the greater number of rebellions in Brazil; some authorities have made the point quite categorically.[47] Certainly it is plausible to see Africans as providing a basis for rebellions. Under any circumstances, as has been said, revolts were hard to organize and even more difficult to carry out, if only because success was so unlikely, that is, suicidal. But rebellions were especially difficult to organize under a system of slavery like that in the United States, where the slaves were principally native-born and thus almost entirely bereft of their African culture or identity. For some sense of slave unity, coupled with alienation from the master's society, would seem to be essential to the mounting of a revolt. But virtually all of the slaves in the United States were natives, raised from birth to be a part of the system. Native-born slaves were united by little more than their common degradation, while divided by their many personal connections with the whites among whom they lived. In Brazil, on the other hand, the presence of thousands of newly arrived Africans, who were resentfully hostile to their new masters and society while also united by their common African tribal culture, provided a basis for slave rebellions that was clearly lacking in the United States, especially after the Revolution.

There is substantial evidence to support the view that newly imported Africans were closely associated with rebellion. Stanley Stein points out for the coffee county he studied in Rio de Janeiro province that just as the number of imported Africans reached a peak, a rash of attempted uprisings occurred. At that time, too, many Brazilians believed that Africans were a prime source of discontent and rebellion. Government officials sought to suppress African customs such as dances, languages, and religious rites, which they recognized might serve as a nucleus for a plot or a revolt. Newspapers in nineteenth century Brazilian cities like Rio de Janeiro, Recife, and Bahia deplored the African dances of the slaves, even to the point of demanding the intervention of the police. Not surprisingly, the survival of African rites and customs was particularly evident in the cities, where the slaves

[47] See, for example, Mörner, *Race Mixture*, p. 76 and Robert Brent Toplin, "Upheaval, Violence, and the Abolition of Slavery in Brazil: The Case of São Paulo," *Hispanic-American Historical Review*, XLIX (November, 1969), 640–41.

had the greatest freedom of movement and the strongest likelihood of meeting with slaves from their own nation and who spoke their African language.[48] The public authorities were well aware, apparently, of the dangers inherent in permitting slaves of the same nation from Africa to be together. Hence they sometimes encouraged rivalries among the African nations in order to forestall that commonality indispensable for a revolt. One foreign traveler believed that national differences among the slaves was the primary protection against rebellions in Brazil. "The race of blacks carried from Africa to Brazil," wrote the German Carl Seidler, "is varied and this must contribute much to the fact that in spite of the great numerical superiority of the blacks, one never hears talk of a general uprising against the whites." For if there was an uprising, Seidler went on, the enmities carried over from Africa would bring many blacks to the side of the whites. During the colonial period, too, it was widely believed that only divisions among the African nations of the slaves prevented uprisings. Masters, it was said, deliberately purchased slaves of different nations to forestall rebellion.[49]

Perhaps the strongest reason for ascribing a central role to the presence of Africans in accounting for the revolts in Brazil is provided by the great rebellions in Bahia in the first third of the nineteenth century. For there the usual divisiveness among the Africans was overcome by special circumstances, principally a common African nation and a common religion. Given the difficulties of rebellion, it is not surprising that this series of revolts is not only without analog in the United States, but is without duplication in any other part of Brazil or in any other period of Brazilian history. Although not all of the eleven revolts or conspiracies that have been identified were of equal intensity or size, those of 1813, 1830, and 1835 involved considerable numbers of armed slaves, by United States standards, and all required gov-

[48] Stein, Vassouras, p. 145; Viotti da Costa, Da Senzala, p. 232; Cardoso and Ianni, Côr e mobilidade social, pp. 126–27; Luna, Negro na Luta, pp. 222–23.

[49] Carneiro, Ladinos e Crioulas, p. 67; Viotti da Costa, Da Senzala, pp. 235, 252, 308; Bastide, ed., Relações raciais, p. 172; Carl Seidler, De Anos no Brasil, trans. Bertaldo Klinger (São Paulo, n.d.), p. 239; Russell-Wood, Fidalgos and Philanthropists, p. 141; Charles Ralph Boxer, The Golden Age of Brazil, 1695–1750 (Berkeley, 1962), pp. 176–77, 313.

ernment troops to suppress them. Some six hundred slaves, for example, were implicated in the revolt of 1813 and before the smaller revolt of 1830 was suppressed more than fifty blacks had been killed and forty taken prisoner. In that revolt the rebels opened a slave pen in the city, releasing a hundred slaves and wounding another eighteen who refused to follow their fellows. In the last and greatest of the series, that of 1835, forty slaves were killed and some 281 slaves and freedmen captured by the authorities. Originally, sixty of the rebels were condemned to hanging, but pardons reduced the number who were actually executed to five. (The mildness of the Brazilian response sharply contrasts with the bloodletting that followed upon the smaller Nat Turner rebellion in Virginia, where seventeen rebels were hanged. In 1822 as a result of the Denmark Vesey *conspiracy*, in which *no* whites lost their lives, thirty-five blacks were hanged for participating in a plot, the very existence of which has been recently questioned.) [50]

At the time and since, it has been widely recognized that African-born slaves were at the center of the Bahian revolts. Hausa Negroes dominated in four of the early ones while Yoruba (Nâgo) Negroes were the principal actors in five of the later revolts. In the revolt of 1809, Hausas and Yorubas actually cooperated in the conspiracy, Pierre Verger points out, though in Africa they had been enemies. In Christian, European Brazil, Verger observes, they were united by the "ties of Islam." The documents captured from the rebels of 1835, significantly, were written in Arabic script, and though Raymond Kent casts some doubt on the traditional view that the revolt was a kind of religious holy war, there is no doubt that many of the rebels were Muslims. Religious instruction in Islam was apparently provided in the houses of some of the free Negro conspirators, with the lessons being taught in an African language, for some of the captured rebels did not even know the Christian names of their fellows. Thus a common African national culture, language, and

[50] Moura, *Rebeliões da Senzala*, pp. 181–82, 184. On the severity of the United States revolts see Ulrich B. Phillips, *American Negro Slavery* (New York, 1918), p. 481; Clement Eaton, *The Growth of Southern Civilization 1790–1800* (New York, 1961), p. 75. The existence of the Vesey plot is called into question in Richard C. Wade, "The Vesey Plot: A Reconsideration," *Journal of Southern History*, XXX (May, 1964), 143–61.

religion provided the indispensable cement of organization as well as incentives to revolt. It is relevant, too, that slaves who came to Brazil on the same ship from Africa thereafter viewed themselves as having a special fellowship or relationship, which they called *malungo*, or comrade.[51]

Events that followed the revolt of 1835 make even clearer the conviction of contemporaries that recently arrived Africans were prone to rebellion. Bahian officials concluded, for instance, that many of the Yorubas, who had been at the heart of the revolt, would have to be sent back to Africa, if such outbreaks were to be prevented in the future.

Consequently, the provincial legislature provided for the founding of a colony in Africa and some 147 Africans were forcefully repatriated, with as many as seven hundred passports being actually provided for blacks, slave or free, who wished to return to Africa. The government also prohibited the further importation of African war drums. The provincial president's report, which told of the Africans' departure, clearly reflected the whites' fear of the Africans. "The evil [of the revolt] has been seriously diminished," the president wrote, "and the fear of a new insurrection is now less justified. However, if that danger is not imminent, it is still not dispelled, and as long as these barbarians, our inevitable enemies, live among us, they will never desist from their black designs." Almost twenty years later a British consul in Bahia reported that Bahian officials still feared that rebellion would be ignited by the Africans in their midst. The Bahian chief of police,

[51] Raymundo Nina Rodrigues, *Os Africanos no Brasil,* 2nd ed. (São Paulo, 1935), pp. 82–94; Ramos, *The Negro in Brazil,* pp. 30–31, 36–37; Donald Pierson, *Negroes in Brazil* (Chicago, 1942), pp. 39–49; The religious element in the Bahian revolt of 1835 is central in the explanations of Roger Bastide, *Les Religions africaines au Brésil* (Paris, 1960), p. 146 and Pierre Verger, *Flux et Reflux de la Traite des Negres entre Le Golfe de Benin et Bahia de Todos os Santos du XVIIᵉ au XIXᵉ siecle* (Paris, 1968), pp. 326–27. On *malungo* see Arthur Ramos, "O Espirito associativo do negro brasileiro," *Revista do Archivo municipal de São Paulo,* XLVII (1938), 107. In offering a general explanation for the relatively large number of slave revolts in Jamaica, Orlando Patterson, *Sociology of Slavery* (London, 1967), pp. 273–76, emphasizes the high proportion of slaves to whites (about ten to one) and the large number of African-born slaves. "It is significant," Patterson writes, "that almost every one of the revolts of the seventeenth and eighteenth centuries was instigated and carried out by African slaves."

the consul wrote to his home office, wanted to send them back to Africa, though they were legally entitled to remain in Brazil. "The prisons are full of free Africans" he wrote, by which he meant slaves brought into the country after the closing of the slave trade in 1831. Although technically free under Brazilian law, such Negroes were not so treated by Brazilians. The Africans were being kept in jail not only out of fear of rebellion, but in order to intimidate other Africans to return to their native land.[52]

The presence of large numbers of newly arrived Africans was not the only factor that set Bahia off from other areas of Brazil. The city also enjoyed a connection with Africa no other Brazilian, much less United States, port could match for directness and closeness. During the eighteenth and early nineteenth centuries, for example, at least four official embassies came from West African states to visit Bahia, not to mention the shuttling of lesser individuals and many goods between Bahia and West Africa. Pierre Verger has thoroughly documented the remarkable exchange of customs, language, and even architecture between Bahia and West Africa. If an African culture of some development and endurance is essential to the triggering of slave revolts, then the steady movement of people, goods, and ideas from West Africa to Bahia and back again during these years is significant in explaining the Bahian revolts.[53]

That there were no more revolts in Bahia after 1835 may also be related to the West African connection. The early nineteenth century saw a shift in the sources of slaves for Brazil from West Africa to the Congo and Angola regions. Negroes of these regions were less aggressive and of a less advanced culture than those from West Africa. Neither slaveholders at the time nor later historians in Brazil have found the Angolan Negroes as prone to violent resistance to slavery as the Hausa and Yoruba. Perhaps most significant was the fact that the Angolans lacked the unifying force of a common religion—Islam, which, as we have seen, was widespread among the West Africans who came to Bahia.

[52] Carneiro, *Ladinos e Crioulas,* p. 69; Verger, *Flux et Reflux,* pp. 355–58, 537–38.

[53] Viotti da Costa, *Da Senzala,* p. 301; Verger, *Flux et Reflux,* Chapters VII and XVI and plates 31–52 present striking evidence of the movement of culture between Bahia and West Africa.

One authority, Luiz Vianna, has pointed out that once the Muslim religion was no longer prominent among the slaves of Bahia even insurrectionary plots severely declined. Thus in 1855 the police of the city of Bahia, fearing a slave uprising, searched the homes of blacks for signs of a plot. The investigators found not "the least plan of an insurrection," Vianna reports.[54]

Finally, one other element distinguishes these revolts from others in Brazil or in the United States. They broke out in or around the city of Bahia (São Salvador). In an urban milieu slaves enjoyed the maximum opportunity to move about freely, which was essential for organizing and carrying out rebellions. An urban environment also increased the likelihood that slaves of the same nation (and religion) would be able to get together.

Thus a number of factors conducive to rebellion coincided in Bahia, which did not come together elsewhere in Brazil and certainly not in the United States. It was this special concatenation of events and circumstances, it would seem, that accounted for the unusual number and violence of the slave revolts at that one place and in that relatively short space of time. Caio Prado, the eminent modern Brazilian historian, after noticing the unimportance of revolts in Brazil as compared, for example, with Haiti, calls attention to the diversity of African nationalities among the Brazilian slaves as one of the principal reasons for the small number. But, he goes on, that obstacle to revolt was not present in Bahia, "where the mass of slaves came to have a certain national unity (as well as the more elevated cultural level of the Sudanese)" and there "we encounter the greatest number of agitations and servile revolts." [55]

Rebellions may have been larger and more numerous in Brazil than in the United States, but the explanation has little or nothing to do with the difference in the laws of the state or in the prac-

---

[54] Philip D. Curtin, *The Atlantic Slave Trade. A Census* (Madison, Wis., 1969), p. 242 observes that in the nineteenth century "West Africa appears to have supplied a smaller proportion of Brazilian slave imports than it did in the eighteenth century." Also, after the early years of the nineteenth century British naval patrols effectively cut off the slave trade emanating from areas north of the equator. Luiz Vianna Filho, *O Negro na Bahia* (São Paulo, 1946), pp. 144–46.

[55] Prado, *Historia economica*, p. 142.

tices of the church. Much more significant in accounting for the difference in rebelliousness was the fact that in Brazil the continuance of the slave trade kept alive that sense of identity that was the tinder from which revolts could be ignited and the fuel with which they could be sustained.

That the slave trade stayed open in Brazil long after it was closed in the United States differentiated the two systems of slavery in still another way. Brazilian slaves and free Negroes maintained a connection with Africa that was almost entirely absent in the United States. Some slaves in Brazil, for example, after they had bought their freedom or otherwise gained manumission, elected to return to Africa. Not an inconsiderable number of former Brazilian slaves returned to West Africa to become important figures in society there, and some of them participated in the slave trade. So intimate was the connection between Brazil and Africa that until 1905 at least—almost twenty years after abolition—ships plied between Bahia (São Salvador) and Lagos, in present-day Nigeria, "repatriating nostalgic, emancipated Negroes and returning with West Coast products much prized by Africans and their descendants in Brazil." [56]

In the United States, on the other hand, efforts on the part of groups like the American Colonization Society to repatriate former slaves to Africa generally met with a frigid response from blacks. The great majority of slaves, after all, even in the early years of the nineteenth century, had been born in the United States and the memories of Africa were so dim as to provide little basis for the kind of migration and connection that occurred in Brazil. Efforts to arouse an interest in Africa among blacks in the United States have historically met with very little response until recently. There are many reasons for this lack of interest in or even aversion to Africa, but certainly one of them is the closing of the slave trade early in the history of slavery in the United

[56] David A. Ross, "The Career of Domingo Martinez in the Bight of Benin," *Journal of African History*, VI (1965), 83; Gilberto Freyre, *Nordeste* (Rio de Janeiro, 1937), pp. 130–31; Viotti da Costa, *Da Senzala*, pp. 56–57n.; Donald Pierson, "The Educational Process and the Brazilian Negro," *American Journal of Sociology* XLVIII (May, 1943), 695n.; Gilberto Freyre, *Ordem e Progresso*, 2nd ed. (Rio de Janeiro, 1962), p. 572, note 33. Verger, *Flux et Reflux* and José Honorio Rodrigues, *Brazil and Africa* (Berkeley, 1965) treat extensively the connections between Brazil and Africa.

States as compared with Brazil.[57] It has also meant that so-called African survivals are commonplace in modern Brazil, especially in Bahia, but almost undiscoverable among Negroes in the United States.

Slave Rearing As Consequence

The endurance and even expansion of United States slavery, without any substantial additions from importations, is unique in the world history of slavery. Neither in antiquity nor in Latin America was a slave system sustained principally by reproduction of the slave population. The highest estimate reported for the smuggling of slaves into the United States after the official closing of the slave trade in 1808 was 270,000. For the fifty years prior to 1860 that works out roughly to 5,000 per year. Large as this figure is, it cannot account for the rather steady rate of growth in the slave population recorded in the census. For example, in the 1790's, prior to the federal closing of the slave trade, the increase was a little less than 28 per cent; in the decade of the forties, a half-century later, the increase was slightly more than 28 per cent. The average *annual* increase for the 1790's was 20,000 slaves, whereas that for the 1840's was 70,000. Both average figures far exceed even the highest estimate for annual importations from abroad. Thus these high annual increases can be accounted for only by recognizing that the principal source of the slave population in the United States during the nineteenth century was natural increase.[58]

One consequence—as well as cause—of the dependence of

[57] On the attitudes of blacks in the United States toward colonization and Africa in general see P. J. Staudenraus, *The African Colonization Movement 1816–1865* (New York, 1961), Edwin S. Redkey, *Black Exodus. Black Nationalist and Back-to-Africa Movements, 1890–1910* (New Haven, Conn., 1969), and Hollis R. Lynch, "Pan-Negro Nationalism in the New World, Before 1862," reprinted in August Meier and Elliott Rudwick, eds., *The Making of Black America* (New York, 1969), I, pp. 42–65.

[58] Curtin, *Atlantic Slave Trade*, pp. 73–74 concludes that between the closing of the slave trade in 1808 and the end of slavery in 1865 only about 54,000 slaves were smuggled into the United States. Figures on slave population are conveniently collected in J. D. B. De Bow, *Statistical View of the United States*. . . . (Washington, D. C., 1854).

United States slavery upon natural increase was that the ratio between the sexes was virtually equal—at least in the nineteenth century. The first census to differentiate slaves by sex was that of 1820. At that date the ratio of the sexes was 95 women to each 100 men, suggesting that a near balance between the sexes must have obtained even before the closing of the slave trade in 1808. By 1830 the ratio was 98 to 100 and by 1850 it was more than 99 to 100. All of these ratios, significantly enough, are close to those for the white population in 1800, which counted 95 women to 100 men. The ratio in 1850 was the same, though there had been some fluctuation in between.

The pattern among the slaves is no different if each state's sex ratio is examined. By 1860, for example, each of the southern slave states, with the single exception of Louisiana, contained a surplus of males over females that was nowhere over 3 per cent of the total. Even in Louisiana, where the heavy demands for physical labor in the sugar mills was undoubtedly influential, the male surplus reached only 3.6 per cent. Again, this ratio among the slaves was closer to an absolute balance between the sexes than that which obtained among the whites themselves in five of the southern states, where the surplus of males ran between 4 and 8 per cent of the white population. At that time it was widely recognized—even in Brazil—that the states of the upper South, such as Virginia, Kentucky, and Maryland, were "breeding" states, that is, raisers and sellers of slaves to the states farther south. Yet these figures on the ratios between the sexes among the slaves suggest that, in general, all the slave states, even those in the Deep South, maintained the kind of balance between the sexes that was conducive to rearing slaves.

To speak of raising slaves in the United States South, however, ought not to be equated with arrangements on a stock farm, or at least not entirely so. It is true that examples have been found of plantations in which the women slaves far outnumbered the men, suggesting systematic breeding. And some planters have left personal records that clearly demonstrate that they bought females in order to translate the offspring into cash. Newspaper advertisements, too, sometimes suggested breeding as a possibility. A Charleston newspaper in 1838, for example, carried an advertisement offering to sell a woman slave of twenty years of age, with two children, aged two and four. She was described as "very prolific in her generating qualities, and affords a rare opportunity for any person who wishes to raise a family of strong and healthy servants for their own use." (That slave breeding was not condoned by the mores is suggested by the closing words, which sought to hide the possibility that the slave's "generating qualities" might be converted into cash through the *sale* of the children.) [59] On the whole, however, examples of deliberate breeding are rare.

Much more commonplace was the recognition and expectation that the pairing off of the sexes would quite naturally result in offspring. The concern for pairing is quite evidently assumed in a semiliterate overseer's letter to his master in 1835: "I wish the three girls you purchest had been all grown. They wold then bin a wife a pese for Harise & King & Nathan. Harris has Jane for a wife and Nathan has Edy. But King & Nathan has sum difuculty hoo wold have Edy. I promist King that I wold in dever to git you to bey a nother woman sow he might have a wife at home. He is envious that you wold git a nuther woman, as he has quit his wife that he had at Netoles, thinking that he wold git Edy for a wife. I am willing to take Vilet at the same price give for her and pay you the expence in bringing her from Mobile, or eny other expence you were at. As she is too young for eney of your men a wife and you hav small girls enough for your young boys, and then you can by a woman in her place for King a wife." [60]

Perhaps the most accurate description of the way in which so-called breeding of slaves actually took place was given by Edmund Ruffin, a Virginian planter who was much interested in agricultural reform and ultimately became a vehement secessionist. In one of his pamphlets on reform Ruffin observed that one source of income for Virginia farmers was "the breeding and selling of slaves." To say this, he went on, "is not meant to convey

[59] For some examples of apparently deliberate efforts at slave breeding see Stampp, *Peculiar Institution,* pp. 246–50 and Joe Taylor, *Slavery in Louisiana,* p. 102. In a judicial case in Mississippi in 1858 a planter, the plaintiff, was described as "an unsuccessful farmer, generally buying his corn and meat, but . . . he succeeded very well in raising young negroes." Quoted in Catterall, ed., *Judicial Cases,* III, p. 356. The quotation from the Charleston newspaper is in Frederic Bancroft, *Slave-Trading in the Old South* (Baltimore, 1931), p. 74.

[60] Quoted in Ulbrich Bonnell Phillips, *Life and Labor in the Old South* (Boston, 1929), p. 278.

the idea that any person undertakes as a regular business the breeding of slaves with a view to their sale; but whether it is intended or not, all of us, without exception, are acting some part in aid of a general system, which taken altogether, is precisely what I have named. No man is so inhuman as to breed and raise slaves, to sell off a certain proportion regularly, as a western drover does with his herds of cattle. But sooner or later the general result is the same. Sales may be made voluntarily, or by the sheriff—they may be made by the first owner, or delayed until the succession of his heirs—or the misfortune of being sold may fall on one parcel of slaves, instead of another: but all of these are but different ways of arriving at the same general and inevitable result. With plenty of wholesome, though coarse food, and under such mild treatment as our slaves usually experience, they have every inducement and facility to increase their numbers with all possible rapidity, without any opposing check, either prudential, moral, or physical." [61]

By pairing off the sexes in the way that Ruffin suggests, masters did more than disguise the fact that they were indeed breeding people. They also lessened discontent thereby and provided a check upon the slave's inclination to run away. A slave with offspring gave hostages to good behavior and docility.

If the kind of breeding that went on in the United States under slavery seems unexceptional and expected, the situation in Brazil reveals how unusual it really was. Gilberto Freyre, it is true, writes of the Brazilian master's interest in the "generative belly" of the female slave and in the size of the male's sexual organs on the assumption that there was a connection between size and procreative powers. But other writers on slavery and commentators at the time make it clear that slave breeding on the scale achieved in the United States was not important to Brazilian slaveholders. Stanley Stein, for example, discovered a genuine reluctance among slaveholders in Vassouras to bother with breeding and rearing slaves. In fact, the very hours male and female slaves could be together, other authorities observe, were deliberately limited. Some masters consciously restricted slave reproduction by locking up the sexes separately at night. An Englishman

[61] Quoted in Lewis Cecil Gray, *History of Agriculture in the Southern United States to 1860*, 2 vols. (Washington, 1933), II, pp. 661–62.

who testified before a Select Committee of the House of Commons in 1849 noted the high mortality of slaves in Brazil who entered the country through the African slave trade. Nevertheless, he continued, the number of women brought into the country was so few "that the generating process is not thought of, and the men worked out." [62] The reasoning of the slaveholders, as a contemporary reported it, was quite straightforward: "One buys a Negro for 300 milreis, who harvests in the course of the year 100 arrobas of coffee, which produces a net profit at least equal to the cost of the slave; thereafter everything is profit. It is not worth the trouble to raise children, who, only after sixteen years, will give equal service. Furthermore, the pregnant Negroes and those nursing are not available to use the hoe; heavy fatigue prevents the regular development of the fetus in some, in others the diminution of the flow of milk, and in almost all, sloppiness in the care of children, from which sickness and death of the poor children result." [63]

Undoubtedly the steady stream of slaves from Africa accounts, at least in part, for the lack of interest in slave breeding in Brazil prior to 1851, when the trade ended. Within five years after the closing of the trade, for example, a book appeared in Brazil advising planters to follow the example of Virginians, who were alleged to be such efficient breeders of slaves that infants were bought while still in the mother's womb! [64] But such exhortations do not seem to have had much effect, for over ten years after the closing of the slave trade W. D. Christie, the British minister at Rio de Janeiro, although he was incensed at Brazilian complacency over the persistence of slavery, still had to admit in a letter to his home government in 1863 that "the slave population is decreasing, though not considerably." Moreover, he pointed out, "The mortality among the children of slaves is very great; and Brazilian proprietors do not appear to have given nearly so much attention as might have been expected, from obvious motives of self-interest,

[62] Gilberto Freyre, *O Escravo nos anuncios de jornais Brasileiros de Seculo XIX* (Recife, 1963), p. 75; Stein, *Vassouras*, p. 155; T. Lynn Smith, *Brazil, People and Institutions* (Baton Rouge, 1963), p. 103; Ribeyrolles, *Brasil pitoresco*, II, p. 32; Conrad, "Abolition of Slave Trade," p. 58, quotes the witness before the English Parliament.

[63] Quoted in Nabuco, *Abolicionismo*, pp. 89–90.

[64] Viotti da Costa, *Da Senzala*, pp. 129–30.

to marriages among the slaves, or to the care of mothers or children." [65]

Infant mortality among slaves was indeed amazingly high. As one antislave-trade newspaper wrote in 1849, slaves "give us almost no children because the mortality among them is frightful in the first years, due to a thousand circumstances which are not strange to us." Even after the slave trade ended, the death rate of slave children was horrendous. One authority on the coffee country places it as high as 88 per cent. The census of 1870 revealed that in the city of Rio de Janeiro the mortality of slave children even exceeded births by 1.8 per cent and even that shocking figure must have been a minimum for the country as a whole because most slaves in Rio were domestics and presumably better cared for than agricultural slaves. Rio Branco, the Brazilian statesman who later gave his name to an important emancipationist law, calculated that on the basis of excess of slave deaths over births alone, slavery would die out within seventy-five years. [66]

One undoubted consequence of the continuance of the foreign slave trade was that Brazilian planters made no effort to balance the sexes among the slaves. Because male slaves were stronger and could serve in a greater variety of jobs than females, they constituted the overwhelming majority of the importations into Brazil. "What was wanted principally was labor," Perdigão Malheiro wrote in 1866, "not families." On some plantations there were no female slaves at all and on most, the males far outnumbered the females. One authority has estimated that for each Negro woman imported three or four males were brought in. The statistics that Stein compiled for Vassouras support that estimate, for he discovered that 70 per cent or more of the African-born slaves between 1820 and 1880 were males. The records of cap-

---

[65] Christie, *Notes on Brazilian Questions*, p. 102n.

[66] Quoted in Conrad, "Abolition of Slave Trade," p. 58; Maria Graham, *Journal of a Voyage to Brazil and Residence There, During Part of the Years 1821, 1822, 1823* (London, 1824), p. 289, quotes a mistress of slaves as saying "that not half of the Negroes born on her estate lived to be ten years old. It would be worthwhile to enquire into the cause of this evil and whether it is general."; Viotti da Costa, *Da Senzala*, p. 256; Gouveia, *História da Escravidão*, p. 208.

tured slave ships in the 1830's and 1840's show ratios of one to four and one to five, in favor of males.[67]

The heavy imbalance between the sexes meant that once the slave trade was closed, Brazilian slavery began to decline, unlike the situation in the United States, where it flourished as never before *after* the closing of the foreign trade. The paucity of women, not to mention the Brazilian masters' lack of interest in breeding, insured that the reduction in the foreign supply of slaves would not be easily or quickly made up.

That same imbalance in Brazil may help also to explain the somewhat greater number of runaways in that country. In the United States, as has been suggested already, with slaves more or less divided into family units, for a male slave to run away meant serious personal loss, since he probably would have to leave woman and children behind. Such a consequence was much less likely in Brazil, where most slaves did not live in family units. Rugendas, the German artist visiting Brazil, recognized the pacifying effect of family life upon slave restlessness when he pointed out that masters encouraged marriage between slaves "for they know by experience that it is the best way of holding them on the plantation and the strongest guarantee of their good conduct." A similar remark was quoted from a planter in São Paulo who said, in talking about a restless slave, "it is necessary to give that Negro in marriage and give him a piece of land in order to calm him down and cultivate responsibility in him." [68]

A Harsher Slavery

If the reader has gradually been concluding from the foregoing that the physical treatment of slaves in Brazil may well have been harsher than that in the United States, he is on the right track. Such a conclusion, however, it ought to be said, is not the traditional one. Modern historians and contemporaries alike have generally concluded just the opposite. Although recognizing that

[67] Perdigão Malheiro, *Escravidão*, II, 65n.; Rodrigues, *Brazil and Africa*, p. 159; Stein, *Vassouras*, p. 155; Conrad, "Abolition of Slave Trade," p. 55.
[68] Rugendas, *Viagem pitoresco*, p. 180; Bastide, ed. *Relações raciais*, p. 81.

slavery, wherever and whenever it occurred, was a heavy burden upon those who lived within it, most commentators have concluded, on balance, that in modern times, at least, those burdens were generally heavier under United States slavery than in Brazil or Latin America.[69] A definitive or scientific comparison, of course, is out of the question. The documentation for one thing is at once overwhelming in amount and subjective in content. In attempting to make a judgment on harshness about United States slavery alone, where the documentation is readily accessible, historians have been unable to agree. For every act of cruelty cited from the sources, a counter act of mildness or kindness can be found. The calculus on that level is endless as well as fruitless. A similarly interminable balancing of atrocities against acts of paternalism would occur were one to follow a similar approach in regard to Brazilian slavery. Acts of torture and cruelty are well documented, and Gilberto Freyre, who has often been charged with emphasizing the mildness of slavery in Brazil, does not hide the cruelties sometimes committed by masters nor the harsh consequences of slavery in general.[70] In short, to simply cite examples of cruelty or kindness from the two societies will not advance us very far in thinking about the nature of slavery in the two places. If, however, general classes of evidence are used in making a comparison as to physical treatment, the methodological difficulty is largely circumvented. The effort is, moreover,

[69] See, for example, Elkins, *Slavery*, pp. 77–78; Caio Prado, Junior, *Formação do Brasil Contemporaneo Colonia*, 7th ed. (n.p., n.d.), p. 275; Williams, "The Treatment of Negro Slaves," pp. 332–36; H. B. Alexander, "Brazilian and United States Slavery Compared," *Journal of Negro History*, VII (October, 1922), 349–64. Travelers also subscribed to this view; see for example, Koster, *Travels in Brazil*, II, pp. 207–208; Rugendas, *Viagem pitoresco*, pp. 168–69; Jean Baptiste Debret, *Viagem pitoresca e historica ao Brazil*, 2 vols., trans. Sergio Milliet (São Paulo, n.d.), I, p. 264. Debret noted that though in Brazil "the slave is treated with greater humanity, the necessity of maintaining discipline among a numerous black population" resulted in the institutionalization of whipping, that is, the establishment of public whipping posts. In the big cities the slaves are beaten at the police station. Thus every day between 9 and 10 one can see the line of Negroes to be punished. After the beating the Negro returns to jail to have his wounds washed with vinegar and pepper to avoid infection."

[70] Sayers, *Negro in Brazilian Literature*, p. 218; Freyre, *Escravo nos anuncios*, pp. 130–31; Koster, *Travels in Brazil*, I, p. 312; Thomas Ewbank, *Life in Brazil* (New York, 1856), pp. 77, 118–19.

worth making, for a comparison does throw some light on the similarities and differences in the two systems of slavery.

There are several general reasons that suggest Brazilian slavery was physically harsher than North American. Perhaps the most persuasive is that slavery in the United States was able to endure and even expand on the basis of reproduction alone. At the very least, that fact offers testimony to a better standard of physical circumstances and care than a system of slavery that did not reproduce itself. It is true, to be sure, that the imbalance of the sexes in Brazil played a part in keeping down reproduction, but the recognized high mortality of slave children and the cost involved in caring for them probably account for the general reluctance to rear slaves in the first place. Masters had little incentive to breed slaves, which required that women be released from work to rear children, so long as the foreign slave trade promised to supply labor needs for the future.

Moreover, Brazilian planters seem to have been convinced that slave women either did not bear children often in captivity or that slave children were difficult to raise. In the middle of the eighteenth century, Charles Boxer tells us, planters complained that slave women were not fecund—a complaint, Boxer points out, that was still being heard 130 years later, after the slave trade was effectively closed. Actually the problem lay not with the women, who as mistresses of white planters experienced little trouble in conceiving and raising children, but with the poor care that planters provided.[71] After the closing of the slave trade, at a time when one would have imagined planters would take more interest in rearing slaves, Perdigão Malheiro was still citing the alleged sterility of slave women as one of the reasons why slave children were not being raised in Brazil as frequently as in the United States.[72] Some slave owners were quoted, too, as believing that it was easier to raise three or four white children than one black child, the difference being attributed to the "greater fragility of the black race."[73] In 1862—over ten years *after* the closing of the slave trade, it will be noted—a French visitor reported that "most simple hygienic measures are almost always neglected

[71] Boxer, *Golden Age*, p. 174.
[72] Perdigão Malheiro, *Escravidão*, I, p. 166.
[73] Quoted in Viotti da Costa, *Da Senzala*, pp. 257–58.

by the owners of slaves, and the mortality of 'negrillons' is very considerable, especially on the plantations of the interior." [74] Brazilians, in short, simply did not take care of their slaves well enough for them to reproduce, or at least for the children to survive, even when they had the incentive provided by the closing of the African trade.

A second general measure for comparing treatment of slaves in the United States and Brazil is that certain types of harsh treatment common in Brazil rarely occurred in the United States. A number of Brazilian sources, both during the colonial period and under the Empire in the nineteenth century, for instance, speak of the use of female slaves as prostitutes. In some cases their masters even lived off the earnings of such slaves. The practice, moreover, was sufficiently extensive for the Crown in the colonial period to legislate against the practice, though without success. [75] This use of slave women as a source of income is virtually unknown in the history of slavery in the United States.

Another striking practice of Brazilian slavery that has little or no counterpart in the United States was the use of iron or tin masks on slaves, in order to prevent slaves from eating dirt or drinking liquor. The practice of using masks was sufficiently common in Brazil for pictures of slaves wearing them to appear in books of travel along with other references. [76] Slaves in the United States also suffered from what we recognize today as dietary deficiencies that drove them to eat clay, and certainly many of

[74] Élisée Reclus, "Le Brésil et la Colonisation, II," *Revue des deux Mondes* XL (July–August, 1862), 391. Curtin, *The Atlantic Slave Trade*, p. 73 independently arrives at the same suggestion made in the text, namely that historians have overlooked the implications for the comparative history of slavery to be derived from the fact that the slave system of the United States was unique in its ability to sustain itself through natural reproduction.

[75] Boxer, *Golden Age*, pp. 138, 165; Gilberto Freyre, *The Masters and the Slaves*, trans. Samuel Putnam (New York, 1946), p. 455.

[76] Ewbank, *Life in Brazil*, pp. 270, 437–38; D. P. Kidder and J. C. Fletcher, *Brazil and the Brazilians* (Philadelphia, 1857), p. 132; Debret, *Viagem pitoresca*, I, pp. 147–48; Seidler, *Dez Anos no Brasil*, pp. 237–38; for a picture of masked slaves see Viotti da Costa, *Da Senzala*, p. 240, and Debret, *Viagem pitoresca*, I, plate 10. Masks are also referred to in Viotti da Costa, *Da Senzala*, p. 289; Freyre, *Escravo nos anuncios*, p. 100; Arthur Ramos, "Castigos de Escravos," *Revista do Arquivo Municipal de São Paulo*, XLVI (May, 1938), 99.

them were addicted to liquor. Yet in the whole literature of United States slavery—and certainly northern abolitionists would have leaped upon such examples if they had been as common in the United States as they were in Brazil—I have yet to see a picture of a slave with a mask. Published references to the use of the mask for slaves in the United States are extremely rare, though they do occur.[77]

Then there are two practices common among Brazilian slaves that have already been mentioned, but which are germane to a comparison with United States slavery. The first is the widespread practice among Brazilians, attested to by official and unofficial sources, of freeing ill, old, or crippled slaves in order to escape the obligations of caring for them. "It is very common in Brazil for the masters to abandon the old and infirm slaves, for they cannot work," wrote F. A. Brandão, a mid-nineteenth century Brazilian commentator on slavery in his country. Maria Graham in the early nineteenth century also observed that in Bahia "it is not uncommon to give a slave his freedom when he is too old or too infirm to work; that is, to turn him out of doors to beg or starve." Even the efforts at stopping the practice by law were slow in coming, and the laws that resulted were ineffective. In the literature of slavery in the United States, on the other hand, such charges were rarely heard from travelers, and historians have scarcely mentioned the issue and then only to discount it. "Only one instance has been noted of slaveholders shirking this responsibility [of caring for the old and incapacitated]," writes Charles Syndor in his thorough study of slavery in Mississippi. The instance was that of an idiot slave woman who was immediately taken in by a neighbor and eventually by the county.[78]

The second practice of Brazilian slavery that has already been mentioned and which might be recalled here is that because of the heavy imbalance of the sexes most slaves in Brazil had neither sexual outlets nor the comforts of even a slave family relationship. To the extent that these deprivations constitute an element in

[77] Theodore Weld, *American Slavery As It Is: Testimony of a Thousand Witnesses* (New York, 1839), p. 76.

[78] Brandão, *Escravatura no Brasil*, 57n.; Graham, *Journal of a Voyage*, p. 144; Gouveia, *História da Escravidão*, p. 179; Perdigão Malheiro, *Escravidão*, II, p. 220; Viotti da Costa, *Da Senzala*, p. 263; Christie, *Notes on Brazilian Questions*, pp. 218–19; Sydnor, *Slavery in Mississippi*, p. 250.

the calculus of comparative treatment, the lot of the United States slave was easier than that of the Brazilian.

Finally, one other measure of comparative treatment might be mentioned, though it is not entirely clear how the facts ought to be interpreted. Suicides were apparently much more common among Brazilian than North American slaves. Nowhere in the secondary or primary literature on slavery in the United States, for instance, is much made of slave suicides, though, of course, they occurred. Ulrich B. Phillips, for example, mentions that in the course of the eighteenth century slave trade Ibo Negroes had a reputation for committing suicide when taken into slavery—an observation that suggests suicide was not ignored by planters or traders when it was commonplace. On the other hand, suicides appear quite frequently in reports of travelers in Brazil. Visitors from the United States, significantly enough, were especially struck by the number of self-inflicted deaths by Brazilian slaves. "Suicides continually occur and owners wonder," wrote the American visitor Thomas Ewbank in the 1840's. Newspapers were constantly reporting such deaths, he goes on, citing from the newspaper three suicides by slaves in as many days. Another visitor from the United States a little later also commented on slave suicides, which, he observed, "are almost unknown in our southern states," but are "very frequent occurrences in the cities of Brazil."

As already pointed out, the meaning of the greater number of suicides is not entirely clear. Generally the travelers assumed it meant harsher treatment, a not unreasonable conclusion. Yet more frequent suicides could also have been the result of the larger number of Africans among the slaves. For as one of the North American visitors suggested, the African's "high spirit, refusing to bow to the white man," causes him to commit suicide.[79] In any case, a higher incidence of suicide among slaves in Brazil does not suggest a milder form of slavery there than in the United States.

Admittedly beset with pitfalls as the making of comparisons

[79] Ewbank, *Life in Brazil*, pp. 281, 440; Kidder and Fletcher, *Brazil and the Brazilians*, p. 132; Maria Thereza Schorer Petrone, *A Lavoura canavieira em São Paulo* (São Paulo, 1968), pp. 123–24 also notices suicides among slaves in the sugar growing areas of São Paulo state. Richard Graham of the University of Texas kindly brought to my attention this reference.

of physical treatment may be, the effort nonetheless has some value. It provides yet another insight into the nature of the two slave systems, particularly as those slave systems are related to differences in race relations after slavery. For treatment of a slave, even physically, constitutes evidence of the way in which masters viewed their slaves and evidence of the way slaves learned of their master's conception of them. Stanley Elkins has contended, on the contrary, that a comparative analysis of treatment is not germane to a comparison of the impact of slavery on the Negro, for "in one case [Latin America] we would be dealing with cruelty of man to men, and in the other [the United States] with the care, maintenance, and indulgence of men toward creatures who were legally and morally *not* men." [80] This argument, however, is not persuasive when it is recognized that the law in *both* Brazil and the United States, as we have seen, defined the slave as simultaneously a man and a thing. Under such circumstances, physical treatment can no longer be confidently separated from attitudes as Elkins tries to do. Thus we have no way of knowing, *independently of the treatment itself,* what the master's attitude toward a slave was, for under the law in both Brazil and the United States he can be viewed as either a thing or as a human being. Only particular circumstances or evidence will make clear whether a particular example or class of harsh treatment means degradation beneath the level of a human being or constitute merely punishment of a fellow human being. Hence the way in which a master treats a slave, particularly when the slave is a member of a physically identifiable class, becomes a part of the historian's evidence for ascertaining the attitudes white men had toward black men who were slaves. It also constitutes evidence for ascertaining the ways in which blacks were conditioned to think of themselves. When a master muzzles a slave, for example, he is literally treating that slave like a dog. At the very least, the master's behavior is evidence for concluding that the master is in the process of thinking of the slave as being on a level with a dog; at the most, his behavior suggests that the source of, or impetus for the particular behavior is the belief that the slave was, from the beginning, no better than a dog and so deserves no better treatment. In either case the master's treatment of the

[80] Elkins, *Slavery,* p. 78n.

slave is part of the evidence to be evaluated in ascertaining white men's attitudes toward black slaves. Equally important for our search for the origins of differences in race relations is the real possibility that a slave who is muzzled or who sees other black men muzzled may well be led to think of himself as no better than a dog and therefore quite worthy of being muzzled. In short, the treatment accorded black slaves in both societies is relevant to the question of how white men think about black men. Simply on the basis of the comparison of physical treatment, it would appear that there is no reason to be confident that Brazilian slavery protected the humanity of the Negro who was a slave. On the contrary, insofar as physical treatment was concerned, it would seem that Brazilian slavery was less likely than United States slavery to give either the master or the slave an awareness of the Negro's humanity.

A second reason for making a comparison of physical treatment is to call attention to the importance of the slave trade in accounting for another of the differences between Brazilian and United States slavery. Brazilians simply did not have to treat their slaves with care or concern when new slaves were readily obtainable from outside the system. That the continuance of the slave trade had the effect of making the lot of the slave hard was clearly recognized in Brazil after the trade was stopped. Perdigão Malheiro in 1866, fifteen years after the closing of the trade, for example, asserted that the ending of the traffic had improved the treatment of slaves in Brazil. No longer, he wrote, do you "meet in the streets, as in other not remote times, slaves with their faces covered with a wire mask or a great weight on the foot." Slaves are now so well dressed and shod, he continued, "that no one would know who they are," by which he meant that they could not be distinguished from free blacks, because in the past slaves did not wear shoes. Two visiting Americans noticed the same change even earlier. "Until 1850, when the slave trade was effectually put down, it was considered cheaper, on the country plantations," wrote Kidder and Fletcher in 1857 "to use up a slave in five to seven years, and purchase another, than to take care of him. This I had, in the interior, from intelligent native Brazilians, and my own observations to confirm it. But, since the inhuman traffic has ceased, the price of slaves has been enhanced, and the selfish motives for taking greater care of them have been increased." [81]

But it needs to be added that the closing of the slave trade in Brazil in 1850 had at least one worsening effect upon the lot of slaves. It undoubtedly stepped up the internal slave trade, thereby enhancing the likelihood of the breakup of slave families. Prior to 1850 the steady movement of slaves into the country from Africa probably kept to a minimum the movement of slaves already in the country. By the same token, United States slaves prior to 1850 probably experienced more disruption of families than Brazilian simply because the foreign slave trade was closed at the opening of the century and the opening of the southwest to cultivation of cotton stimulated the demand for slaves, who had to be drawn from the older regions. Moreover, simply because there were more slave families in the United States, as we have seen, disruption was undoubtedly greater than in Brazil.

When the effects of the closing of the slave trade are thus explored it is readily evident that the question of harshness is more a function of the availability of slaves from abroad than a matter of different culture or social outlook. If on balance United States slavery was indeed milder, as the foregoing argues, then a large part of the explanation ought to be charged to the earlier closing of the slave trade. For once the trade was closed, slavery could survive as a going labor system only so long as it could replenish itself, and that required some attention to physical care of the slaves. Why the slave trade was closed earlier in the United States than in Brazil is a question we will return to later in this chapter.

To Arm a Black Slave

Despite the differences in slave systems already discussed, the most striking has not yet been mentioned. In the attitudes toward the arming of slaves, the two systems could not have been more divergent. One of the earliest signs of discrimination against Ne-

[81] Perdigão Malheiro, *Escravidão*, II, pp. 114–15; Kidder and Fletcher, *Brazil and Brazilians*, p. 132.

groes in seventeenth century Virginia, Maryland, and even New England was the legal denial of arms to blacks, whether free or slaves. No such discrimination, incidentally, was made against white indentured servants. The discrimination against Negroes was evident even before slavery was written into the laws of Virginia and Maryland. Not until 1660 did statute law speak of Negroes as slaves, though some may well have been. The precise legal status of the first Negroes who came to the English colonies in the 1620's and 1630's is not clear and probably never will be, given the paucity of evidence on the subject. But that discrimination against Negroes took place long before slavery was spelled out in the statutes there is no doubt. Denying blacks the opportunity to arm themselves was only one of the several ways the early laws discriminated against blacks, whether free or servants, but that subject will be more fully explored in Chapter V.

The situation in Brazil constitutes a dramatic contrast with that in the United States. Almost from the beginning of settlement, the Portuguese, and then the Brazilians permitted not only Negroes, but slaves themselves to be armed. Arthur Ramos, a well-known authority on the history of the Negro in Brazil, has even suggested that the whites encouraged the slaves to arm themselves.[82] During the war against the Dutch invaders of Brazil in the seventeenth century, not only did large numbers of slaves fight for the Dutch, but in the course of that struggle Henrique Dias established his fame as a black military leader. The Dutch occupation of northeastern Brazil lasted for a quarter of a century, during which time warfare between them continued. Negroes, slave and free, also fought against the French invader at the beginning of the eighteenth century when Rio de Janeiro came under attack.[83] In fact, in all the armed conflicts within Brazil itself, in the eighteenth and nineteenth centuries, blacks, both slave and free, were to be found bearing arms. Sometimes the black slaves fought on both sides, as they did in the war of independence in 1823–24. Even bandits and magnates in Minas Gerais during the mining boom used armed slaves to exert their power. When fights in Minas occurred in the early eighteenth

[82] Ramos, *Negro in Brazil*, p. 157.
[83] Charles R. Boxer, *The Dutch in Brazil, 1624–1654* (Oxford, 1957), p. 166; João Dornas Filho, *A Escravidão no Brasil* (Rio de Janeiro, 1939), pp. 224–25; Boxer, *Golden Age*, p. 89.

century between the miners and "invaders" from São Paulo in the so-called war of the Emboabas, Negro slaves fought in considerable numbers against the *paulistas*.[84] In southern Brazil, during the revolt there against the central government, called the war of the Farrapos, 1835–45, slaves also took part, and the Imperial armies threatened to punish those slaves who fought with the rebels. Perhaps the most striking example of the role of the armed slave in the wars of Brazil, aside from the Dutch episode of the seventeenth century, was the participation of slaves in the Paraguayan War of 1865–70. When the war was over, some 20,000 slaves were given their freedom for their participation in the struggle.[85]

When comparable situations arose in the United States, the responses were quite different. During the American Revolution, for example, Henry and John Laurens, leading figures in South Carolina, proposed in 1779 that slaves be enlisted to help counter the military successes of the British in the southern colonies. It was understood that the survivors would be freed. Although the Laurenses were joined by a few other South Carolinians and the Continental Congress approved the plan, it was voted down overwhelmingly by the South Carolina legislature. The Laurenses raised the issue again in 1781, but once more the proposal was rejected by the South Carolina and the Georgia legislatures. During the Civil War, when the slave South was once again faced with a struggle for survival, it again steadfastly refused to use slave soldiers until the very last month of the war. As Jefferson Davis told the Confederate Congress in November, 1864, so long as whites were available to fight there was no need to enlist the Negro, "who has merely been trained to labor, and as a laborer under the white man, accustomed from his youth to the use of firearms. . . ." But, Davis continued, "should the alternative ever be presented of subjugation or of the employment of the slave as a soldier, there seems no reason to doubt what should be our

---

[84] Ibid., pp. 79, 116–18, 194, 201; Carneiro, *Ladinos e Crioulas,* pp. 68, 84–85; *Dornas, A Escravidão,* p. 148; Bastide, *Les Religions africaines,* p. 106; Moura, *Rebeliões da Senzala,* pp. 53–56.

[85] Nestor Ericksen, *O Negro no Rio Grande do Sul* (Porte Alegre, 1941), pp. 25–27; Cardoso, *Capitalismo e Escravidão,* pp. 153–54n.; Ianni, *Metamorfoses,* pp. 175–76; Viotti da Costa, *Da Senzala,* p. 401; Rodrigues, *Brazil and Africa,* pp. 45–52.

decision." Davis' conception of the black man as a soldier was low, but he did at least acknowledge that under certain circumstances blacks might have to be armed. General Howell Cobb of Georgia, however, was less practical and more ideological; he recognized that to arm the slaves was to contradict the white South's conception of the Negro. Consequently, even as late in the history of the Confederacy as the end of 1864, he denounced the recommendation that the slaves be armed as "the most pernicious idea that has been suggested since the war began. . . . Use all the Negroes you can get for all purposes for which you need them," he told the Confederate Secretary of War, "but don't arm them. The day you make soldiers of them is the beginning of the end of the revolution. If slaves make good soldiers," he shrewdly pointed out, "our whole theory of slavery is wrong." Generally, the Confederacy refused to enlist even free Negroes when they offered their services at the beginning of the war.[86]

The fact that slaves in Brazil were frequently armed and that in the United States they rarely were is obviously a significant difference between the practices of slavery in the two places. Moreover, to permit Negroes as slaves and free men to be armed and to fight in behalf of the national cause surely affected the way in which whites felt toward blacks, whether slave or free. Such a practice, as Gilberto Freyre has pointed out, helped to integrate the Negro into the nation. Indeed, it was just that consequence that Howell Cobb feared when he warned against arming the slaves in the waning days of the Confederacy. A glimpse of the process of integration as it took place in Brazil is provided by the example of eight slaves who were sent into the army from the province of Espírito Santo in 1827 in place of the

[86] John Alden, *The First South* (Baton Rouge, 1961), pp. 37–40; Benjamin Quarles, *The Negro in the American Revolution* (Chapel Hill, N.C., 1961), pp. 60–67. During the Revolution a few slaves were enlisted by their masters in the New England states. For the quotation from Davis and Cobb, see Charles H. Wesley, "The Employment of Negroes as Soldiers in the Confederate Army," *Journal of Negro History*, IV (July, 1919), 246–47. Wesley also cites examples of free Negroes' offering their services to the Confederacy in 1861. For an example of the refusal of such offers see D. E. Everett, "Ben Butler and the Louisiana Native Guards," *Journal of Southern History*, XXIV (May, 1958), 202–204. Wesley also notes that as late as November, 1864 the Confederate Secretary of War turned down a request from a Confederate officer from Georgia to raise a regiment of Negro troops.

master's son. In this way, it was said of the mulattoes, "they have the honor of serving the nation, as soldiers." As the Brazilian sociologist Octavio Ianni has observed concerning the use of Negro slaves in the Paraguayan War, whites could not help but obtain a new and broader view of the Negro's capabilities once the blacks had served as defenders of the nation. Howell Cobb defined the interaction between the white man's conception of the Negro and the arming of the blacks even more directly and succinctly. "You cannot make soldiers of slaves or slaves of soldiers," he told the Confederate Secretary of War at the end of 1864.[87] Inasmuch as the arming of slaves affected white men's perceptions of blacks and their capabilities after slavery, it is relevant here to inquire why slaves were so freely armed in Brazil while in the United States they were generally denied arms.

At the outset we can dismiss the idea that it was because of the state or the church's interest in protecting the humanity of the Negro. For as we shall see, the Portuguese government, like the English colonial governments, forbade blacks and mulattoes to bear arms. Rather it was the quite dissimilar history of the Portuguese and English colonies that holds the key to the explanation. Sixteenth and seventeenth century Brazil was a tiny, sparsely settled colony, desperately clinging to the coastline, yet attractive to foreign powers because of its wealth, actual and potential. The French in the sixteenth and again in the eighteenth century and the Dutch in the seventeenth century sought to wrest the colony from Portugal by actual invasion. Because the mother country (even during the dual monarchy with Spain, 1580–1640) was too weak or unconcerned to offer much assistance, all the resources of the sparsely settled colony had to be mobilized for defense, which included every scrap of manpower, including black slaves.

The recourse to armed slaves, it is important to recognize, was undertaken reluctantly, for the Portuguese, like any other slave-holding people, could easily anticipate the dangers that might arise from arming their own slaves. As Arthur Ramos writes, Negroes were first used in the sixteenth and seventeenth century only as a kind of skirmishing guard, being denied a place in the

---

[87] Freyre, *Nordeste*, p. 145; de Novaes, *A Escrivadão . . . no Espírito Santo*, p. 57; Freyre, *Escravo nos anuncios*, p. 245; Ianni, *Metamorfoses*, p. 217; Wesley, "The Employment of Negroes," *Journal of Negro History* (1919), pp. 246–47.

regular army. But as the need for soldiers persisted and even grew, and a new generation of Brazilian-born Negroes entered the scene, the whites came to demand that they serve in the armed forces. That the acceptance of Negro troops was more the result of circumstances than of ideology is shown by the fact that the Negro troops were usually segregated until the nineteenth century and even when they were no longer set apart, "whites tended to occupy the military posts of major responsibility." Moreover, the slaves who fought against the Dutch under Henrique Dias were not freed until 1657, years after the expulsion of the Dutch and in violation of the Crown's promise of immediate manumission. Henrique Dias himself complained to the King that despite his royal decorations for valor and his many wounds incurred in the royal service, "I am treated with little respect, with unspeakable words to my person, and no one recognizes me as a soldier." [88] Use of Negroes as soldiers in the colonial period in Brazil, in short, was not the result of the prior acceptance of the colored man as an equal, but of the need of him as a fighter. It ought not be forgotten, either, that down through the eighteenth century the law forbade Negroes and mulattoes to carry arms. Indeed, it was not until 1755 that the Overseas Council changed the penalty for that crime from ten years in the galleys to a hundred lashes.[89] Presumably the reason for the change was that masters would thereby not lose the service of their slaves who violated the law.

The history of Negroes and arms in the British colonies of North America is almost the reverse, for conditions and circumstances of settlement and economic development there differed markedly from Brazil. In the first seventy-five years of the seventeenth century, when the necessities of defense and economic development might have dictated the arming of slaves, there simply were very few Negroes in North America. In the colonies of Virginia and Maryland, which were to become the first slave-using provinces of English America, the great majority of unfree workers, until the 1680's at least, were white indentured servants. Not until 1715 did Negro slaves constitute as much as a quarter

[88] Ramos, *The Negro in Brazil*, pp. 151–54; Luna, *Negro na Luta*, pp. 30–31.

[89] Mörner, *Race Mixture*, p. 52; Rodrigues, *Brazil and Africa*, p. 49.

of the population of Virginia. Meanwhile, throughout the seventeenth century, the white population, servant and free, was more than adequate for defensive purposes against the threat of foreign invasion or attacks. One of the reasons the white population was adequate is that England exported more people in the seventeenth century than did Portugal; moreover, it had more people to begin with. But even those numbers might not have been adequate if the English colonies had had to sustain the kinds of massive attacks made upon Brazil. The fact is that the few weak and ineffectual foreign invasions that threatened English America did not occur until the eighteenth century, when the colonies were well established. During Queen Anne's War, at the opening of the eighteenth century, a combined French and Spanish fleet demanded the surrender of Charleston, but the ineffectual invasion was easily crushed by the English. Similarly, when the Spanish briefly invaded the new English colony of Georgia in 1742 they were quickly repulsed by Oglethorpe at the battle of Bloody Marsh; the next year Oglethorpe was sufficiently strong to confront the Spanish before the walls of their stronghold at St. Augustine in Florida. Thus, neither at the beginning nor at the close of the formative seventeenth century were English colonists under any significant pressure to use Negroes or slaves as defensive troops.

As a consequence they could indulge their acute awareness of their own different appearance, religion, and culture from Africans, by permitting their social institutions to reflect this awareness. Even the New England colonies of Massachusetts and Connecticut, with only a few hundred blacks in their midst, excluded by law in the seventeenth century all Negroes, whether slave or free from service with arms.[90] The law of the English colonies thus reproduced the law of Brazil regarding the arming of blacks, but unlike the Portuguese, the English could honor the prohibition in practice for there were no foreign threats to their survival to cause the practice to override the principle.

Actually, there is one exception to the foregoing summary of

[90] Edward McCrady, *The History of South Carolina Under the Proprietary Government, 1670–1719* (New York, 1897), pp. 396–401; E. Merton Coulter, *A Short History of Georgia* (Chapel Hill, N.C., 1933), pp. 45–48; Winthrop Jordan, *White Over Black* (Chapel Hill, N.C., 1968), pp. 122–28 surveys the legal discriminations against free blacks in the English colonies.

the English colonists' practices in the arming of slaves, but it is the exception that proves the rule. South Carolina as a newly established colony and close to the Spanish domains was the most vulnerable of the English colonies. Hence in the early eighteenth century, Negro slaves were made liable for armed service in the case of foreign attack. In 1704, for example, the legislature enacted a law "for Raising and Enlisting such slaves as shall be thought Serviceable to this Province in time of Alarms." Similar acts were passed in the course of Queen Anne's War with Spain and France. And in later threats to the colony, during wars with France and Spain, the legislatures made other authorizations to enlist slaves in the armed forces. Extant records indicate that in 1747, at least some slaves were enlisted by the province. Yet the overall conclusion would seem to be that the need for arming the slaves was always slight, even in South Carolina, and occurred only very occasionally.[91] Thus not even South Carolinians gained much experience with armed blacks as the Brazilians perforce did. Yet the comparison with the situation in Brazil suggests that if the foreign threats had been graver, perhaps a quite different attitude toward blacks might have been encouraged in South Carolina. Conversely, in the light of the English experience, it would seem that an important ingredient in the evolution of Brazilian attitudes toward blacks was the threats from foreign foes, which compelled the arming of the slaves to help repel attack and to throw out invaders. For as we have already observed, when whites see Negroes, even as slaves, fighting alongside them they cannot help but have their conception of blacks affected.

Who Identifies with Negroes?

Further revealing of differences in attitudes toward Negroes and slaves in the United States and Brazil are the responses that the two societies made to the threat of slave insurrections. In both

[91] Warren B. Smith, *White Servitude in Colonial South Carolina* (Columbia, S.C., 1961), p. 98. See also McCrady, *South Carolina under Proprietary Government*, pp. 477–78, where in 1708 it was said that each captain of a company of militia was "obliged by an act of Assembly, to enlist, train up and bring into the field for each white, one able slave armed with a gun or lance, for each man in his company."

societies, it should be said, fear of slave revolts was widespread. One of the measures that whites in the southern United States took to forestall slave insurrections was to place restrictions upon free Negroes, who were widely believed to be fomenters of slave conspiracies and revolts. Thus the uncovering in 1822 of a plot among slaves, believed to be organized by the free Negro Denmark Vesey, caused South Carolina and other southern states to enact new and more stringent limitations on the free movement of Negroes. South Carolina, for example, required that all free Negroes entering its port as seamen be lodged in the public jail for the duration of their stay in port. Although the attorney general of the United States declared such restrictions on the citizens of other states or foreign nations a violation of the United States Constitution, South Carolina did not rescind its law and ultimately every one of the Deep South states that had ocean or gulf ports passed similar laws. Fear of the free Negro as a potential instigator of slave revolts was also a principal reason for the restrictions placed upon manumission in every one of the southern states during the nineteenth century. The most common limitation, significantly enough, was the requirement that all newly manumitted Negroes leave the state. Several of the southern states, at the very end of the antebellum era, so feared the influence of the free Negro that they enacted laws prohibiting manumission entirely; at least one state passed a law requiring the enslavement of all free Negroes found within the state after a certain date.[92] White society in the southern United States saw a connection between the Negro slave and the free Negro; the important thing was, not that one was free and the other a slave, but that both belonged to the same race.

In a fundamental sense, Brazilian slavery was racially based, also. Only Negroes (and early in the colonial period, Indians) were slaves, though in Brazil, as in the United States, there was an occasional slave who was fairskinned and had blue eyes, so that he was a white in everything but status.[93] In Brazil, however, the inferior status of slavery did not become as closely associated with race or skin color as it did in the United States.

[92] Stampp, *Peculiar Institution,* pp. 232–35; John Hope Franklin, *From Slavery to Freedom* (New York, 1947), pp. 218–19.

[93] Stampp, *Peculiar Institution,* p. 194 and Freyre, *Escravo nos anuncios,* p. 195 cite instances of blond, blue-eyed slaves in newspaper advertisements for runaways.

Although slaveholders in the United States viewed the free Negro as a potential threat to the slave system, their counterparts in Brazil envisioned the free Negro as a veritable prop to the system of slavery. Many, if not most of the *capitães de mato*—the bush captains or slave catchers—for example, were mulattoes or Negroes. "The men whose occupation it is to apprehend runaway negroes are," wrote Koster at the opening of the nineteenth century, "almost without exception, creole blacks." In the middle of the century the French traveler Expilly commented that "the *capitão de mato* is always a man of color, but free." And on the eve of abolition Anselmo Fonseca, the Bahian abolitionist, pointed out that the three props of slavery were the overseers, the *capitães de mato* and the public whippers of slaves. "Certainly two-thirds of the individuals who descend to such ignoble tasks," Fonseca complained, "are, in this province, and probably in the whole country, black men or of color." [94] Moreover, many free blacks and mulattoes showed little, if any interest in abolition and some, according to the abolitionists, even actively opposed the end of slavery.[95] In Brazil, in other words, more important than race in differentiating between men was legal status. The mere fact that a man was a Negro or a mulatto offered no presumption that he would identify with slaves.

The contrast is also evident in the ways in which slavery was

[94] Koster, *Travels in Brazil*, II, p. 221; Expilly, *Mulheres e Costumes*, p. 242; Fonseca, *Escravidão, O Clero*, pp. 150–51; Rugendas, *Viagem pitoresca*, 182; Ianni, *Metamorfoses*, pp. 61–62; Viotti da Costa, *Da Senzala*, p. 29. "Louisiana was apparently the only state in which free Negro overseers (as distinguished from Negro foremen) were ever employed. Eleven free colored overseers were listed in New Orleans in 1850. Four years later the number had risen to twenty-five, of whom twenty-two were mulattoes," writes William Kauffman Scarborough, *The Overseer, Plantation Management in the Old South* (Baton Rouge, 1966), p. 19.

[95] Viotti da Costa, *Da Senzala*, p. 433 quotes Joaquim Nabuco, the great Brazilian abolitionist, as saying in 1884 that free Negroes were not supporting abolition and "many are found on the opposite side." Fonseca, *Escravidão, O Clero*, pp. 145–54 cites a number of examples of men of color who mistreated their slaves and of one who publicly supported slavery; see also Freyre, *Ordem e Progresso*, p. 322. Oracy Nogueira, "Relações raciais no município de Itapetininga" in Bastide, ed., *Relações raciais*, p. 408 tells of a newspaper in São Paulo state in 1874 that favored abolition and whose editor was a mulatto, but that also called upon the police to take action to destroy a nearby *quilombo* that was harassing the neighborhood.

defended in the two countries. At the height of the slave system in the United States, slavery was increasingly defended on racial grounds. From the outset, to be sure, the most common justification for slavery was the need for labor. But then during the 1830's as cotton became king, more and more southerners took up the argument that slavery was not only a necessary evil, as Thomas Jefferson had said, but a positive good. One of the reasons for accepting slavery as good was that Negroes were considered racially inferior to whites and therefore natural slaves. Sometimes the argument was couched in social terms, as in James Hammond's famous "mud-sill" speech in the Senate in 1858. "In all social systems there must be a class to do the menial duties," he argued, "to perform the drudgery of life. . . . Fortunately for the South, she found a race adapted to that purpose to her hand. A race inferior to her own, but eminently qualified in temper, in vigor, in docility, in capacity to stand the climate, to answer all her purposes. . . . We do not think that whites should be slaves either by law or necessity. Our slaves are black, of another inferior race. The *status* in which we have placed them is an elevation. They are elevated from the condition in which God first created them, by being made our slaves." At other times the racial defense of slavery was put in clear biological terms, with an assist from the Bible. "Aside and apart from Scripture authority," wrote Samuel Cartright in 1857, "natural history reveals most of the same facts, in regard to the negro that the Bible does. It proves the existence of at least three distinct species of the genus man, differing in their instincts, form, habits, and color. The white species having qualities denied to the black—one with a free and the other with a servile mind—one a thinking and reflective being, the other a creature of feeling and imitation, almost void of reflective faculties and consequently unable to provide for and take care of himself. The relation of master and slave would naturally spring up between two such different species of men, even if there was no Scripture authority to support it." [96] Cartwright's article appeared originally in a New York newspaper and

[96] The Hammond and Cartwright statements can be found in Eric Mc-Kitrick, ed., *Slavery Defended: The Views of the Old South* (Englewood Cliffs, N.J., 1963), pp. 122–23 and 147, respectively. A broader discussion is provided in William Sumner Jenkins, *Pro-Slavery Thought in the Old South* (Chapel Hill, N.C., 1935), Chapter VI.

then was republished in books circulating in the South as well as the North. As these quotations attest, many hours of mental labor and many pages of print were consumed in developing and propagating a racial defense of slavery in the United States.

No such effort was made in Brazil. It is true, to be sure, that a racist conception of Negroes was not unknown in nineteenth century Brazil. Charles Expilly, the French traveler in the 1860's, provides probably the most explicit examples of racial arguments in defense of slavery. He quotes one slaveholder as saying that one could free slaves "today, and tomorrow, instead of using this freedom, they will rob and kill in order to satisfy their needs. Only by terror do they reform services. . . . I believe, gentlemen, Negroes would be baffled by freedom. God created them to be slaves." A little later in his account Expilly quotes the planter as saying, "The Africans represent an intermediate race between the gorilla and man. They are improved monkeys, not men." A priest is also cited as justifying slavery on the grounds that St. Thomas Aquinas claimed "that nature intended certain creatures for physical and moral reasons to be slaves." [97]

Yet it is essentially accurate to say that defenders of slavery on clearly racist grounds were as rare among public supporters of slavery in Brazil as they were common in the United States. For example, in the debates in the Brazilian Parliament concerning the treaty with Britain in 1827, closing the international slave trade, only one member of that body made a statement clearly asserting the racial inferiority of Negroes, though at the time other kinds of defenses of slavery were certainly made. A French writer in 1862 summarized well the Brazilian attitude when he said that slaveholders in Brazil "do not believe themselves obliged, like their American colleagues, to invent for the Negro a new original sin, nor to erect a system of absolute distinction between the races, nor to place an insurmountable barrier between the offspring of descendents of slaves and of those of free men." Even an opponent of slavery in the midst of the great abolitionist campaign of the 1880's could testify to the lack of racism in the slaveholders' defense. "No one in this country," wrote Rui Barbosa in 1884, "ever deified slavery. No one openly defended it as in the seceding states of the American Union, as

[97] Expilly, *Mulheres e Costume*, pp. 381–83; see also Stein, *Vassouras*, pp. 133–34; Viotti da Costa, *Da Senzala*, pp. 354–55.

the cornerstone of the social edifice. [This was a reference to Alexander Stephen's famous "cornerstone" speech as vice president of the Confederacy.] No one, as there, anathematized emancipation as a disturber of a providential design. All are, and all have been emancipationists, even those who opposed the repression of the traffic, and saw in it an economic convenience, or a more tolerable evil than the extinction of the Negro commerce."[98]

Brazilians, in short, were not backward in defending slavery. But their most commonly voiced defenses were in behalf of the rights of property (slaves) and that the prosperity of the country depended upon slave labor. A number talked of slavery as a "necessary evil," as some North Americans had done in the early years of the Republic. Sometimes a slaveholder would admit publicly that he would be willing to see slavery abolished. In 1886, for example, as slavery was coming under increasingly powerful and effective attack, a member of the Brazilian Parliament from the coffee district—the region then most heavily and obviously dependent upon slave labor—asserted that the planters in his district would have no objection to emancipation if they could be assured of a new, adequate supply of labor.[99] He was probably alluding to white European immigrants, who were then coming into Brazil. Such a demonstration of the willingness of slaveholders to accept emancipation was unknown in the United States during the antebellum years. Even a more dramatic contrast with the North American scene is that many of the Brazilian abolitionist leaders, who held elective office, represented slaveholding constituencies. Joaquim Nabuco, who is credited with inaugurating the campaign that resulted in the final emancipation in 1888, for example, came from the state of Pernambuco, where, except for a single election, he was regularly elected to Parliament. No such willingness to contemplate the wholesale increase in the free black population was even thinkable among public figures in the slaveholding regions of the United States. There

[98] Rodrigues, *Brazil and Africa*, p. 151; Reclus, "Le Brésil et la Colonisation, II," *Revue des deux Mondes* (May, 1862), pp. 386; Rui Barbossa, *Projecto N. 48 Sessão de 4 de Agosto de 1884* Camara dos Deputados (Rio de Janeiro, 1884), p. 11.

[99] Viotti da Costa, *Da Senzala*, pp. 354–56; Cardoso, *Capitalismo e Escravidão*, p. 280; Florestan Fernandes, *A Integração do negro na sociedade de classes* (São Paulo, 1965), I, p. 200n.

were a few antislavery southerners in the United States, to be sure, but none of them was elected to Congress or any other public office from the South. In nineteenth century Brazil even defenders of slavery sometimes spoke with apparent approval of the high positions achieved by some Negroes and mulattoes in their country.[100] One would find it very difficult indeed to identify a slaveholder or defender of slavery in the United States who would utter publicly a statement of praise of free Negroes as a class. Even an outspoken southern opponent of slavery, Cassius Marcellus Clay of Kentucky, never concealed his belief in the inferiority of the Negro.

The Hidden Difference

What may we conclude from this examination of slavery in Brazil and the United States? That there were in fact differences in the practices of slavery in the two countries there can be no doubt. That Brazil kept the foreign slave trade open longer than the United States was not only a difference, but a cause for several other differences, as we have seen. The two countries also differed markedly in their attitudes toward arming slaves and toward defending slavery on grounds of race. The explanations for these differences, however, are not to be found in differences in the laws of the two home governments nor in the attitudes and practices of the respective national religious persuasions. Neither the church nor the state in Brazil displayed any deep concern about the humanity of the slave and, in any event, neither used its authority to affect significantly the life of the slave. As we will see in Chapter V, even when the Portuguese Crown sought to provide some protection for the Negro as a human being, it was not always obeyed by white masters in Brazil. Much more persuasive as explanations for the differences are the demographic and economic developments and geographic circumstances in the two countries, that is, the differences in their respective historical experiences.

At the same time, there is yet something else that might be gained from this comparison. For there is a pattern behind some of the differences that becomes clear only as the individual dif-

[100] Viotti da Costa, *Da Senzala*, p. 358.

ferences are viewed together. Behind several of the divergencies in practice and ideology is the clear implication that in Brazil the slave may have been feared, but the black man was not, whereas in the United States both the slave and the black were feared. Thus the willingness of Brazilians to manumit slaves much more freely than North Americans is a result of their not fearing free blacks in great numbers, regardless of the fears they may have entertained about slave uprisings. Thus Brazilians did not feel it necessary to restrict manumission as North Americans did. In the United States, slavery was always a means of controlling dangerous blacks as well as a way of organizing labor. That is why most plans for emancipation, prior to the great abolitionist crusade, looked to expatriation to Africa or some other place once the Negroes were freed. Winthrop Jordan, in *White Over Black*, points out that the "earliest American suggestion of colonization included an observation that it was not safe to have Negroes free in America." The "warning" was published in 1715.[101] As late as the Civil War, President Abraham Lincoln was still seriously considering the founding of a settlement in Central America for the blacks who would be freed by the war. Only the impracticality of resettling four million people caused him to give up the idea.[102]

United States fear of Negroes is also highlighted in the contrast between the willingness of Brazilian slaveholders to use blacks as slave catchers and overseers, whereas in the United States, few white men, much less slaveholders, were prepared to put Negroes in such positions of authority. Nor is it accidental that a racial defense of slavery was developed in the United States and largely absent from Brazil. Such a defense followed almost logically from the fear of blacks and was quite consonant with the refusal to permit free blacks to be overseers and slave catchers. Although when one looks at the United States experience alone the development of a racial defense of slavery seems quite natural, the Brazilian experience compels us to realize that the development of such a defense was not a simple function of slavery, but the result of a special attitude on the part of whites toward blacks— an attitude derived from a particular history. It would be difficult

[101] Jordan, *White Over Black*, p. 561n.

[102] For a full discussion of Lincoln's attitudes toward free Negroes and his plans for their future see Benjamin Quarles, *Lincoln and the Negro* (New York, 1962), especially pp. 108–23.

for Brazilians to develop a racial defense of slavery when they used these same blacks as overseers and slave catchers, that is, as defenders of the system.

Finally, the fear of Negroes on the part of North Americans emerges nowhere more forcefully than when one asks why the slave trade remained open in Brazil down to 1851, but was closed in most of the United States before the end of the eighteenth century. If one examines official explanations for the closing of the slave trade, the fear of being overwhelmed by blacks stands out as a significant, if not the chief motive.

Long before the Revolution, Englishmen in North America had been seeking ways to limit the number of blacks in their midst, both slave and free. As early as 1735, the Governor and Council of South Carolina petitioned the Crown: "The Importation of Negroes we crave leave to Inform your Majesty is a Species of Trade, that is exceedingly increased of late in this Province where many Negroes are now Train'd up to be Handycraft Tradesmen; to the great Discouragement of your Majesty's white Subjects who came here to Setle [sic] with a view of Employement [sic] in their several Occupations but must often give way to a People in Slavery, which we daily discover to be a great Obstruction to the Settlement of this Frontier with white People." Then in February, 1750 a report of a committee in charge of security, health, and convenience of the people of Charleston recommended that in view of the excessive number of slaves "some proper Restraint may be put to this growing Evil, to reduce the present number, And that all due encouragement may be given to white Inhabitants to reside in the said Town, it is proposed that all White Persons who will accept of servile Labour, such as Porter, etc. shall have the preference to all Jobs that offer and be entitled to an additional Hire per Diem." The next year the legislature passed a law to raise revenue to encourage white immigration. "The best way to prevent the mischiefs that may be attended by the great importation of negroes into the province," the law read, "will be to establish a method by which such importation should be made a necessary means of introducing a proportionate number of white inhabitants." [103]

---

[103] Quoted in W. B. Smith, *White Servitude in . . . South Carolina*, pp. 34–36; the colonial and early republican laws are quoted at length in W. E. B.

South Carolina was not alone in its concern. In 1772 the Virginia legislature begged the Crown to permit it to stop the slave traffic into the province because "the importation of slaves into the colonies from the coast of Africa hath long been considered as a trade of great inhumanity, and under its *present encouragement*, we have too much reason to fear, *will endanger the very existence* of your majesty's American dominions." After the Revolution, in 1786, North Carolina placed a tax on slaves on the ground that "the importation of slaves into this state is productive of evil consequences, and highly impolitic." The widespread fear of Negroes also explains why all but one of the North American slave states had already prohibited the importation of slaves before the federal prohibition was enacted in 1808.

In Brazil, on the other hand, the slave trade came to an end not only much later, but only after great pressure had been applied from outside the society. Although there were also some Brazilians in the nineteenth century who advocated the closing of the infamous traffic, the principal force came from the British government. In 1827, on pain of commercial restrictions, Britain compelled the Brazilian government to agree to the closing of the trade. But from the outset the Brazilians showed that they were not going to stop a traffic so important to them and especially when agreement to do so was exacted under duress. Thus for almost a quarter of a century thereafter the British navy harassed Brazilian shipping while the foreign office harassed the Imperial government in an effort to put teeth into the treaty of 1827. Success was meager. As we have seen already, it was during that twenty-year period that several hundred thousand fresh slaves entered Brazil from Africa.

The trade was definitely ended in 1851 by Brazilian action. Behind that decision lay twenty years of British harassment and humiliating violation of Brazilian sovereignty. At times the Royal Navy, in its zealous suppression of the hated traffic, actually chased slavers through the harbors and inlets of Brazil. It was not fear of

---

DuBois, *The Suppression of the African Slave Trade to the United States of America 1638–1870* (New York, 1896), pp. 215–29. Don B. Kates, Jr., "Abolition, Deportation, Integration: Attitudes Toward Slavery in the Early Republic," *Journal of Negro History*, LIII (January, 1968), 33–47 contains many expressions by white Americans of their opposition to free Negroes' remaining in the United States.

being inundated by blacks that wrote an end to the trade in Brazil, but the desire on the part of Brazilians to put a stop to British hectoring and to have their country take its place among those nations that refused to participate in a business no longer considered civilized.[104] Besides, in a country in which most of the people were black or brown, fear of being overwhelmed by colored people could hardly have been an important consideration.

The overall conclusion that emerges from this comparison of slave systems is that the differences are not fundamental to an explanation of differences in contemporary race relations. It is evident that differences in the practices of slavery in Brazil and the United States can be quite adequately accounted for by the accidents of geography, demography, and economy and the underlying differences in attitudes toward Negroes rather than by differences in the laws and practices of church and state regarding slavery. In short, the differences were a result of historical circumstances in the New World, not of inherited moral intent or law. As a part of the whole complex of interacting events and circumstances, to be sure, the practices of slavery certainly played a part. But as a causal factor in the shaping of race relations slavery was itself a consequence of deeper differences rather than a primary explanation. If we seek the basic origins of the diverging racial patterns of Brazil and the United States, clearly we must look behind the practices of slavery.

Before we can hope to explain the differences in race relations, however, we need to be more precise about what we are attempting to explain. What, in fact, are the central differences between race relations in the United States and in Brazil? In an effort to identify these differences, the next two chapters are devoted to a comparison of contemporary race relations in the two countries. Then, in Chapter V we will return to our search for a historical explanation for the principal differences that emerge from that comparison.

[104] Richard Graham, "Causes for the Abolition of Negro Slavery in Brazil: An Interpretive Essay," *Hispanic American Historical Review*, XLVI (May, 1966), 129 lists the large literature on the preeminent role of the British in compelling Brazil to put a stop to the African trade. See especially Leslie Bethell, *The Abolition of the Brazilian Slave Trade* (Cambridge, 1970), Chapters 10–12.

III

The Outer Burdens of Color

All are equal before the law. There will be no privileges or distinctions by reason of birth, sex, race, profession or of country, social class, wealth, religious belief or political ideas.

—Article 113, Brazilian
Constitution of 1934.

All persons born or naturalized in the United States, and subject to the jurisdiction thereof, are citizens of the United States and of the State wherein they reside. No State shall make or enforce any law which shall abridge the privileges or immunities of citizens of the United States; nor shall any State deprive any person of life, liberty, or property, without due process of law; nor deny to any person within its jurisdiction the equal protection of the laws.

—Section 1, Article XIV, United
States Constitution, ratified
1868.

To a North American, the position and place of Negroes in Brazil can seem only different. On the streets of Brazilian cities, blacks, browns, and whites mingle without apparent attention to color, whether in public or private places. At the primary schools the spectrum of colors runs from white to black, with no evidence of distinction in groups or playmates. Signs designating facilities for "Colored" and "Whites Only," which were common in the southern states of the United States until very recently and which the North knew in the nineteenth century, have no history in Brazil. Furthermore, the mingling of the races in Brazil carries no historical burden of violence. The race riot as it has been known in the United States for well over a century is unknown in Brazil. Brazil has certainly known violence in the past as in the present, but the violence has *crossed* lines of color rather than followed them. The lynch mob has a long and hideous history in the United States; at its height—or depth—lynching snuffed out the lives of over two thousand Negroes between 1882 and 1903 alone. In some particularly brutal years during the 1890's the annual total of deaths of blacks by lynching reached almost two hundred. In the 1970's that particular form of racial violence has passed from the scene, but as recently as a generation ago, lynch mobs still claimed at least a few black victims each year. The lynch mob, like the race riot, is virtually unknown in Brazil, although in some sections of the country Negroes and mulattoes make up considerably more than a majority of the population. No state of the United States, not even Mississippi, has ever counted as high a proportion of colored people as have the states of Bahia or Pernambuco. In Bahia in 1950 the white population was no more than 30 per cent.

Brazilians are extremely proud of what their leading sociologist, Gilberto Freyre, has called their "racial democracy." One prominent Brazilian has been quoted as saying that the problem of color prejudice "does not exist in São Paulo certainly; it does not exist in Bahia. It is new, it is imaginary, it is not real." [1] Even a sociologist like Florestan Fernandes, who has done more than any other Brazilian scholar to call into question the validity of Freyre's assertion of racial democracy admits that Brazil is probably the most racially tolerant nation in the world.[2]

This very tolerance, especially in the face of the blatant racism of the United States, tends to make Brazilians either complacent about, or oblivious to the realities of the relations between whites and blacks in their country. E. Franklin Frazier, the United States Negro sociologist, noted this fact after he returned from a visit to Brazil just before World War II. "There is, in Brazil," he observed, "little discussion of the racial or the color situation. It appears that there is an unexpressed understanding among all elements in the population not to discuss the racial situation, at least as a contemporary phenomenon." [3] Another North American, T. L. Smith refers to the "veritable cult of racial equality" in Brazil. The cult includes among its votaries the principal intellectuals of the country, whose unwritten creed has two tenets. "(1) Under no circumstances should it be admitted that racial discrimination exists in Brazil; and (2) any expression of racial

[1] Thales de Azevedo, *Les Élites de couleur dans une ville brésilienne* (Paris, 1953), p. 93.

[2] Florestan Fernandes, *A Integração do negro na sociedade de classes* (São Paulo, 1965), II, p. 293.

[3] E. Franklin Frazier, "A Comparison of Negro–White Relations in Brazil and the United States," in G. Franklin Edwards, ed., *E. Franklin Frazier on Race Relations* (Chicago, 1968), p. 98.

discrimination that may appear always should be attacked as un-Brazilian."[4] One consequence of the cult, as Smith rightly observes, is that the grosser forms of discrimination against Negroes are prevented or firmly objected to.

The very existence of the cult, moreover, suggests that Brazil may not be as free of prejudice as the cultists would like to have others believe. As Emilio Willems, now a sociologist at Vanderbilt University, but long a resident in Brazil, has written, the alleged absence of prejudice in Brazil "is put with an insistence that certainly would be unnecessary if there were actually no doubt about it."[5] Recently several Brazilian sociologists have been even more insistent upon the existence of prejudice within their society. Florestan Fernandes, for instance, who admits that Brazilians are among the most racially tolerant people in the world, emphasizes that tolerance is not equality. "The victims of color prejudice and discrimination are treated with relative decorum and civility as persons," he recognizes, "but as if they were only half persons. Their material and moral interests are not taken into account. What is important immediately and fundamentally is 'social peace.' . . ." The widespread denial of prejudice in Brazil Fernandes calls "the prejudice against prejudice."[6] Professor L. A. Costa Pinto has called the Brazilian denial of prejudice "crypto-melanism" or "the fear of confessing to and the desire to hide the importance one really gives to the question of race and color."[7]

It is the purpose of this and the next chapter to spell out in some detail the nature of the relations between the races in Brazil, especially as they compare with those in the United States. But before we move into an examination of concrete examples, two general observations need to be made if we are to avoid misinterpreting the comparison. The first is that relations between the races vary from region to region in Brazil as they do in the

[4] T. Lynn Smith, *Brazil People and Institutions* (Baton Rouge, 1963), p. 66.

[5] Emilio Willems, "Race Attitudes in Brazil," *American Journal of Sociology*, LIV (March, 1949), 403.

[6] Fernandes, *Integração do negro*, II, p. 293.

[7] Luis A. Costa Pinto, *O Negro no Rio de Janeiro* (São Paulo, n.d.) p. 325.

United States. The second is that the Brazilian definition of a Negro differs from that in the United States. Let us turn first to the question of regional diversity.

The Geography of Color Prejudice

The fullest and most important examination of race relations in Brazil written in English undoubtedly is Donald Pierson's *Negroes in Brazil*. Although first published in 1942, the book has been partly brought up to date by Pierson in a long introduction to a new edition published in 1967. But the principal conclusion Pierson makes in the book has not changed. "Prejudice exists in Brazil," he writes, "but it is *class* rather than *race* prejudice." [8] By that he means that the principal barrier that keeps blacks at the bottom of the social economic ladder—a fact that Pierson admits in his book—is their general poverty. The validity of Pierson's conclusion is a central issue, but discussion of it will be taken up later. Here it is pertinent to notice only that Pierson's study, which has been widely used in analyses of race relations in Brazil, is actually based upon evidence drawn from a small and indeed very special part of the country. The state of Bahia, in northeastern Brazil, where Pierson carried on his field work, is located in that section of the country where Negroes have been and still are most numerous and culturally influential. (His research actually centered on the city of Salvador, or Bahia, as it is usually known, after the state of which it is the capital; its proper name was once Cidade de São Salvador da Bahia de Todos os Santos, or the City of the Holy Savior of the Bay of All Saints.)

All authorities acknowledge that the relations between the races are the easiest in the *Nordeste* or Northeast, of which Bahia is the largest state. For one thing, racial mixture in Bahia has probably progressed farther than in any part of Brazil. In the census of 1940, for example, the ratio of blacks to mixed bloods in the state of Bahia was 1 to 2.55, whereas in the state of Minas Gerais, it was 1 to 1 and in Maranhão and Piauí there were more Negroes

---

[8] Donald Pierson, *Negroes in Brazil. A Study of Race Contact* (Carbondale, Ill., 1967), p. 349.

than mulattoes.[9] There are so many so-called whites in Bahia with mixed ancestry that the term *branco da Bahia* is the name throughout Brazil for a person with a small amount of Negro blood. Pierson examined the photographs of the first five hundred people listed as white at the Identification Bureau of Bahia. To him, as a North American, only 68 per cent appeared to be of white ancestry exclusively. A light mulatto who came to Bahia from a state farther west summed up the special place of Bahia in the regional patterns of Brazil. He said that during the nine years he had lived in Bahia he had been struck by "the mutual respect between persons of different 'quality' [that is, of different color], for in his state persons of color would be treated with contempt." Other informants in Bahia agreed that even at the "highest levels of society" in Bahia a colored person does not generally "suffer humiliation." [10] Bahia or the Northeast, then, represents the area or zone in which prejudice against colored people is slightest.

South of the Northeast at least three other zones of race relations can be identified: the area around Rio de Janeiro, São Paulo state, and the region comprised of the states south of São Paulo. As a rule of thumb, the farther south one travels in Brazil the more intense the degree of prejudice. E. Franklin Frazier, for example, who found that it was hard to discern in Bahia a color line at all, reported that in the states south of Rio (that is, São Paulo, Santa Catarina, Paraná, and Rio Grande do Sul), the color prejudice came close to what he, as a Negro, was familiar with in the United States. There was no legal discrimination, he added, but the social practices were clearly discriminatory.[11] Brazilian Negroes notice the difference even between Rio and São Paulo. A Negro maid who was taken by her employer from São Paulo to Rio refused to return with him when the visit was over, preferring to remain in Rio. "You can understand," she said, "here Negroes are people." A young mulatto woman who came to São Paulo from Rio was shocked by the attitudes of her neighbors toward

[9] Azevedo, *Les Élites de couleur*, p. 22.

[10] Ibid., p. 32.

[11] E. Franklin Frazier, "Some Aspects of Race Relations in Brazil," *Phylon*, III (Third Quarter, 1942), p. 292.

Negroes. In short order she came to hate the city, contending, "It is the worst place for Negroes. In Rio there was greater tolerance than here," she explained. Yet a white personnel manager in a São Paulo industrial firm asserted that São Paulo was quite "moderate" in its attitudes toward blacks compared with the attitudes of whites in the states to the south.[12]

The degree of difference in attitudes toward blacks among the four regions or zones is not of central importance here, though it bears upon later analysis. (Nor is the number of regions—four —of importance, other than to illustrate the diversity of outlooks. It is possible to point to several other regions of Brazil in which attitudes toward blacks on the part of whites might differ from these, but materials for drawing conclusions are not as abundant as for the four regions referred to here. Moreover, to add other regions unnecessarily complicates a pattern already complicated enough.) The purpose of mentioning the different degrees of prejudice here is simply to stress that relations between whites and blacks in Brazil do vary from region to region and that to generalize about race relations on the basis of one part of the country or another can be confusing and misleading. This variation in regional race relations has been one major source of the varieties of interpretations of race relations in Brazil. Generally, those students, like Pierson, who emphasize the absence of race or color prejudice in Brazil draw their conclusions from evidence gathered in the Northeast, Bahia and Pernambuco in particular. It is not accidental, either, that Gilberto Freyre, who has celebrated Brazil's "racial democracy," is from Recife, in Pernambuco. On the other hand, those who have played down or denied racial democracy in Brazil, like Florestan Fernandes and Roger Bastide, have made their studies in São Paulo.

The regional variation in Brazil might be compared to that which is well recognized in the United States. No one will deny that the treatment of the Negro in New England, for example, has been less discriminatory than that in, say, the Middle West. Furthermore, most Americans would acknowledge, I think, that prejudice and discrimination, not to mention violence against

[12] Roger Bastide, ed., *Relações raciais entre negros e brancos em São Paulo* (São Paulo, 1955), p. 138; Fernandes, *Integração do negro*, II, p. 303, 323.

blacks, have their greatest incidence in the South. Beneath the regional variations in each country, however, lies a norm that is truly characteristic of each country. We shall in this and the next chapter note regional variations in discussing concrete examples, especially in regard to Brazil, if only because these regional differences often have been ignored in previous analyses of race relations. But it should be understood that the regional variations in each country are only variations on a central theme. It is the central themes that we are ultimately comparing.

Who Is a Negro?

Up to now the word *Negro* has been used without definition, yet the most fertile source of confusion, if not error, in comparing race relations in the United States and Brazil is that the conception of the Negro differs in the two countries. Historically, in the United States any person with Negro ancestry has been considered a Negro, even if he appeared to be a white. In the days of slavery as later, in the days of legal segregation, a Negro was defined in law and in custom as anyone with a certain amount of Negro ancestry—usually one-eighth. But there have been instances in the twentieth century when any amount of Negro ancestry would cause a person to be legally a Negro. Thus a statute of Virginia enacted in 1924, for purposes of its antimiscegenation law, defined a white person as ". . . such person as has no trace whatever of any blood other than Caucasian; but persons who have one-sixteenth or less of the blood of the American Indian and have no other non-Caucasian blood shall be deemed a white person." [13] Because appearance did not decide the matter, persons with blue eyes, fair skin, and sandy or blond hair, like Walter White, for many years head of the NAACP, could be considered a Negro. Simply because White acknowl-

[13] Quoted in J. Kenneth Morland, *Race, Values and American Unity* and *Stetson University Bulletin* (Leland, Fla., 1969), p. 5n. The exception for Indian blood was made in order to permit the descendants of Pocohantas to take advantage of that ancestry and white status at the same time. Charles S. Mangum, Jr., *The Legal Status of the Negro* (Chapel Hill, N.C., 1940), Chapter 1 surveys in detail the legal definition of the Negro from the days of slavery to the 1930's.

edged his Negro ancestry, regardless of his appearance, he was a Negro. Also because of this definition, whites could suddenly become "Negroes," as happened not only in a work of fiction like Sinclair Lewis' *Kingsblood Royal* but in real life as well. By this genetic or biological definition, thousands of Negroes also "pass" into the white world each year, remaining there as long as they wish to keep their secret or are able to. Historically in the United States words like *mulatto, quadroon,* and *octoroon*—all of which describe different degrees of Negro ancestry—have been used. But in fact they have been no more than descriptive; they carry no social or legal significance. There are only two qualities in the United States racial pattern: white and black. A person is one or the other; there is no intermediate position.

Although all Americans, white and black, grow up with and accept without question that definition of a Negro, there is no inherent logic in it. There is no reason why a person with half his ancestry white and half black should be defined as a Negro. With equal logic he could be defined as a white, or more precisely as a half white, half black. Brazilians are more logical, for they do not follow the North American definition of a Negro. In fact, no other country in the New World, with the exception of Canada, follows the United States in defining a black man as anyone with a measurable amount of Negro ancestry or "blood." In Brazil, for example, a Negro is a person of African descent who has no white ancestry at all. If a person has some indefinite amount of white as well as Negro ancestry he is something else. He is not white, to be sure, though he may be a *mulato,* or a *moreno,* or a *pardo.* For as we shall see in a moment, Brazilians are not color-blind. Indeed, they see, socially, more color distinctions than North Americans, who can see only two: white and black. Brazilians do not concern themselves about the genetic background of a person,[14] but they look at hair and lips as well as skin color in categorizing someone. In Bahia, Pierson writes, one often hears "He is a bit dark, but his hair is good."[15]

Anthropologist Harry Hutchinson has spelled out the great variety of color gradations that he found in the community of Vila Reconcavo, located across the bay from Salvador, in the state of

[14] Pierson, *Negroes in Brazil,* p. 128.
[15] Ibid., p. 140.

Bahia. Although these gradations are not necessarily typical of all of Brazil, they do illustrate the diversity of colors and the valuations that are placed upon them in a community of the Northeast, where racial tensions are weakest in Brazil.[16] The lowest level is composed of the *pretos* (blacks) or *preto retinto* (dark black). Somewhat above the *preto* is the *cabra*, who is slightly less black. (The word *cabra* also means goat in Portuguese, incidentally.) Still moving upward, we come next to the *cabo verde* (Cape Verde), who is lighter than the *preto*, but still quite dark, but with straight hair, thin lips, and narrow, straight nose. Then comes the *escuro*, literally, "the dark one," but he is still lighter than *preto*. The *mulato* is divided into two classes, *mulato escuro* (dark mulatto) and *mulato claro* (light mulatto). *Pardo* (light mulatto) is not used in speech in Vila Reconcavo, though it is used in other parts of Brazil and in the census. The *sarará* has light skin and red or blond hair, which is kinky and curled. Some *sararás* would pass in the United States as white. The *moreno* has light skin and straight hair, but is not viewed as a white. Just beneath the white is the *branco de terra* (literally, "white of the land," or *branco da Bahia* elsewhere in Brazil.) Though everyone recognizes that they have some Negro blood, *brancos de terra* are always spoken of as white and receive from everyone the same treatment accorded whites. The whites themselves are divided into blond and brunettes, depending on the color of their hair.

This amazing array of terms and gradations is testimony to the Brazilian emphasis upon appearance rather than upon genetic or racial background, which is the key to the North American definition of the Negro. It is also testimony to the fact that in Brazil there is a continuum or spectrum of colors from white to black, rather than a dichotomy as in the United States. For purposes of ease of discussion, we shall speak of black, or Negro, mulatto, and white, which terms, in themselves, are in striking contrast with the simple black–white devision in the United States. But it should be understood that *mulatto* in Brazil really stands for a whole range of color types between black and white. Most accurately, distinctions among people in Brazil are between

[16] Harry William Hutchinson, *Village and Plantation Life in Northeastern Brazil* (Seattle, Washington, 1957), p. 118.

lighter and darker, not simply between Negro and mulatto or mulatto and white.

This fundamental difference in the definition of a Negro in Brazil and in the United States extends beyond the spectrum or hierarchy of colors. It determines the form that prejudice and discrimination take. In the United States a Negro's social position in society as a whole is largely unaffected by his class. (*Within the Negro community*, however, his occupation, income, education, and other indicia of class are the principal determinants of his position, as they are for whites, but that is another question.) It is this genetic definition of the Negro that causes some sociologists to speak of the Negro's *caste* position in the United States.[17] The word *caste*, it is true, has a number of connotations not applicable to the situation in the United States; for example, in India, the concept's place of origin, caste carries religious significance as it does not in the United States. But the term does have the great advantage of making clear the difference between the position of the Negro and that of all white people in the American social structure. Classes exist in the United States, but it is not impossible or even especially difficult for an individual or his children to rise or fall from one class to another. All the indicia of class affiliation can be acquired, that is, money, education, a prestigious house, or a distinguishing profession. For the Negro in the United States, however, it is not possible to shed his ancestry and it is that which defines him and limits his social mobility at the same time. Caste aptly differentiates the rigid and unalterable limitation placed upon the Negro alone from those limitations or barriers, however difficult to surmount they may be, for any particular non-Negro individual, which are only those of class.

Because ancestry as such is not important in Brazil, though color obviously is, commentators on the Brazilian racial scene do not speak of a caste system as they rightly do in discussing the United States. In Brazil, to put the matter simply, if abstractly, a person is located in the social hierarchy on the basis of both color *and* class, a phenomenon that Charles Wagley has

[17] Gunnar Myrdal, *An American Dilemma* (New York, 1942), Chapter 31 discusses the word *caste* as a description of the position of the Negro in United States society. The weaknesses as well as the sound reasons for using this East Indian word in this context are canvassed in that chapter.

called "social race." Color is important, but it is not decisive, as it is in the United States. A rich mulatto is accepted by whites to a degree that a poor mulatto is not. Marvin Harris, an American anthropologist who has long studied race relations in Brazil, has succinctly summarized the relationships between color and class in defining status in a backcountry town in Bahia state. His scheme, like Hutchinson's terminology, is derived from the study of a community in the Northeast, but it is applicable more or less to Brazil as a whole. Its principal value is that it serves to differentiate in a clear and concrete fashion the bases of social hierarchy in Brazil from those in the United States.[18] In Brazil,

A "Negro" is anyone of the following:	A "white" is anyone of the following:
Poverty-stricken white	White who is wealthy
Poverty-stricken mulatto	White of average wealth
Poor mulatto	White who is poor
Poverty-stricken Negro	Wealthy mulatto
Poor Negro	Mulatto of average wealth
Negro of average wealth	Negro who is wealthy

Two conclusions stand out in this comparison of who is Negro and who is white. First, to be of Negro ancestry is certainly a handicap; not as severe a one as in the United States, perhaps, but a handicap nonetheless. Second, as the Brazilians say, "money whitens," although it takes a good deal to whiten a full-blooded Negro, even in Bahia. (Once "whitened" by money, a "Negro" becomes a "*mulato*" or "*pardo*," regardless of his actual color. A significant commentary on the meaning of *Negro* or blackness in itself.) One informant in Recife, which is also in the Northeast, put the whitening process this way: "When a black (*preto*) at-

---

[18] Marvin Harris, "Race Relations in Minas Velhas, A Community in the Mountain Region of Central Brazil," in Charles Wagley, ed., *Race and Class in Rural Brazil*, 2nd ed. (New York, 1963), p. 72. One type of explanation that is typical, if not actually the most popular among Brazilian Negroes for color prejudice, is that quoted by Fernandes, *Integração do negro*, II, p. 362: "It is a mixed prejudice of race and class. It is not only of race, because there are whites who accept the Negro. It is not only of class because certain restrictions affect all Negroes, even the rich. As a mixed prejudice it is a color prejudice."

tains a prominent position—he has a ring on his finger. [The ring of a profession.] The black will be easily accepted. In that case, however, it is not the black, but the ring of the black that they accept." The same principle is illustrated by the humorous story of a light-skinned mulatto in the same city who had three daughters. One of the daughters had a white boyfriend who was a factory worker; because he was white the father accepted him as a son-in-law. The second daughter had a boyfriend who was a Negro, studying to be a lawyer. After the wedding of the two couples the father told the third daughter: "A worker only if he is white: a Negro, only if he is a doctor." [19] An even better illustration of the way in which class mitigates color is an incident that took place in a São Paulo restaurant. Among the customers were two well-dressed mulattoes and a white man in working clothes, sitting at separate tables. The waiter gave equally solicitous attention to the mulattoes, the white, and the rest of the patrons. The two mulattoes were obviously old customers because they talked freely with the manager and other customers. Then a young black man in workingmen's clothes came into the restaurant, only to be stopped by the waiter from sitting at a table. The youth protested, exclaiming, "What is this, the Esplanada?" [20]

The story reveals a number of things about Brazilian race relations. For one thing, the presence of the middle class mulattoes as accepted customers means that colored persons as such were not excluded, but the failure to accept the working class black cannot be attributed simply to class, because the white worker had been admitted. In short, a black had to be better, socially speaking, than a white in order to achieve the same acceptance; but he could be accepted, as he would not have been in, say, a restaurant in Georgia fifteen years ago. Finally, one other revealing aspect in the incident: the young Negro made his protest in class terms, not racial terms, for his exclamatory query is whether the restaurant is trying to put on the high social airs of a well-known luxury hotel in São Paulo. This failure of blacks who are discriminated against to react immediately in racial terms is also

[19] René Ribeiro, *Religião e relações raciais* (n.p., n.d.), pp. 123–24.

[20] Oracy Nogueira, "Preconceito de marca and preconceito racial de origem," *Anais do XXXI Congresso Internacional de Americanistas* (São Paulo, 1954), 428–29n.

characteristic of Brazilian race relations, as we shall have occasion to observe in more detail a little later.

Some North American observers, seeing the ability of wealth or education to whiten, and being themselves used to the rigid caste situation in the United States, in which no amount of money could gain a Negro or even a mulatto entrance to certain public, much less private places, have concluded that in Brazil there are in fact no race or color barriers. Donald Pierson, as we have already noted, has concluded that there are only class barriers restricting the mobility of Negroes and mulattoes in Brazil. It is not necessary, however, for color to be conclusive for it to have an effect upon opportunities open to a Negro or upon his life style. Ugliness, as Marvin Harris remarks, has low social value even when it accurately describes a millionaire's daughter; her ugliness may not singlehandedly determine the prospective husbands available to her, but it is not without influence either. In Brazil, as we shall see later in this chapter, blackness carries at least as low social value as ugliness and considerably more tangible social disabilities.

From the Brazilian definition of the Negro it follows that the mulatto or mixed blood in general, occupies a special place, intermediate between white and black; he is neither black nor white. No such place is reserved for the so-called mixed blood in the United States; a person is either a black or a white. Thus the mulatto in Brazil represents an escape hatch for the Negro, so to speak, which is unavailable in the United States. Historically it has been the mulatto who has risen in Brazilian society, not the Negro. The great men of color of the nineteenth century, such as Luis Gama and José do Patrocinio among the abolitionists, André Rebouças, the famous engineer, and Machado de Assis and Cruz e Souza among the writers, were all mulattoes.[21] As we shall see later, that fact in itself is important in comparing the race relations in the two countries. Right now, however, it is necessary only to look at several concrete examples to illustrate the fact and simultaneously expose some of the consequences that flow from it.

[21] Fernando de Azevedo, *Canaviais e engenhos na vida política do Brasil*, 2nd ed. (São Paulo, 1958), p. 126n.

First look at the following explosion from a white Brazilian, in which the social mobility of the mulatto is obviously the source of his anxiety. "I am going to get out of Bahia and go to São Paulo," complained a prominent white to Pierson. "This town is too full of mulattoes and mulatto traits. . . . This place is full of envy, ill will, and egotism, all mulatto characteristics. The mulatto is not like the black; he is a person without character. He has no honor. He's always envious, he's jealous, he's so busy 'maintaining himself,' pushing himself in where he isn't wanted, that he can't tend to his business or his job; he can't do anything except make of himself a general nuisance." [22] The diatribe is not only the classic indictment of the parvenu, but it makes a distinction between Negroes and mulattoes that has no meaning to North Americans. In the United States, mulattoes are no more a threat to the established class than Negroes.

An even more revealing outburst of white, middle-class hostility toward the mulatto is one also reported from the Northeast, this time from Recife. Here the antagonism is tempered and tortured by religious considerations, but the class issue also slides over into racial conceptions, despite the speaker's efforts to rule out race.

"You know that as a *Catholic intellectual,* trained in the doctrine of the church, I do not have, I cannot have, I ought not to have any racial prejudice. For us, all men are metaphysically equal; they are all given the same possibilities of salvation and all are redeemed by the blood of Christ in the mystery of the Redemption. I confess that as a Catholic and as an intellectual I never supported, doctrinally, any prejudice in that sense. I do not believe that the superiority of the race is in the color of the epidermis or in the turned up nose. I believe, however, that there are superior and inferior races. . . . My testimony will not be that of the intellectual without prejudice, brought up in the doctrine of the church. It will be only that of the man, grandson of the masters of the *engenho* [sugar mill] and full of prejudices. . . . I never felt any violent reaction against the fact that a colored man travelled with me on the same train, sat next to me at the same table, in the same movies, etc. . . . What irritates me is the mulattoist philosophy. . . . It is the mulatto wanting to

[22] Pierson, *Negroes in Brazil,* p. 231.

take the place of the white, dressing like him, wanting to marry with the white, driving his own automobile. It is the meddlesome mulatto . . . wanting to imitate people of quality. To that my reaction is strong. I have an invincible antipathy for that mulatto-ness. I assert, however, that color does not prevent my admiring and esteeming those mulattoes whom I consider good people, better than many whites who have gone off the deep end. A man like X, for example, is not spiritually a mulatto. He has the char-acter of a white. Against mulattoes of this level I feel no preju-dice. A very dark Negro with the face of an old monkey like . . . X, does not arouse antipathy in me. On the contrary, twenty years ago I knew that black and considered him white and a good man. . . . I feel, however, a certain prejudice in regard to mulattoes who exercise offices of direction or functions of com-mand. In this country there are sufficient whites to govern and to command. I do not believe that the Negro or the mulatto can or ought to govern and command white people . . . inferior people. They are good for work. They have souls. They ought to be baptized. Ought to be saved and to go to heaven. But to be equal to white, no. . . . The Catholic intellectual subscribes to none of this, which the man in him ends by saying . . . I believe that in this the intellectual is right—but it is the man who lives and feels." [23]

Although there are many insights into Brazilian attitudes toward race in that statement, here we can content ourselves with calling attention to the distinction between mulattoes and Ne-groes once again. As the speaker himself makes evident, the basis of the distinction in his mind is that the Negro does not get out of his place, whereas the mulatto does. It is the mulatto, once again, who is socially mobile, not the Negro.

The greater opportunity that mulattoes enjoy for social mo-bility also encourages them to dissociate themselves from Negroes. This tendency is observable even when a mulatto has a strong intellectual interest in the life and culture of Negroes. Ruth Landes, a North American anthropologist working in Bahia in the 1940's on a study of the *condomblé* (Negro dances of African origin), noticed that her mulatto colleague, Edison Carneiro, a Brazilian student of the Negro, clearly did not identify with the

[23] Ribeiro, *Religião e relações raciais,* pp. 215–16.

blacks he so assiduously studied. They, in turn, viewed him with genuine affection, but as a patron and not as a fellow black. Landes, as a North American, could not avoid noticing what seemed to her an incongruity in this sharp separation. Carneiro himself, of course, was oblivious to her concern. In his mind there was no reason to assume an identification between himself and the Negroes; he was a mulatto, educated, and a gentleman, and therefore not a Negro. More recently Rodrigues Alves, the Brazilian writer, provided another example of the way in which mulattoes are differentiated from blacks, especially in Bahia. Alves pointed out that if one goes into an office and sees that the chief is a Negro and hears him say "I am a Negro," the chief's aid will say, "No, Sir, you are not a Negro, you are a *moreno*." [24] Both these instances are more or less neutral examples of the mulatto's dissociation from Negroes. Later we shall have the occasion to look at some examples in which the dissociation is more stressful and anxiety-producing. Whether benign or stressful, however, the mulatto escape hatch is one of the distinguishing aspects of the Brazilian racial scene when compared with the United States. These persons who are neither black nor white play the central role in differentiating the race relations of the two countries.

Although Brazilians do take color into consideration in ranking people, as we have seen, they do not refer to genetic or biological origins. As a result, insofar as there is prejudice or discrimination against Negroes in Brazil, it is based upon color rather than racial origins. "In Brazil," Professor L. A. Costa Pinto has written, "a defined and strong racist philosophy, giving support and moral sanction to racial discrimination does not exist." By that he means that Brazilians do not justify prejudice or discrimination against Negroes on grounds of innate genetic inferiority. They do refer to what they think of as cultural deprivation—the African heritage—and the burdensome historic experience of slavery to justify their placing low social value on Negroes. Sometimes, admittedly, it is difficult to distinguish between the justifications derived from cultural and historical experiences and those of race, but in general the distinction between United States and Brazilian ex-

---

[24] Ruth Landes, *The City of Women* (New York, 1947), pp. 59–60; *80 Anos de Abolição* Serie Cadernos Brasileiros (Rio de Janeiro, 1968), p. 39.

planations holds. Oracy Nogueira has called the distinction the difference between a prejudice of mark (Brazil) and a prejudice of origin (United States).[25] This terminology has the advantage in regard to Brazil since it can include within a single term elements such as hair quality, general physical appearance, and even educational background as well as color. All of these elements enter into the Brazilian basis of stratification. It is superior, for that reason, to the more common term often applied to Brazil, that of *color prejudice*. Yet the latter term is more convenient and will be used here, though it should be understood that it includes more than color. The phrase *racial prejudice* will be reserved for the United States, because of the genetic or biological basis for the definition of a Negro.

As we have already noted, many Brazilians and some North American scholars have asserted that there is no color or racial prejudice in Brazil, only class prejudice. Recently, however, a number of Brazilian students of race relations have begun to revise that view, arguing that color carries rather severe disabilities in their country. Undoubtedly the leader of this group, whose research has centered at the University of São Paulo, is Roger Bastide. Bastide taught and worked at São Paulo for many years, but has since returned to his native France, where he now teaches at the Sorbonne. His work in Brazil has been continued by a number of younger sociologists at the University of São Paulo, notably Florestan Fernandes, Oracy Nogueira, Octavio Ianni, and H. F. Cardoso, to name only the oldest. Their studies in the history of slavery and contemporary race relations in southern Brazil have been a major contribution. Professor L. A. Costa Pinto in Rio de Janeiro has also been a leader in the reevaluation of the place that race and color play in the lives of blacks and mulattoes in Brazil.

[25] Costa Pinto, *Negro no Rio de Janeiro*, p. 344; Oracy Nogueira, "Preconceito de marca e preconceito racial de origem," *Anais do XXXI Congresso Internacional de Americanistas* (São Paulo, 1954). The Negro leader Abdias do Nascimento was quoted in *Jornal do Brasil*, May 12, 1968 as putting the difference between United States and Brazilian attitudes toward blacks in this fashion: "There is no problem of races; here the problem is color—the black who looks white and assumes the behavior of the white has no more difficulties." In the United States, of course, such a black would also have his ancestry kept a secret in order to "pass" as a white.

Nor have the Brazilians been alone in this reevaluation. Particularly valuable have been the studies of race and class in Brazil sponsored by UNESCO, four of which have been published under the general direction of Charles Wagley, an anthropologist at Columbia University. All of these studies recognize in varying degrees that the racial situation in Brazil differs from that in the United States, but all also acknowledge, as many Brazilians do not, that a form of color prejudice and discrimination exists in Brazil.

Before we turn to an examination of the nature and extent of color prejudice in Brazil, it is worth clarifying the distinction between prejudice and discrimination. Both prejudice and discrimination imply the inferiority of the person or group against which they are directed. But they are not the same thing; prejudice is an attitude, whereas discrimination is an action. As a moment's reflection makes evident, one may occur without the other. A person may be prejudiced against Negroes, but not act on it, at least not consistently. Conversely, a person may act in such a way as to discriminate against a Negro, but not be doing so consciously or as a reflection of prejudice. Most often, of course, both occur together: a prejudiced person acts in a discriminatory manner and discriminatory behavior reflects prejudice. But in a country like Brazil, where color and class so closely coincide and where the thrust of social values and public attitudes is hostile to discrimination, prejudice and discrimination do not always coincide. We will see in some of the examples in this and the next chapter that individuals may well admit to prejudice, but their behavior belies it, just as there are examples of discriminatory behavior on the part of persons who deny having any prejudicial attitudes.[26]

[26] James W. Vander Zanden, *American Minority Relations,* 2nd ed. (New York, 1966), p. 9 reports on a well-known United States example of prejudice that did not result in discriminatory behavior. It concerns a sociologist who traveled around the United States in the 1930's with a Chinese couple, stopping for service at hundreds of hotels, auto camps, tourist homes, and restaurants. Only once were they refused service. Six months later the sociologist wrote each of the establishments they had visited and asked if Chinese guests were welcome. Over 90 per cent of the managers replied they would *not* accommodate Chinese, despite their having actually done so six months earlier.

Permutations of Prejudice

The existence of color prejudice in Brazil has been implied in what has been said up to now. The purpose of this section is to show that pejorative attitudes toward blacks is rather widespread in Brazil. The best place to begin is with that section of the country in which the absence of prejudice is most often asserted, that is, the Northeast. "That there is no prejudice of color in Bahia is an affirmation only partly true," one recognized Brazilian authority on race relations has recently written. "The colored people are still considered as forming a part of a biological and social category characterized by traits which cause them to be considered inferior to the whites. Some are convinced that Blacks and Whites are different in intellectual capacity, personality, morality, and aptitude for progress. They declare that if Bahia does not progress, it is the fault of the Blacks." The most obvious form the prejudice takes is in the stereotypes that whites have of Negroes in Bahia. They "are more or less the same as those which are encountered in the rest of the country," Thales Azevedo has written, "judging by the representations of the black in Brazilian literature." Negroes are seen as ugly, evil smelling, savage, superstitious, and lazy, much as they are stigmatized "in the United States." [27] In the sayings and folklore of the Northeast, perjorative judgments on blacks are common:

> The white drinks champagne
> The *caboclo* [mixture of Indian and white] port wine:
> The mulatto drinks cheap rum
> The Negro urine of the pig.[28]

Even Donald Pierson, in his study of the Negro in Bahia, includes a list several pages long of derogatory statements about Negroes. Writing in 1942, Pierson cautioned his readers not to take seriously these canards, likening them to the disparaging thrusts at Irishmen and Swedes common in the United States in

[27] Azevedo, *Les Élites de couleur*, pp. 70–71, 103.
[28] Roger Bastide, *Brasil, Terra de Contrastes*, trans. Maria Isaura Pereira de Queiroz (São Paulo, 1959), p. 47.

the nineteenth century.[29] It can be left to the reader, however, to judge whether he himself, as a North American, knows as many insulting remarks about any nationality in the United States as are here given about Negroes—and I have not reproduced the full list provided by Pierson. One ought also to consider whether such clearly unfavorable judgments can be without effect upon whites or blacks, as Pierson implies. In any event, here are some of the sayings:

Negroes aren't born; they just appear.
Negroes don't marry; they just live together.
Negroes don't eat; they bolt their food.
Negroes don't dry themselves; they just shake the water off.
Negroes don't comb their hair; they curry it.
The Negro if he doesn't soil things on entering, soils them
　　before he leaves.

The Negro was born to be a dog
And to spend his life barking.
The Negro will not go to heaven,
Even though he prays,
Because his hair is kinky,
And it might stick Our Lord.

The white man is a son of God,
The mulatto is a foster-child,
The *cabra* has no relatives,
The Negro is a son of Satan.

The white man goes to heaven,
The mulatto stays on earth,
The *caboclo* goes to Purgatory,
The Negro goes to Hell.

The white man sleeps in a bed,
The mulatto in the hall,
The *caboclo* in the parlor,
The Negro in the 'privy.'

Not all uncomplimentary remarks about Negroes are confined to folklore; a teacher in Bahia voiced a similar downgrading of blackness. Using the word from slavery times to describe a young

[29] Pierson, *Negroes in Brazil*, Appendix B, pp. 362–65.

slave, the teacher said, in the hearing of the class, "That *moleque* has no sense. Not only is he black, but he is not studious." In the same school a dark colored student, although highly respected by his fellow students, was not elected president of his class because a white student suggested that "a young man so black" would not carry sufficient prestige before the educational authorities and the public. As a result the black student was elected vice-president.[30]

René Ribeiro, in his study of race relations in Recife, found prejudice rather weakly defined. Nevertheless he quotes examples of denigrating attitudes toward Negroes. One informant, for example, said that when a child refused to take milk in her coffee the mother told her that if she drank coffee plain, she would become a Negro. At other times the mother would exclaim, "God save me from having a Negro in the family." Among the middle class in Recife a major fear is the loss of station that would result from marrying someone darker. To do so, one informant said, would be to "disgrace the family." Nor would this same informant permit her daughter to marry a Negro, even if it meant a lessening of her daughter's happiness and even though "all are equal before God." She conceded there might be a conflict between her views and Christianity, but one cannot overcome "social prejudice," she said, carefully avoiding the tabooed word *race*. The church generally has no objection to the marriage of people of different colors, but individual clerical objections are known in the Northeast, as in the case of a priest who refused to marry a certain couple, saying, "I do not marry a black with a white. It is an outrage." Sometimes whites object to a Negro priest, especially in the backcountry. One black priest in the Northeast, upon arriving at his new church, found that none of the people in the town would come except the very old and the children. He was told that the people were proud of being white, "very full of quality," as one of them expressed it. The priest left for another parish.[31]

Given the existence of prejudice in the Northeast it is not surprising to find rather vehement expressions of it in the rest of Brazil. Indeed, it is not far wrong to say that Brazilian culture

[30] Azevedo, *Les Élites de couleur*, p. 70.
[31] Ribeiro, *Religião e relações raciais*, pp. 116, 118, 127, 130–31.

is pervaded with a low conception of blacks. And in some instances it comes strikingly close to views or conceptions commonly expressed in the United States. Both societies, for example, have a folktale about the origin of the Negro's black skin. The similarities are striking, but on balance in this particular instance the Brazilian example is the more denigrating to blacks.

In one of his Uncle Remus stories, Joel Chandler Harris tells "Why the Negro is Black." [32] The story begins with the observation by the little white boy that Uncle Remus' palms are white, like his own. When the boy asks him about it, Uncle Remus replies that at one time everyone was black. "Niggers is niggers now," he says, "but de time wuz w'en 'uz all niggers tergedder." Then there came a time, he goes on, when "de news come dat dere wuz a pon 'er water some'rs in de naberhood, w'ich ef dey'd git inter dey'd be wash off nice en w'ite, en den one un um, he fine de place en make er splunge inter de pon', en come out w'ite ez a town gal. En den, bless grashus! w'en de fokes seed it, dey make a break fer de pon', en dem w'at suz de soopless, dey got in fus' en dey come out w'ite; en dem w'at wuz de nex' soopless, dey got in nex', en dey come out merlatters; en dey wuz sech a crowd un um day dey mighty nigh use de water up, w'ich w'en dem yuthers come 'long, de morest dey could do wuz ter paddle about wid der foots en dabble in it wid der han's. Dem wuz de niggers, en down ter dis day dey ain't no w'ite 'bout a nigger 'ceppin de pa'm er der han's en de soles er der foot."

From the folklore of São Paulo, Florestan Fernandes reports a very similar story, entitled "Origins of the Races." [33]

Long ago all men were black. One day God resolved to reward the courage of each one without telling them; he ordered them to cross a river. The quickest, and he who had the most faith, quickly carried out God's order, crossing the river by swimming. When he emerged on the other side he was completely white, which was beautiful.

The second when he saw what had happened to his brother, also ran to the waters of the river, doing the same thing that he had

[32] Joel Chandler Harris, *Uncle Remus* (London and New York, n.d.), pp. 165–66.

[33] Quoted in Florestan Fernandes, *Mudanças sociais no Brasil* (São Paulo, 1960), p. 357.

done. But the water was dirty and he came out on the other side only yellow.

The third also wanted to change color, imitating his two brothers. But the water was much dirtier and when he arrived at the other side, he saw with disgust that he was only a mulatto.

The fourth was very sluggish and lazy, when he arrived at the river, God had already made it dry. Then he moistened his feet and hands, pressing them over the river bed. It is in this way that the black has only the palms of the hand and the soles of the feet white, and he is less than the others.

It is noticeable that the Brazilian version, with its blatant praise of the white man, is more prejudiced than the North American version. A longer form of the same story, this time from Espírito Santo, which is a state just north of Rio de Janeiro, reflects the concern of Brazilians with the physical features of the Negro, other than color.[34]

God, in order to complete the work of creating the world, made man and woman, who were placed in Paradise. But the devil, during the completion of the work, was envious and jealous. He suggested that he was capable of making the same prodigy. God, in order to punish him for such audacity, called him and ordered him to make another man.

Proudly, the devil began the work, conscious of his power. Egoist! He amassed the black clay, in imitation of what God had done and, after hours and hours of work, completed a beautiful statue, equal to that of Adam.

He blew upon his work of art in order to give it movement; but it remained black; more black, indeed, than the original clay. What disillusionment! He pressed for a dispensation in order to better the situation. To do this the artisan resolved to wash his man. He carried him to the edge of a river and began to wash him. But he scrubbed and washed him so much that the hair became kinky, without, however, the skin's getting any lighter.

Horrible!

He gave him a slap, a tremendous slap that knocked the figurine to the ground, thickening the lips and flattening the nose.

More furious than ever, the unfortunate artisan took up his black

[34] Quoted in Maria Stella de Novaes, *A Escravidão e a abolição no Espírito Santo* (Vitoria, Brazil, 1963), pp. 94–95.

figure and carried it to the beach. He attempted to drown it with a push that knocked it into the water. It must be destroyed! But the waters refused it and the black ended on all fours, with the soles of his feet and the palms of his hands in the wet sand.

Amazed, the devil then saw his creature get up. Unconcerned, gay, and happy, with a flat nose, large lips, and kinky hair, the soles of his feet and the palms of his hands much lighter than the skin of his body.

In this tale the Negro is clearly the product of the devil and of the devil's arrogance and defiance of God. Moreover, the Negro's appearance, which is looked upon as a deformity and is also explicable as the work of the devil. Although the story does not attempt to account for the so-called happy-go-lucky character of the Negro, it repeats that stereotype. The story well illustrates Florestan Fernandes' conclusion that in the folklore of São Paulo the Negro is seen as etiologically inferior, biologically superior, and socially inferior to the white. By *etiologically inferior* Fernandes means that the Negro's color is the work of the devil, whereas white skin is the handiwork of God, as the story makes clear. The biological superiority is evidenced by the white's belief that the Negro is physically strong and capable of extraordinarily heavy, but lowly work. "The Negro is like a cat, he has seven lives," says one proverb. "The Negro is like a bad chamber pot, it does not break," is a dubious compliment paid to the Negro's durability and strength. As one traditional *paulista* said, "The blacks are better than the whites at hard work, because of the brute force required." The belief in the Negro's social inferiority is reflected in sayings like "The Negro does not eat, he gulps;" "he does not dine, he eats; he does not sing, he shouts." [35]

Common sayings, sometimes identical with those heard in Bahia, also denigrate the Negro in São Paulo. "Blacks are not people" is used to explain why a Negro lives or acts as he does. "I soon knew he was a black" suggests that Negroes do not behave like whites. "If the Negro does not make a mess when he enters, he does when he leaves," conveys the conviction that the Negro is not only incompetent, but dirty.[36] One writer from the

[35] Fernandes, *Integração do negro,* I, pp. 232–33; Bastide, ed., *Relações raciais,* p. 111.
[36] Fernandes, *Integração do negro,* II, p. 298.

Northeast, who is sympathetic toward the cause of Negro equality, referred to Negroes as the "cursed race," which, he explained, derives from the belief that Noah cursed Cham for making fun of him while drunk. "The Negroes (*Chamistas*)," he goes on, "are considered descendants of Cham." [37] (It is worth recalling that one of the defenses of slavery in the Old South of the United States was that Negroes were inferior because they bore the curse of Ham upon them. Similarly, the São Paulo saying, "A good Negro is born dead," [38] comes close to the United States frontier judgment on the only good Indian.)

Even those sayings that seek to excuse an individual Negro from the alleged ineptitude of his race, clearly convey the white's low estimation of the Negro: "he is black, but he has the soul of the white"; "he is Negro, but he is better than many whites"; "poor fellow, he cannot help that he is a Negro"; "he is black on the outside only." [39]

Much more vicious, in rhetoric at least, are the statements collected by Marvin Harris in the rural backcountry of the state of Bahia. There, where Harris says white men are convinced that Negroes are their inferior, the folk sayings take on a strong racist form: [40]

> Everything about a Negro is no good including his house which hasn't even got a ceiling. The only good thing he has are his teeth which God gave him so that he could tear *rapadura* [a hard brick of crude sugar] apart.
>
> They are foul-smelling but there's no incense in the world that can make them smell better. No matter how little time I spend with them, I can't stand it.
>
> The Negro isn't human. God has nothing to do with him and the Negro has nothing to do with the saints.
>
> The Negro is an ass and a brute. He's the cousin of the orangutan, the monkey, and the chimpanzee. He isn't a person. All he's good for is to make black magic.

[37] Affonso de Toledo Bandeira de Mello, *O Trabalho Servil no Brasil* (Rio de Janeiro, 1936), p. 86.

[38] Fernandes, *Integração do negro*, II, p. 298.

[39] Bastide, ed., *Relações raciais*, p. 111; Fernandes, *Integração do negro*, II, p. 298.

[40] Harris, "Race Relations in Minas Velhas," Wagley, ed., *Race and Class*, p. 55.

Harris notes that derisive terms will be used for blacks and that whites will make fun of them to their faces, but not consistently nor with hatred or malice. A white will call a Negro a "miserable nigger, what an ugly creature," but smile broadly while saying it. Many folktales in the area portray the black as naive and easily tricked by whites. One of the favorites is of the Negro who finds diamonds or gold and runs to tell the white, who then defrauds the hapless black of his find. When these stories are told by blacks, they emphasize two elements: the unfortunate, child-like simplicity of the Negroes and the greed and chicanery of the whites. "The whites, on the other hand," writes Harris, "simply ignore the implicit criticism of their honesty and conclude laughingly, 'How stupid the black is!' "[41] This, too, suggests the white's conception of Negroes. Many of the stereotypes that whites have of Negroes are contradictory. Thus blacks appear simultaneously as honest and dishonest, stupid and cunning, lazy and hardworking. But no matter how the stereotypes may contradict one another—and they often do in the United States as well—they are all in agreement in denigrating the Negro and his blackness.

On the floor of the United States Congress, a member was speaking: "If God Almighty had intended the two races to be equal He would have so created them. He made the Caucasian of handsome figure, straight hair, regular features, high brow, and superior intellect. He created the Negro, giving him a black skin, kinky hair, thick lips, flat nose, low brow, low order of intelligence, and repulsive features." That was in 1908. By 1938 the appeal was to civilization rather than to God, but the message was the same. "America must stand for white supremacy," said Senator Allen J. Ellender from Louisiana, "for if we do not, I say to you, that our civilization will deteriorate as did that of Egypt, of India, of Haiti, and of other countries of the world in the past. That is what may happen to us, and I am not willing to silently permit it. . . ." Even during a war against racism, Senator Theodore Bilbo from Mississippi in 1944 continued the appeal to civilization but with the alleged support of science and history thrown in. "Historical and scientific research," he argued, "has established three propositions beyond all controversy:

[41] Ibid., p. 53.

"First, The white race has founded, developed, and maintained every civilization known to the human race.

"Second, The white race, having founded, developed, and maintained a civilization, has never been known, in all history, to lose that civilization as long as the race was kept white.

"Third, The white man has never kept unimpaired the civilization he has founded and developed after his blood stream has been adulterated by the blood stream of another race, more especially another race so widely diverse in all its inherent qualities as the black race." [42] Behind such statements stands a whole body of literature asserting the biological inferiority of the Negro.

Such an obsessive concern with racial purity and racial mixture is absent from the writings of Brazilians, if only because race is a much less clear-cut phenomenon to them; indeed, as we have seen, it figures hardly at all in their social thought. Yet expressions of what North Americans recognize as racism are not entirely absent from Brazilian writings. The pronouncements of Oliveira Vianna do not have many imitators in Brazil, but he was a respected Brazilian sociologist of the past generation. In his best known book, *Evolução do povo brasileiro* (1933), he wrote: "The pure Negroes will never be able, not even the most advanced representatives of the race, to be assimilated completely into white culture; their capacity for civilization—their 'civilizability' so to speak, does not extend beyond merely imitating, more or less imperfectly, the habits and customs of the whites. Between the Negro's mentality and that of the Caucasian lies a substantial and irreducible difference which no social or cultural pressure no matter how long it may be continued, can possibly overcome." The Negro succeeds in rising into the upper class, he continues, "only when he loses his purity and mixes with the white." [43] Although Oliveira Vianna makes the same claim to a racial basis for civilization that people like Ellender or Bilbo have made in the United States, there is an important difference. Oliveira Vianna did not want to keep the races pure as Bilbo did and as Ellender still does—he actually desired mixture, for in it he saw hope for the black. Yet his conception of the Negro as such is

[42] Quoted in I. A. Newby, ed., *The Development of Segregationist Thought* (Homewood, Illinois, 1968), pp. 5, 130, 142.
[43] Quoted in Pierson, *Negroes in Brazil,* p. 213.

undoubtedly racist. Interestingly enough, Oliveira Vianna was a mixed blood. He used the mulatto escape hatch with a vengeance!

Oliveira Vianna's works are scholarly, not popular works, but the kind of racial stereotypes that he advanced has also appeared in more widely disseminated works. For example, the depiction of Aunt Nastacia in Monteiro Lobato's well-known children's book, *Viagem ao Ceu,* published in 1934, is nothing less than that of the Negro mammy as she used to appear in the United States in the form of Aunt Jemima. The sketches of Aunt Nastacia show her with a fat, shapeless body, thick lips, large eyes, large flat feet, and a kerchief on her head. As a personality she is loving, hard working, superstitious, fearful, subservient, and ignorant. From such books children, principally middle- and upper-class whites, learn how to perceive blacks. In other ways black children are instructed quite directly on the low value of their color. At an early age little black boys are called *urubu* (a black vulture) or *anu* (a small black bird). White children who do not perform a household task well are laughingly threatened with marrying a Negro when they grow up. None of these remarks are said with hatred or malice; yet they betray once again the pervasive disapprobation accorded blacks and blackness in Brazilian society. It is not only a source, but an extension of the prejudice, however innocent the intention of those who use the terms.[44]

Marvin Harris, in his study of a backcountry town in the state of Bahia, cites another way in which Brazilian children are exposed to derogatory stereotypes of Negroes. His example is from the textbook used in the town's public school as of 1950. "Of all races the white race is the most intelligent, persevering, the most enterprising," the text asserts. "The Negro race is much more retarded than the others." All six teachers in the school, who also happened to be white, accepted the statement when asked about it, Harris reports.[45] In 1950 a study of six primary school textbooks by Dante Moreira Leite showed, Florestan Fernandes writes, "how our school literature spreads and maintains ethnocentric evaluations unfavorable to the 'black.' The authors of the

[44] Nogueira, "Preconceito de marca, *XXXI Congresso . . . de Americanistas,* p. 421n.

[45] Harris, "Race Relations in Minas Velhas," Wagley, ed., *Race and Class,* p. 52.

school books which are analyzed," Fernandes is careful to observe, "probably enlist themselves among the advocates of *racial democracy*. Yet, inadvertently, they project images of 'the blacks' which produce the opposite effect." [46]

The white Brazilian's stereotype of blacks appears in a variety of ways. A joke going around Rio de Janeiro reflected the stereotype of the Negro as criminal. Two persons are talking. One says to the other, "When two whites pass me running, I think there go two athletes training; when two Negroes pass me running, I know at once—they are fleeing from the police!" [47] A Negro journalist in Rio in 1951 complained about the large number of Negro criminals' pictures in the newspapers, saying that on the basis of the pictures one would not know that there were "other ethnic groups with these evil attributes in Brazil." [48] The same complaint was made against the newspapers in São Paulo by a Negro woman, who stated "Everyone thinks that only the Negro robs her mistress. In the newspapers are published pictures of five black women thieves and only one of a white girl. The white woman also drinks and goes into the street, but they berate only the black woman." [49] Carolina Maria de Jesus tells of a black friend who was furious about a white policeman who beat a Negro and tied him to a tree. "There are certain whites who transform blacks into whipping posts," she commented in her diary. Very recently, in 1968, at a conference on the Negro held in Rio de Janeiro, Marcos Santarrita, the journalist and novelist from Bahia, also gave testimony to the effects of stereotypes on police behavior as far as Negroes were concerned. "The color of the skin of a citizen makes a very great difference, for example, to our police," he pointed out. "A white can drive around the city of Rio de Janeiro years on end without ever having to present his documents to the police, but a Negro will have to do it at the first occasion in which a Black Maria passes near him, especially at night. (In an interview a while back with a magazine the Bahian actor Antonio Luiz Sampaio declared that when he first came to Rio he was stopped almost daily in Copacabana to show

[46] Fernandes, *Integração do negro*, II, p. 298n.
[47] Costa Pinto, *Negro no Rio de Janeiro*, p. 166.
[48] Ibid., p. 175n.
[49] Virginia Leone Bicudo, "A Influencia do lar nas attitudes de preferencia e de rejeição dos escolares," *Anhembi*, XIII (December, 1953), p. 29.

his documents. 'A well dressed black, with money, hardly impresses the police,' he concluded.) A white without documents, although he may be setting out from a district very prone to investigation, if he is more or less well dressed will receive a quite different treatment from that given to a Negro in the same circumstances." [50]

Stereotypes of the Negro as criminal are not the only kind that can have significant social consequences. Employment officers in São Paulo often believe that the Negro is lazy or irresponsible. "They only work when they need money," said one. "With time they learn. But they do not like to submit to a schedule or to daily labor." They do not have the capacity for organized labor," asserted another. "They like freedom more than whites. Because of this one cannot count on them for work." Another kind of stereotype is illustrated by a little street drama staged by two reporters from the Brazilian magazine *Realidade* in 1967. One of the reporters, a Negro, stood on a busy corner in São Paulo, pretending to be ill, leaning against a wall and holding his head and so forth. Though he put on the performance for seven minutes, while a secret camera photographed him, no one came to help him though some white people who observed him were heard to comment contemptuously on the drunken Negro. When a white reporter, dressed in exactly the same middle class fashion as the black put on a similar act at the same place, passers-by stopped almost immediately to help and to offer to call a doctor—for he was obviously sick. When the reporters staged their two little

[50] Carolina Maria de Jesus, *Child of the Dark* (New York, 1963), p. 96; "80 Anos de Abolicao," *Cadernos Brasileiros*, X (May–June, 1968), 171. Bastide, ed., *Relações raciais*, pp. 187–89 notes that Negroes are well represented on the police force in São Paulo, though they are generally found only in the lower levels. Yet they are still complained against for brutality and special strictness toward Negroes. Negro women, he goes on, are often picked up as prostitutes, though white women seldom are; Negro men are held longer than white men who have been picked up by mistake. But the real evil is that Negroes are not interfered with when they fight among themselves or engage in prostitution among blacks. John Dollard *Caste and Class in a Southern Town*, 3rd ed. (Garden City, N.Y., 1957), pp. 279–81, noted a similar tendency among southern police to condone or ignore black crime so long as it was confined to blacks, thereby, in effect, encouraging it. Certainly blacks under such circumstances received less than their just protection against lawlessness and violence.

dramas later in Rio the contrast in whites' attitude was equally striking.[51]

As a result of their own stereotypes, whites are sometimes taken by surprise in dealing with Negroes. A Negro who had worked as a façade mason in Bahia ever since he was a boy obtained a job in São Paulo. The boss insisted that he be put on a week's trial because he could not believe that a Negro could perform such a skilled task.[52] Whites are also surprised to find that Negroes are dentists or owners of decent homes in São Paulo. Door-to-door salesmen, when confronted by a black face at a good home, automatically say "Go call your mistress." Even when told that she is in fact the mistress, the salesman may respond, as one did, "Don't kid me. I have no time to lose. Go call your mistress!" [53]

When Brazilians are confronted with evidence of their own prejudice or discriminatory behavior, they are often defensive, in much the same way as some progressive-minded owners of public accommodations were in the United States, especially prior to the passage of the Civil Rights Act of 1964. A president of a social club in São Paulo that barred Negroes defended the discrimination with these words. "Personally I am not against Negroes. I think that they are human beings like you and me. But the members of the club do not wish to meet Negroes at the club's dances. The girls would not accept them as dancing partners, and the heads of families would take the presence of Negroes as an offense to their personal dignity and to the prestige of the club." Under such circumstances, he wanted his questioner to believe, it was better to exclude the blacks. His own paternalistic approach to the question was neither ambiguous nor unfamiliar to a North American: "Besides, in doing so, we spare them a good deal of trouble and humiliation." [54]

Unlike most white North Americans, however, white Brazilians can believe in the inferiority of blacks and yet associate on a

[51] Fernandes, *Integração do negro,* II, pp. 118–19; Narciso Kalili and Odacir de Mattas, "Existe preconceito de côr no Brasil," *Realidade,* II (October, 1967), 41.

[52] Ibid., I, p. 209.

[53] Ibid., II, p. 206.

[54] Willems, "Race Attitudes in Brazil," *American Journal of Sociology,* LIV (1949), p. 407.

rather intimate level with Negroes. One white Brazilian in São Paulo said that he employed Negroes in his small business, played football with them, took them to his house for a meal, and befriended "those who seemed to deserve his confidence." Yet he had no hesitation in affirming that "the Negro is indeed inferior to the white. Those persons who say that they have no prejudice are hypocrites. But they hide it." When reminded that some people, particularly the wealthy, seem to accept Negroes as members of their families, he compared the treatment the Negroes received with that "the same persons dispensed to their house pets. They treat the Negroes as if they were a beloved puppy or kitten. . . . It is clear," he went on, "that they do not treat the Negro as an equal. Also, they would not think of confusing the Negro with a white." [55]

Upper-class people may associate fairly intimately with Negroes without losing status, but prejudice against Negroes is most noticeable among white Brazilians of the middle class for their association with the black can be threatening. Thus a white chemist in São Paulo admitted that "when I meet a Negro or mulatto I know on the street, because I do know various people of color, and begin to converse, I become preoccupied with the fear that someone I know will pass by. I feel bad if I am seen on the street, or at the entrance to the movies, conversing with a person of color." The simplest solution, she added, is to avoid contacts with black people.[56] A Brazilian of Italian descent said that when a Negro sought to drink and talk with him in a bar he quickly drank up and left; he followed the same practice on buses and trains. An equally candid young journalist said that he knew a well-educated, well-mannered Negro who worked in his office. When they leave the office together, he went on, "I go along talking, keeping up a front. But inside I am thinking: if anyone sees us they will not think that we are colleagues at work." [57]

It is noteworthy that in the three last examples, all of the people have prejudices against Negroes, but apparently they do not act on them, at least not consistently. It is likely that in a society like the United States, where, until recently at least, prejudice was

[55] Fernandes, *Integração do negro*, II, p. 300.
[56] Ibid., II, pp. 306–307.
[57] Ibid., II, pp. 203, 307.

openly accepted among whites, such strong feelings against blacks would also result in discriminatory behavior. The Brazilian experience would suggest that in the future, prejudiced North Americans will hesitate more than they have heretofore to act out their prejudices.

Not all white Brazilians manage to suppress their feelings in the face of blacks. As one Negro dentist complained, his white fellow dentists treat him to his face as an equal, but if any of his clients visit the white dentists, they are critical of his work. Sometimes, in moments of stress, the whites' prejudice breaks out with vehemence. Thus when a white woman was arrested by a Negro policeman for beating two children, she resisted with the challenge: "Where have you seen a Negro arrest a white? Only yesterday you were in the slave quarters. No black is going to arrest me!" [58] At other times the prejudice is admitted only to be immediately excused as a matter of class or of history. Thus in 1950, when the Brazilian Congress was discussing the first civil rights bill ever to be enacted in the country, a newspaper in São Paulo pointed out that outlawing color prejudice, as the bill intended, would not remove the historic barriers to the entrance of Negroes into certain places. "The Negro still is, for many people," the paper observed, "an inferior being, unworthy of rubbing elbows with the white and of disputing with him in society as a peer. So long as the white maintains the economic supremacy which came to him from the former slave masters, and the blacks continue, because of lack of resources, to constitute the poorest classes, prejudice will continue. There can be no laws that destroy that. There have never been any laws that could uproot profound sentiments and change the mentality of a people." [59] The concluding comment is close in word and sentiment to the arguments that were often raised against proposals for civil rights legislation in the United States at about the same time. A favorite observation of President Dwight Eisenhower, for example, was that the hearts of men could not be changed by laws.

Among whites in São Paulo, the view is widespread and quite settled that Negroes are simply socially inferior. In 1952, for

[58] Ibid., II, p. 214.
[59] Roger Bastide and Florestan Fernandes, *Brancos e negros em São Paulo*, 2nd ed. (São Paulo, 1959), p. 303.

example, a mulatto whom everyone concerned conceded to be first rate, was not hired by a club in São Paulo. "L, like all blacks, is disorganized and insubordinate," it was said in explanation. "How could he be a leader and give orders? . . . More than that, in the room would be young white men of good education, including trained lawyers. How could they be commanded by a Negro and receive orders from him?" [60] (In this particular upper-class club, apparently no distinction was being made between a Negro and a mulatto.)

Some whites in São Paulo come close to exhibiting outright racial prejudice, one asserting, "Prejudice does not exist because of color, but because of the particular circumstances of the Negro's being inferior to the white, of always having served the whites as slave, servant, and worker. Color serves to place the person and to act as a kind of point of reference. It simplifies things, condensing in terms of color the ideas which the white has of the Negro." [61]

Suggestive as these examples may be in delineating the character of prejudice, they are only impressionistic. A more precise picture of attitudes toward Negroes and people of color in general in Brazil can be obtained from an examination of some of the attitudinal surveys made in various parts of the country in the last two decades. F. H. Cardoso and Octavio Ianni, for example, made a study of stereotypes held by 552 white students in Florianópolis in the southern Brazilian state of Santa Catarina in the 1950's.[62] The breakdown on some of the unfavorable stereotypes was as follows:

STEREOTYPE	NEGRO	MULATTO	WHITE
Bad smelling, dirty, non-hygienic	73%	27%	—
Ugly	69	31	—
Prejudiced, superiority complex	—	—	100
Wants to be white, envious of white	—	100	—
False, dishonest, thief	34	37	29
Distrustful, inferiority complex	68	32	—

[60] Fernandes, Integração do negro, I, p. 225.
[61] Ibid., II, p. 300.
[62] Adapted from Fernando Henrique Cardoso and Octavio Ianni, Côr e mobilidade social em Florianópolis (São Paulo, 1960), Appendix, Tables I and II.

The breakdown on some of the favorable stereotypes was as follows:

STEREOTYPE	NEGRO	MULATTO	WHITE
Worker, strong	45%	26%	29%
Honest, sincere	33	20	47
Intelligent, studious	17	17	66
Courageous, valiant, agile	56	44	—
Happy, gay, playful	46	41	13
White teeth, good dentition	100	—	—
Neat, clean, hygienic	—	—	100
Religious, charitable	22	26	52

Although the stereotypes held by these white Brazilians are recognizably similar to those held by most North Americans, there are some differences. White Brazilians, for example, recognize their own excessive racial pride while conceding that the Negro is often courageous, if naive. Neither of these stereotypes would be included in the North American conception of the black, where hostility if not hatred is also evident. Also worth noting is the distinction that the Brazilians draw between Negroes and mulattoes, with the latter viewed as more attractive physically— because of his closeness to the white—yet less sympathetic personally. Although these students live in a region of the country viewed as most hostile toward blacks, their conception of the Negro differs very little from that of whites in other regions, as we have seen in looking at Bahia and will see in Rio and São Paulo.

In 1951 Roger Bastide and Pierre van den Berge examined stereotypes among 580 white college students in São Paulo, drawing the list of adjectives, significantly enough, from United States studies of stereotypes of Negroes as well as from Brazilian literature. Of the forty-one unflattering stereotypes of the Negro that were used, twenty-three or more were accepted as accurate by at last 75 per cent of the sample. No person rejected all of them. In some instances the acceptance rates were very high, indicating a high degree of agreement. Ninety-one per cent judged Negroes and mulattoes as unhygienic; 87 per cent found Negroes and mulattoes physically unattractive; 80 per cent thought them superstitious; 77 per cent believed they lacked financial foresight; 76 per cent judged them deficient in morality; 72 per cent simply said they were immoral; 62 per cent ascribed lack of persistence at work to Negroes and mulattoes. On the other hand, 55 per cent considered Negroes intellectually equal to whites, but that left 43 per cent who thought people of color were intellectually inferior to whites. In the light of the stereotypic view of Negroes in the United States, it is surprising that only 22 per cent of the students accepted the notion that Negroes were musically gifted. In the end, when the authors of the study added up the similarities and differences between Brazilian and North American conceptions of the Negro, they found that the agreement outweighed the disagreement between the two groups.

Oracy Nogueira measured the character and extent of prejudice in São Paulo in a slightly different way in 1941.[63] He examined ten thousand help-wanted ads in a São Paulo newspaper, in which he found 1,139 ads that made reference to color. After discounting multiple insertions he found that 245 ads specified white, four asked for colored, and six indicated no preference as to color. Forty-nine of those seeking jobs said that they were white; forty said that they were colored. About 220 ads were placed by people who specified a white employee; each of these people was interviewed and asked his reasons. Forty-eight offered no explanation, thinking the requirement was simply natural; thirty said they believed Negroes to be dishonest, eighteen thought Negroes to be unclean, fourteen said Negroes were not hardworking enough, twelve claimed that they were accustomed to white servants, seven declared they did not want their children in contact with Negroes, four considered Negroes disobedient, and four simply categorically disliked Negroes. Aside from a few miscellaneous other reasons, the remainder—twenty-seven—denied that they were prejudiced against Negroes, though they had specified *white* in their advertisement. From the interviews Nogueira concluded that there was a prejudice against Negro blood, that is, an attitude close to that in North America, as well as a color prejudice against Negroid features among middle- and upper-class *paulistas*.

[63] Richard M. Morse, "The Negro in São Paulo, Brazil," *Journal of Negro History*, XXXVIII (July, 1953), 302 reports the study of newspaper advertisements.

Some years ago an American sociologist, E. S. Bogardus, recognizing that people vary in the intensity of their prejudices according to situations, developed a scale for measuring prejudice under different circumstances. He worked out a seven-point scale, running from the most intimate association—the family—to the least—the nation. Using the Bogardus scale of social distance, René Ribeiro collated the results for college students in the United States, in Recife (in northeastern Brazil) and in São Paulo (in the southern part of the country). The tests were made between 1947 and 1956. His results thus provide us with a revealing comparison of attitudes toward colored people by North Americans and two different groups of Brazilians. His tabulations are on p. 132.[64]

The most obvious conclusion is that intermarriage in all three places is the least acceptable of all the seven options. But in Recife it is more acceptable than in São Paulo, which is what one would expect in the light of the less systematic observations on the difference in attitudes in the northern and southern regions of Brazil. Also noticeable is that in regard to intermarriage, at least, both the *paulistas* and the *nordestinos* make a distinction between Negroes and mulattoes that is almost entirely absent, as we should again expect, among the United States students. On the other hand, the United States students make a distinction when asked whether blacks or mulattoes ought to be excluded from their country, though the direction of that distinction is just the opposite of that made by the Brazilians. In the absence of any hard information on what lay behind these choices, it can be speculated that the North American students' response is consistent with a racial conception, whereas the Brazilian attitude is reflective of a concern with color only. The United States students viewed mulattoes as less desirable because they were a product of a racial mixture, but the Brazilian students, who view lighter color as more socially acceptable, believed mulattoes to be more desirable than blacks.

The remainder of the comparison is in line with what one would expect on the basis of what has been said already. In every category Brazilians are much more willing to accept Negroes and mulattoes than North Americans are. What is surprising and not readily explicable is the considerably higher proportion

[64] Ribeiro, *Religião e relações raciais*, p. 159.

CATEGORIES OF ACCEPTANCE	RECIFE		SÃO PAULO		UNITED STATES	
	Negroes	*Mulattoes*	*Negroes*	*Mulattoes*	*Negroes*	*Mulattoes*
	PER CENT		PER CENT		PER CENT	
1) Relative by marriage	13.0	24.1	9.9	14.0	1.4	1.1
2) Member of club or friend	53.4	56.2	55.5	59.7	9.1	9.6
3) Street neighbor	65.1	62.6	71.9	75.8	11.8	10.6
4) Member of profession	59.0	57.4	73.3	74.9	39.7	32.0
5) Citizen of country	63.0	61.4	74.4	77.4	57.3	47.4
6) Tourist in country	71.9	71.1	85.9	87.3	17.6	22.7
7) Would exclude from country	8.8	7.2	7.0	5.2	12.7	16.8

of *paulistas* than *nordestinos* who will accept blacks and mulattoes in categories below the level of marriage.

Professor Costa Pinto found the same pattern that we have seen in São Paulo and Recife when he tested secondary school children on the Bogardus scale in Rio de Janeiro. It was at the upper end of the scale, specifically in regard to marriage, that the highest intensity of prejudice was to be found. His study also revealed a clear distinction between Negroes and mulattoes on most levels of the scale, suggesting, as he points out, that "whitening" works in Rio as in the rest of Brazil. Using a different social distance scale than Bogardus', he tried to measure further the attitude of white students toward blacks and mulattoes. He asked the white students to choose which member of each of the following pairs they would invite home to study for an examination: [65]

	NUMBER WHO WOULD SELECT:			
PAIRS	White	Mulatto	Black	Indifferent
White and mulatto	216	28	—	70
Mulatto and black	—	128	111	75
Black and white	206	—	35	73

The percentages for all the selections were:
46.9 per cent selected white.
12.6 per cent selected black.
16.2 per cent selected mulatto.
24.2 per cent were indifferent.

Noticeable is the clear preference for white companions. But if a similar comparison were made in the United States it is unlikely that a quarter of the students would declare themselves indifferent, nor is it likely in the United States that the preference for mulattoes over Negroes would be so evident, if present at all.

Interestingly enough, it is in the extreme south of the country that the distinction between mulattoes and Negroes seem to loom greatest in the minds of white students. In Florianopolis in Santa Catarina State, Cardoso and Ianni tested students on a modified social distance scale in which they asked whether the students would like to meet Negroes or mulattoes in the following circum-

[65] Costa Pinto, *Negro no Rio de Janeiro*, pp. 189, 191–92.

stances. (In the original study, p. 163, Cardoso and Ianni put the answers in the negative, but for purposes of comparison I have here transposed them into positive statements of acceptance.) Respondents are also differentiated by sex.

	MALE STUDENTS	FEMALE STUDENTS	MALE STUDENTS	FEMALE STUDENTS
CIRCUMSTANCES	*Negroes*		*Mulattoes*	
Family (Marriage)	13	9	17	10
Dances	29	19	43	30
Neighborhood	65	67	72	76
School	81	82	85	87

The difference here between acceptance of mulattoes and Negroes is dramatic. Once again it is evident that intermarriage arouses the greatest fear among whites, regardless of region. We shall return to this question at the end of the next chapter. The difference in attitudes between men and women is probably related to intermarriage, for once the more intimate relationships, like "family" and "dances," which may lead to or involve marriage, are not at issue, the women reveal somewhat less prejudice than the men.

Finally, there is yet another way of measuring the degree of color prejudice among Brazilians. That is to compare whites' attitudes on marriage with Negroes to attitudes toward marriage with nationalities or ethnic groups other than Brazilian. A poll in 1940 among 1,088 students in public normal schools in São Paulo, of which most were middle-class young women, asked whether they would like to have a member of certain ethnic groups marry into their families. The positive responses indicate that Negroes are least acceptable.[66] Following are the percentages that would accept the various groups:

Japanese: 6 per cent (São Paulo has a significant and prosperous Japanese population.)
Mulattoes: 5 per cent

[66] Morse, "The Negro in São Paulo," *Journal of Negro History* (1953), p. 302.

Jews: 3.8 per cent
Negroes: 2.29 per cent

Among university students in Recife, the acceptance of Jews and Japanese in the family is higher than in São Paulo, but lower than for Negroes or mulattoes. Roughly a quarter of the male students would accept a Japanese or Jew in the family, but less than 10 per cent of the women would accept a Jew and only 3.2 per cent would accept a Japanese. The northeast part of Brazil has very few immigrants as compared with the São Paulo region, a fact that may account for the differences between attitudes toward Jews and Japanese on the one hand and Negroes and mulattoes on the other. That familiarity may be the key to the shaping of attitudes in Brazil is suggested by these students' attitudes toward Russians. Most of them undoubtedly have heard a great deal about Russians. In Brazil during the 1940's the Russians were played up as dangerous communists, but few of the students have had a chance to actually see or know Russians. As a result, Jews and Russians received the highest proportions in category 7 on the Bogardus scale ("wish to exclude from country"). Among men the proportion was 39 per cent against Russians and 37 per cent against Jews. Among women students the proportions were 47 per cent against both Russians and Jews.[67]

If there are differences in attitude toward color between men and women in Brazil, so is there a difference between classes. In the United States it is well recognized that hostility toward Negroes is generally greater among lower-class than among upper-class people. Down through the years, Negro rights organizations have recognized that their best white supporters are from the upper classes and that the greatest opposition to an improving position for Negroes comes from the working class. The relationship between class and prejudice in Brazil seems to be exactly the opposite, a fact that calls for extended analysis and explanation in Chapter V. It is the upper and middle classes who seem to harbor the strongest prejudices against blacks and mulattoes in Brazil. "In the tenements there is no prejudice," one overoptimistic Negro from São Paulo said. "Everyone is treated as

[67] Ribeiro, *Religião e relações raciais*, p. 163.

equals, as Brazilians. Only the old Brazilians have prejudice, out of ignorance. They created it, attempting to denigrate the Negro." [68] Another Negro also emphasized the prejudice of the upper classes, though he thought all classes reflected it. "The newspapers print daily ads by persons who want white employees. These ads generally are from fancy districts. Prejudice grows with money." [69] Among some old families in São Paulo even a forthright avowal of racial superiority is not unknown, but most middle-class families hide their prejudice while avoiding inviting Negroes home or having close friendships with them. Negro and mulatto doctors and dentists in São Paulo, for example, are accepted by their white colleagues at the office, but they are not invited home. Undoubtedly part of the avoidance of blacks and mulattoes among middle- and upper-class whites, as we have suggested already, stems from fear of loss of social status.

Yet prejudice against blacks and mulattoes is evident among the poor and in the Northeast, too. A Negro of a poor class in Recife eloped with a white girl of the same class. The girl's mother opposed the match, saying he was an "uppity" Negro and that she did not want her "daughter to marry a Negro." The mother even tried, unsuccessfully, to send the girl away. The young man's mother also objected, predicting that "in the first spat she will throw up your color at you." In fact, the girl soon left the Negro for a common-law relationship with a mulatto.[70] A white worker in São Paulo observed that "Prejudice against the Negro is very strong, even though it is said that the Brazilian has no prejudice. It exists even among poor persons. But it is much less than that revealed by rich people. The poor have less prejudice because they must live among the blacks, at work and as neighbors." The acceptance, he went on, is greatest at work because many whites avoid inviting blacks to their homes.[71] And it is true that the general absence of segregation in housing in Brazil means that whites and blacks do live side by side if they are poor. In the *favelas* in the hills around Rio, for example, whites as well as blacks are to be seen, though blacks predominate. Roger

[68] Fernandes, *Integração do negro*, II, pp. 336–37.
[69] Ibid., II, p. 327.
[70] Ribeiro, *Religião e relações raciais*, p. 111.
[71] Fernandes, *Integração do negro*, II, p. 321.

Bastide, in writing about São Paulo, says that there is little prejudice at the very lowest economic level: they work, play, and live together. At the level of factory workers, however, separation begins to appear. They too work together, it is true, but when the factory lets out, the colors separate. They may mix in bars and on the streets, but at home they do not. Negroes invite Negroes home and whites whites, he notes. And when recreational clubs are established at factories, the Negroes are barred from the balls and dances. As one Negro observed, "at work only class counts; but after work color reappears." [72]

Cardoso and Ianni tried to test systematically the degree of prejudice by class in Florianópolis, in southern Brazil. To obtain an admittedly rough measure of class origins they divided the students they tested into three groups, depending upon the fathers' occupations. They called the groups *low, middle,* and *high class.* They then asked the students to state whether they would accept a Negro or a mulatto in one of five situations.[73] (Once again, for purposes of compatibility with previous tables of prejudice, I have transposed a negative into a positive response.)

PERCENTAGE WILLING TO ACCEPT A NEGRO OR A MULATTO IN THE FOLLOWING CIRCUMSTANCES

| | NEGRO | | | MULATTO | | |
	Low	*Middle*	*High*	*Low*	*Middle*	*High*
Family	14	9	11	20	10	12
Dances	34	26	17	45	37	30
Cinema	74	64	69	79	74	78
Neighbor	72	67	63	81	74	70
School	86	79	81	90	84	85

As in other measures of prejudice that we have examined, the two most intimate relationships (family and dances) arouse the strongest prejudice in all classes. There is a difference in attitude between classes, but the great majority of lower class students

[72] Bastide, ed., *Relações raciais,* p. 137.
[73] Adapted from Cardoso and Ianni, *Côr e mobilidade,* p. 177.

would not want to be related to a black or a mulatto or even to have them attend their dances. The now familiar distinction between blacks and mulattoes is also clearly shown in almost every category of the comparison for all classes.

At the outset of this chapter we noted that prejudice may or may not result in actual discriminatory behavior. Now that we have looked at evidence suggesting the shape and intensity of color prejudice in Brazil as compared with racial prejudice in the United States, let us turn to the comparative evidence for discrimination.

Measures of Discrimination

North Americans have to be careful in drawing conclusions from examples of discrimination in Brazil, for such instances do not always carry the meaning in Brazil that similar behavior would in the United States. For discrimination, like prejudice in Brazil, is less open as well as less acceptable. As a white Brazilian sociologist once said in describing prejudice in his country, "It hides itself in the folds of the collective mind's lack of awareness and reacts, ashamed of itself, at attempts at expression or of exposures to the light of conscience. The reaction is even more vigorous when we suspect some effort to cultivate it. One tolerates the prejudice as an unavowed sentiment of class or social prestige, but an immediate repulsion is felt when someone attempts to raise it to the level of an institution or in the spirit of a caste." [74]

A particularly good example of this peculiarly Brazilian public reaction to expressions of color discrimination was seen at the time of the passage of the Afonso Arinos law in 1951, which provided penalties for discrimination on grounds of color or race in public places. The occasion for the passage of the law was the refusal of accommodations at a luxury hotel in São Paulo to Katherine Dunham, the Negro dancer from the United States. The protests of the North American evoked cries of outrage from the press, and in the Chamber of Deputies, Gilberto Freyre, then a deputy, along with Afonso Arinos, sponsored a bill that was enacted within a matter of months. The incident reveals several things about Brazilian race relations.

[74] Azevedo, *Les Élites de couleur*, p. 97.

First of all, it exemplifies the fact that most white Brazilians, at least publicly, do not condone racial discrimination and that in certain circumstances they are willing to do something quite concrete about it and without much foot-dragging. An example on a smaller scale of the same attitude is illustrated by the story of a dark-skinned mulatto, an army officer, who, while visiting a town in the state of São Paulo, went to a local barbershop to have his hair cut. As a stranger he did not know that this particular barbershop generally did not cater to colored people. When the barber refused to attend him, the mulatto loudly remonstrated, attracting thereby a crowd of onlookers. When the crowd learned about the situation, it invaded the shop, apparently intending to administer a beating to the barber. The frightened barber, fearful of danger to himself and his shop, quickly asserted that he was not discriminatory; his refusal to accept Negroes, he said, was imposed on him by his white customers.

The second point that the passage of the Afonso Arinos law suggests is that color discrimination is a fact in Brazil. The admissions of it on the floor of Congress at the time should have removed any doubts. The prohibition against racial discrimination contained in the 1946 Constitution, it was pointed out, simply was not effective. The diplomatic corps in effect, one person observed, was closed to Negroes, and the navy and air force raised "unjustifiable obstacles to the entrance of Negroes." If the government itself violated the organic law, members of Congress noted, is it to be wondered that commercial establishments also discriminate in employment against Negroes? [75] As one Negro said, whatever the weaknesses in the law, it was clearly worth "something. The government gave a big victory to the Negroes, forcing recognition of the existence of prejudice, which was falsely denied by many whites who were practicing it." [76]

Discrimination in Brazil is not the same as discrimination in the United States. It has rarely been admitted, often disguised as something else, and sometimes not present at all. It is, in short, quite different from the overt, undisguised, and consistent discrimination that has been so common in the United States not only in the South but in the North as well. But the fact of that difference does not mean there is no discrimination against Ne-

[75] Bastide and Fernandes, *Brancos e negros,* p. 303.
[76] Fernandes, *Integração do negro,* II, p. 140.

groes and mulattoes in Brazil. Indeed, the basic fact of life for people of color in Brazil is that they are concentrated at the bottom of the economic and social pyramids. All authorities, even Donald Pierson, agree to that conclusion. It is as true of northeastern Brazil, where blacks by all accounts have the best reception among whites of any area of Brazil, as it is of the far South. By Pierson's own figures, in 1936 80 to 90 per cent of the professors, priests, bankers, lawyers, doctors, and other professionals in Bahia were white, or *brancos da Bahia* (near whites) whereas 93 per cent of the porters, 90 per cent of the laundresses, 83 per cent of baggagemen at the port, and 82 per cent of the stevedores were Negroes. "A Bahian official engaged in income-tax collections," Pierson wrote in 1942, "knew of no rich blacks in the city, but did know of several well-to-do mixed bloods, among whom were a few dark mulattoes. Most incomes in the upper brackets, however, are those of whites." [77] Although whites were a minority in the population of the city of Bahia, 86 per cent of the teachers in the normal school in 1936 were white and 1.6 per cent were black. The remainder were either *brancos da Bahia* or mulattoes. No blacks at all were then teaching in the faculties of law, medicine, or engineering of the university. Pierson provides a table from the census of 1936 in which he not surprisingly shows that 75 per cent of the lower class is composed of blacks, whereas whites make up 1.5 per cent. Of the intelligentsia, the blacks comprise less than half of 1 per cent, whereas the whites contribute almost 84 per cent.

A similar picture emerges from an examination of the census of 1940 in Recife, another northeastern city. There, whites made up about 50 per cent of the population, but only 29 per cent of the so-called poor class and 35 per cent of the working class. They constituted 95 per cent of the middle class. Blacks comprised 15 per cent of the total population, but were 41 per cent of the poor class and 22 per cent of the working class; no blacks at all were then in the middle class.

In the study of Bahia made in the early 1950's, Thales Azevedo found that though blacks made up 20 per cent of the population, they comprised only 2 per cent of the members of the liberal professions; whites, who constituted 33 per cent of the population,

[77] Pierson, *Negroes in Brazil,* p. 183.

occupied 76 per cent of the places among the liberal professions. The mixed bloods constituted 47 per cent of the population, but only 22 per cent of the liberal professionals.

It is possible to argue, as Pierson has done, that the concentration of black people on the bottom of the economic pyramid is an example of class, not color discrimination in the Northeast as in the rest of Brazil. And as we have seen, class is certainly an element in the ranking of people in Brazil. Furthermore, because Negroes are poor as a result of slavery, they do not have the education or the income to attain the education or skills, which will help them to rise from the bottom. Moreover, their children tend to stay on the lower levels of the economy and society for the same reason. Yet the similarity with the social and economic situation of Negroes in a country like the United States, in which racial discrimination is undeniable, causes one to wonder if only class is involved in accounting for the position of Negroes and mulattoes in Brazil. Slavery was abolished in 1888 in Brazil and millions of slaves had been freed before that. Yet the great majority of Negroes and probably a large percentage of mulattoes are among the poor. Although exact figures are not available, it is not unlikely that the proportion of Negroes among the poor in Brazil is greater than the proportion in the United States. (The latest United States government figures cited in the *New York Times*, August 20, 1969, report one-third of U. S. Negroes among the poor, that is, those with an annual income of less than $3,553 in 1968. As recently as 1961, over one-half of the Negro population was counted as below the poverty line in the United States.)

There is more than coincidence between the patterns in the United States and in Brazil to arouse doubt that it is only class disabilities that hold down Brazilian Negroes. Even in the Northeast, there are specific examples of discrimination that are clearly attributable to color rather than class. Thales Azevedo, a *bahiano* who is proud of the racial tolerance of his native city, tells the story of a mulatto boy who was generally given roles in the plays put on in his secondary school that were stereotypic of the low valuation of Negroes, such as fishermen or charlatans. On one occasion the boy was given a romantic part to play opposite a white girl, in which he was to hold her hand. At the last minute, however, he was replaced by a white boy, the director alleging that others had to be given a chance to act, too. The mulatto boy, however, was convinced that he had been removed from the part because it was not considered seemly for a mulatto to play a love scene with a white girl. The incident is informative, aside from its being an example of alleged discrimination. It reveals the covert, even hesitant character of discrimination in Bahia. In the United States the mulatto boy would never have been put in the part in the first place, but in Brazil he was allowed to stay in until just before it was to become public. And even then his removal was disguised as something other than racial discrimination.

Not all forms of discrimination in Bahia, however, are so subtle. The adult theater there makes no bones about its discrimination. The only occupations open to Negroes are as stage hands or as actors in stereotypic roles like old mammies or uncles, or clever, but malicious types who are either ridiculous or socially inferior. Generally even important parts calling for a Negro are played by whites in black face! In order to avoid being taken for someone with Negro blood, white actresses refuse to play the part of Bahians, for all *bahianos* are thought to have some Negro blood. For those parts mulattoes and *morenos* get a chance. On radio and TV, blacks were similarly relegated to roles of social inferiors or undesirables.[78]

Other industries in Bahia also clearly discriminate on grounds of color. Few Negroes, for example, were employed in the banks of the city or in stores dealing with feminine articles like dresses, jewelry, or textiles. Such places almost invariably hired sales people who "look good," which is a euphemism for "white persons or those who approach white." Department stores have been known to put ads in newspapers asking for sales girls in which the qualifications are good health, eighteen years of age, and "white color." One informant reported that his sister, who dressed well and was educated, was denied a job in such a department store because of her color. Clients of such stores, it was said, did not like to be served by dark-skinned persons. Even in stores frequented by members of the working class, light-colored or white sales people were preferred.[79] Ribeiro acknowledges the same demand for light-skinned or white sales personnel in Recife, "in

[78] Azevedo, *Cultura e Situação racial*, pp. 73–74; Azevedo, *Les Elites de couleur*, p. 63.
[79] Azevedo, *Les Élites de couleur*, p. 49.

order not to scare away customers," as one informant phrased it.[80] For much the same reasons, apparently, the upper echelons of the military police in Bahia were white; having to deal with important public officials, who were white, they needed to be able to give a "good impression," that is, not be black.

Education is one of the primary ladders of upward mobility in Bahia, as it is in Brazil in general. Yet Negroes are grossly under-represented in the schools and universities. Their representation is highest in the primary schools, especially those that are without tuition and are supported by the government. (In no educational institution, of course, is there or has there been any segregation by law, as was the case in the United States until recently.) Pierson sampled twenty-two primary schools in Salvador in 1936 and found that nonwhites made up 57 per cent of the total, which is fairly close to 68 per cent, the estimate of their proportion in the population at large. But as one examines proportions above the primary level, the Negroes fall off rapidly. For the secondary schools Pierson found that only thirty-four Negroes and ninety mulattoes attended out of a total sample of 523. Only twelve Negroes and eighty-eight mulattoes were in attendance at the Schools of Law, Medicine, and Engineering, whereas whites numbered 424. Whites also outnumbered blacks and mulattoes together at the normal school in Bahia at that time.[81]

The pattern has not changed since then. According to the census of 1950, whites constituted 30 per cent of the population of the state of Bahia, but they made up 83 per cent of the graduates of secondary schools and 88 per cent of those who completed the superior level. Mulattoes, who constituted about half of the population, made up 15 per cent of the middle-level school attendance and 10 per cent of the superior schools. Negroes, who were 19 per cent of the population constituted about 2 per cent of the middle level and superior level school populations. Of the 137 persons granted a diploma by the faculty of philosophy at the University of Bahia between 1945 and 1950, fewer than 3 per cent were Negroes; a third were mulattoes, and almost two-thirds were whites. One mulatto in Bahia complained that "there is one sector forbidden to blacks and to persons of

[80] Ribeiro, *Religião de relações raciais*, p. 142.
[81] Pierson, *Negroes in Brazil*, p. 188.

color: the university professorship." He himself thought that he had been denied a chair because he was a mulatto, and he was not alone in suspecting discrimination. Only a few mulattoes or *morenos* have served on the faculty of the university. Of the ninety-nine professors in the early 1950's, fifteen were *morenos* or mulattoes; the proportion among the assistants was the same.[82]

The situation in Bahia and in the Northeast in general is the best for the Negro in the whole country, so it is not surprising that in the rest of Brazil blacks and mulattoes make up only a tiny fraction of the student bodies and faculties of institutions of higher learning. In the 1930's, for example, 27 per cent of the children born in the São Paulo charity ward were black, but only 0.6 per cent of the university students were. In 1968 the respected newspaper *Jornal do Brasil* reported a study of thirty schools in the old federal district around Rio de Janeiro. The study revealed that Negroes were still only sparsely represented in educational institutions. Although they comprised an estimated 23 per cent of the population, they constituted 12 per cent of the primary school, 10 per cent of the secondary school, and 3 per cent of the superior school populations.[83] Today, in walking across any major campus in the United States, one can see more black students than I saw at the Federal University in Rio de Janeiro in 1967 even in attendance at a lecture on race relations.

In Bahia everyone recognizes that dark color is discriminated against in social affairs. "The social and professional clubs are to persons of very dark color the most difficult area in which to gain access," reported one informant. Color bars are admitted at the most exclusive clubs, but there is hardly a club that does not permit some opening in the high wall of exclusiveness for a black of extraordinary achievement. All recognize that the Negro who does get into such a club does so because he is a "doctor" and in spite of his color. In one upper class club, whites constituted over two-thirds of the memberships and there was not a single Negro member. In a club of the middle class, almost 40 per cent were white, more than a third were *morenos*, a quarter mulattoes, and

[82] Azevedo, *Les Élites de couleur*, p. 81; Florestan Fernandes, "Mobilidade raciais," *Cadernos Brasileiros*, X (May–June, 1968), 55–56.

[83] Eduardo Pinto, "Preconceito de classe atinge negros 80 anos após Abolição," *Journal do Brasil*, May 12, 1968. I am indebted to Rebecca Bergstresser of Stanford University for this reference.

half of 1 per cent Negroes. On the other hand, in the dancing clubs frequented by workers, domestics, day laborers, and soldiers, the whites were in the minority and the Negroes greater in proportion.

The exclusion of blacks from the upper- and middle-class clubs is done subtly and without overt reference to color. Negroes simply do not try to enter exclusive white clubs because they know that white girls will refuse to dance with Negroes, even in Bahia. As one black pointed out, a Negro in Bahia "does not need barriers because knowing the prejudices of the whites, he does not go into certain places." It is understood by whites and Negroes that blacks who are accepted will behave in a manner acceptable to whites and not be "uppity." [84] In the community of Bahia state, which Marvin Harris studied, there was a social club technically open to all, but tie and coat were needed and the girls danced only with certain men. Hence the only black seen on the dance floor was the son of the wealthy Negro councilman. Harris estimated that as a result of such unstated but effective barriers, about 90 per cent of the Negroes and 10 per cent of whites in the town were excluded from the club. E. Franklin Frazier, writing in 1944 about the upper and middle classes in the city of Bahia, noticed the same kind of barriers. "Prejudice toward black persons," he wrote, "seems to operate most strongly in intimate social relations involving marriage and in the new type of social life which is developing in clubs and hotels. For example, black persons do not attend the weekly dances at the large hotels patronized by Brazilian officials and businessmen as well as foreigners; nor are black men to be found at the tennis clubs and the yacht clubs. They may attend on some special occasion, but they do not move about freely and would not be invited to become members." [85] A middle-class Negro in São Paulo, explaining why he did not experience much prejudice, said, "I know where to go, I do not intrude myself where Negroes are not well received." Another Negro said, "When I go out with my wife, I avoid places where I know that the black is not received." As Roger Bastide has written, the Negro in São Paulo "knows that he can dress well

[84] Azevedo, Les Élites de couleur, pp. 35, 88, 91.

[85] Frazier, "A Comparison of Negro–White Relations," in Edwards, ed., Frazier on Race Relations, pp. 99–100.

and penetrate a barber shop frequented by whites, but he also knows that he will wait for hours, and that in the end will leave poorly barbered, or with his face cut, in order that he remember not to return." A Negro journalist in 1967 reported similar instances of discriminatory hints when he deliberately sought services where Negroes might not be wanted. Thus in a bar in the airport in São Paulo he was charged double for a drink and his hotel room in Recife was small, on the first floor, and contained a broken air conditioner, whereas his white companions were assigned a large, airy room with a working air conditioner.[86] In short, the remark by the contemporary Brazilian humorist Millor Fernandes has wry truth as well as humor in it: "There is no color prejudice in Brazil; the Negro knows his place."[87]

René Ribeiro sums up well the nature of discrimination in the Northeast as a whole in his general statement on the situation in Recife. After noting that there are occasional examples of whites showing public dislike for Negroes, such as refusing to sit next to them on public vehicles or denying them entrance to clubs on the ground of color, he concludes that on balance there "is no fixed pattern of racial segregation rigidly followed on all occasions in all places."[88] The strict and sharp line between the races so characteristic of the United States is absent there; always there are the individual exceptions, the mulatto escape hatch, or the "bleaching" power of class.

Farther south, however, evidence of discrimination on grounds of color is more abundant and the line between the colors is less easily penetrated. Costa Pinto, for example, cites a number of examples of exclusion of blacks from first-class hotels in Rio de Janeiro even though the Negroes in question were well dressed and presumably of the middle class. He even goes so far as to

[86] Fernandes, *Integração do negro*, II, p. 333; Bastide, ed., *Relações raciais*, p. 163; Kalili and de Mattos, "Existe Preconceito . . . ," *Realidade*, October, 1967, 35, 37.

[87] Quoted in Pinto, "Preconceito de classes . . . " *Jornal do Brasil*, May 12, 1968.

[88] Ribeiro, *Religião e relações raciais*, pp. 137–38. Ribeiro notes, too, that, "In educational institutions, especially in women's schools directed by foreign religions there have existed and still exist a certain degree of discrimination, admitting by preference students of white color, although in the course of the present study black and mestiço students have been found in a limited number." Ibid., p. 138.

contend that in Rio there is residential segregation by race. Pointing out that roughly 27 per cent of the population of the city in 1950 was colored, he argues that if the population were distributed without regard to color, each district of the city would count the colored as roughly 27 per cent of its population. In fact, however, he goes on, several of the districts have as much as 40 to 46 per cent Negroes and mulattoes, whereas others have only 10 to 12 per cent. Yet such a distribution is explicable on grounds of class and the need to be near places of employment. A class rather than a racial interpretation seems most likely to be accurate when it is recognized that not a single district contained a majority of Negroes and mulattoes. In short, if there is segregation by race in Rio, it is a far cry from the kind that North Americans are familiar with in Chicago's Southside or New York's Harlem, where the great preponderance of the population is Negro.

More persuasive on the same point, however, are Costa Pinto's figures on the color of the inhabitants of the *favelas*—the shantytown slums set precariously in the steep hills that surround Rio de Janeiro and other large cities. The census of *favelas* taken in 1951 revealed that 7 per cent of the inhabitants of Rio lived in the hill-slums. Although people of color constituted 29 per cent of the population of the city, they constituted 71 per cent of the inhabitants of the *favelas*. A Negro writer estimated in 1968 that blacks constituted less than a quarter of the population in Rio de Janeiro, but that they comprised two-thirds of the people living in the *favelas* of the city.[89]

As in the Northeast, the colored population of Rio is concentrated at the lowest end of the economic and social scale. Although in 1940 about a quarter of the people of the city were colored, that is, mulatto or Negro, only 0.4 per cent of the employers of the city were colored. Help-wanted ads in the newspapers often asked for someone of "good appearance" or asked for a picture to accompany the application. It was said that a person of color in a certain job would be inconvenient "because the place of the Negro is in the kitchen." [90]

[89] Costa Pinto, *Negro no Rio de Janeiro*, p. 257n., Chapter 4 and especially pp. 121–24, 130, 145; Pinto, *Jornal do Brasil*, May 12, 1968 cites the estimate of a Negro writer.

[90] Costa Pinto, *Negro no Rio de Janeiro*, p. 76.

Despite the Afonso Arinos civil rights law of 1951, Negroes comprise today fewer than 2 per cent of the federal employees, according to a survey reported in 1968. Over 80 per cent of the federal employees listed themselves as white. At the time of the survey there was no Negro in the Supreme Federal Tribunal and no Minister of State was a Negro; indeed, the number of Negroes even in the middle echelons of government was few. About 3 per cent of the officers in the armed services are Negroes; among officers of general rank, Negroes are almost nonexistent. (A black general explained the lack of Negroes in the armed services as the consequence, not of discrimination, but because "the number of capable people of black color who seek a military career is very limited." Marcos Santarrita had a different explanation. "In our Armed Forces, also, it is known that it is easier for a camel to pass through the eye of a needle than for a Negro to enter the Command School and Estado Maior.") At the time that report was made in 1968 there was only one Negro diplomat in the Brazilian foreign service and he was not a career officer because the Rio Branco Institute, which trains Brazil's diplomats, has never had a Negro student. Finally, the survey noted that "the number of Negro engineers, doctors, teachers, lawyers, and economists is less than 1 per cent of the total of these professions."

Another article, also published in 1968, reported on the difficulties Negroes of good qualifications confronted in getting jobs in Rio, especially in those fields in which there was contact with the public, such as banking, barbering, public relations, food dispensing, tourism, and retail trades. The newspaper told of a mulatto girl, trained by IBM, presumably for office work, who was unable to obtain a job except as a maid, which she finally took in the absence of any other kind. Some employment agencies accept Negroes only when there are calls for kitchen personnel. Even though the Afonso Arinos law has been on the statute books for seventeen years, one firm was quoted as saying that it would be the final judge of the acceptability of employees' "physical type, residence, education, etc." [91]

[91] Pinto, *Jornal do Brasil*, May 12, 1968; "80 Anos de Abolição," *Cadernos Brasileiros*, X (May–June, 1968), 170; Paulo Cesar de Araujo, "Discriminação racial dificulta empregos," *Jornal do Brasil*, March 11, 1968, 15. I am indebted to Rebecca Bergstresser for the last reference. "It is well known," said Sebastião Rodrigues Alves in 1968, "that in spite of the great number

In São Paulo, as in areas farther north, the Negroes are at the bottom of the economic scale. In 1940 the number of employers among Negroes was one-thirteenth of their proportion in the population as compared with the Japanese and Chinese, whose proportion among employers was double their proportion in the population. Yet most of the Chinese and Japanese came to São Paulo *after* the emancipation of the last slaves in 1888. In a study of the town of Itapetininga in the state of São Paulo, one student found that Negro mobility lagged noticeably behind that of the Italians, who came to the town only in the 1880's. At the time of World War I, Negroes and Italians were in the same organizations, and excluded from the established institutions and social affairs of the community. But by 1930 the Italians were beginning to appear in public office and to be admitted to the social clubs. By 1945 the Italians were accepted by even the old families in politics, at the best clubs, and at other places. The Negroes and *pardos*, however, showed an "almost complete inpenetrability" of the upper reaches of the social structure.[92] This lag between immigrant and Negro mobility is also noticeable in the United States, where it is usually cited as a measure of the special prejudice and discrimination practiced against Negroes. It seems reasonable to infer that discrimination against Negroes is also one of the causes for a similar pattern's developing in São Paulo.

Evidence of discrimination against Negroes in employment is abundant in São Paulo. In 1959 an official in charge of placement admitted that he could not place well-qualified Negroes in office jobs, even in large firms.[93] "As a race and as a people the situation of the Negro in São Paulo," wrote one black in an autobiographical statement in the 1960's, "is the worst possible. Despite the

of Negro enlisted men [in the army] that they remain always relegated to a position of inferiority. As everyone knows, [the Negro cannot penetrate] the Ministry of External Relations; in the Navy and in the Air Force . . . if one finds a young Negro, one soon learns that he is related to someone. Twenty million Negroes cannot be related to whites." "80 Anos de Abolição," *Cadernos Brasileiros*, X (May–June, 1968), 23.

92 Fernandes, *Integração do negro*, II, p. 286; Florestan Fernandes, "The Weight of the Past," in John Hope Franklin, ed., *Color and Race* (Boston, 1968), p. 291 cites the census figures of 1940; Oracy Nogueira, "Relações raciais no municipio de Itapetininga," in Bastide, ed., *Relações raciais entre Negros* . . . , pp. 472–78, 481–503.

93 Fernandes, *Integração do negro*, II, p. 318.

variety of businesses and economic activities in that industrial city, there still are no big businessmen, merchants, high functionaries of government or representatives in the legislature, bankers or financiers 'belonging to the Negro race.' Negroes are only small businessmen, head secretaries, managers of small industries and even then not in proportion to their numbers. The Negro lives in an almost parasitic state on the edge, without a future, without a goal, without power to participate in the objectives which give energy to the whole in a community on the march to progress; they pass with long steps rapidly through history on the road to inglorious death. . . . The situation of the mass of Negroes is more than pessimistic," he concluded. "Socially unadapted, the Negroes obtain only jobs that a defeated man can get: police investigator, member of the police force, washer of automobiles." [94] (Another informant said that 90 per cent of the automobile washers in São Paulo were Negroes.)

Although the statement is bitter, the fact of discrimination in jobs is as well documented in São Paulo as in Rio. Compared with the United States, however, the discrimination is without much public notice, is not consistent, and is generally disguised. At the end of the nineteenth century, one Negro was said to have had to present eight theses in order to gain his professional chair at the Law Academy in São Paulo, though he was highly qualified. Yet, in the end he did get the chair. The color line, as we have had occasion to observe before, is not drawn absolutely as it is in the United States. But that Negroes are denied jobs for reasons of color there is no doubt. One employment officer described his efforts to help Negroes get positions in his firm, and in the process revealed some of the subtle distinctions of color that influence decisions. "The other day they asked me for a white porter. I had only the dossier of a Negro and I did not send it. Later a *nordestino* appeared. I though he was white, but asked some of my colleagues who observed him, whether they would confirm me or not. They concluded that he was white. Nevertheless the firm did not hire him." [95] Sometimes colored applicants find out that though the job is alleged to be filled, it is in fact still open. "They refused me because of color," cried one mulatto, "I became almost crazy with that." [96]

[94] Ibid., II, p. 270.
[95] Ibid., II, p. 383.
[96] Ibid., I, p. 119.

Although employment in certain industries in São Paulo is undoubtedly discriminatory, residential patterns are not. A study of housing patterns in thirty-six small cities in the state of São Paulo, conducted by the anthropology department of the university, for example, found that in nineteen of the cities there were recognizable Negro districts, but no evidence that color prejudice was the cause. Nowhere, for example, did blacks live exclusively in any district; low rents and closeness to work were more likely explanations for the patterns than color prejudice.

The same survey did turn up examples of color discrimination in other ways. Twenty of the thirty-six cities, for instance, reported that Negroes were excluded from certain barbershops, but in eight of them poor whites were barred as well! Eight of the cities reported that Negroes were excluded from certain bars and two of them reported that the best hotels in the city barred blacks. Nowhere, however, were any punitive measures taken against blacks who stepped across the color line, except that they were denied service. The law neither supported nor condoned such discrimination. In twenty-three of the thirty-six cities there were associations—usually social clubs—from which Negroes were barred, though none of the clubs, significantly, has formal, stated barriers against blacks. Furthermore, only sixteen of the clubs were prepared to justify the informal bars. Six of the presidents of the clubs referred to the low social level of Negroes and only four alluded to color as the basis for exclusion.

The informal, often inconsistent, yet effective character of discrimination in Brazil is well illustrated by another kind of behavior. In the central parks of São Paulo cities, where people congregate for relaxation, talk, and exercise, the area is more or less divided informally by class, with each group respecting the other's preserves. Sometimes the division is also by color, even within the lower class. Twenty-two of the thirty-six small cities of the state reported that division by color existed, but, significantly enough, no sanctions were taken against colored persons who invaded a white section of the park, as for example, certainly would be the result if an invasion took place in a similar situation in the United States.

In 1968, Correia Leite, the Brazilian Negro leader, told of his being denied service in a restaurant in Campinas, a city in São Paulo long known for its hostility toward Negroes. Although many mulattoes were being served, Correia Leite's party was not attended because two of its members were dark-skinned, though the restaurant was not fancy. Interestingly enough, the next day when an investigation was ordered, the owner asked to be forgiven for his discriminatory behavior.[97]

Cardoso and Ianni have concluded for the Far South of Brazil that even in the 1950's the occupational structure of Negroes in Florianopolis is close to what obtained in the past: most blacks were still domestics and laborers with a few in the middle range of occupations, like government service. "Almost all of the Negroes and mulattoes one encounters," they concluded, "are still concentrated in the lower levels of the population. A small number, particularly mulattoes, begins to penetrate the middle class. And only some, also mulattoes, are attaining the liberal professions." Negroes tend to live in the less desirable places in the hills and are barred from certain hotels and clubs. At least one restaurant refused service to a Negro from the Northeast, who was visiting the town and did not know the local mores. Even sports tend to be segregated on an informal basis, though generally sports is an important avenue of social mobility for blacks in Brazil, as it is in the United States. Rowing is considered a white sport and Negroes or dark mulattoes are discouraged from participating in it. "It is said that the whites consider crew an elegant sport and one for whites." [98]

Such are the outer burdens of color borne by Negroes and mulattoes in Brazil. If they were the only ones, they would be heavy indeed, though certainly not as severe as those that have been heaped upon blacks in the United States. But they are not the only ones, for if we are to understand the nature of prejudice and discrimination in Brazil we must turn our attention to the inner burdens, which are also part of the cost of color.

[97] Willems, "Race Attitudes in Brazil," *American Journal of Sociology* (1949), 405–407; *80 Anos de Abolição* (Serie Cadernos Brasileiros, Rio de Janeiro, 1968), p. 32.

[98] Cardoso and Ianni, *Côr e mobilidade,* pp. 112–20, 176, 180–81, 189, 217–18.

IV

The Inner Burdens of Color

It was with the black woman that the white man from the cradle, when he was caressed, in bed when he was sexually satiated, that he learned his terms of love: *negrinho-negrinha, meu preto-minha preta, pretinha-pretinho, minha nega-meu nego.* One hears them from every mouth, from that of the college graduate to that of the exploited worker.

—Luiz Luna, *O Negro na Luta Contra a Escravidão,* 1968.

Those African Ladies are of a strong, robust Constitution; not easily jaded out, able to serve them [bachelors and widowers] by Night as well as Day. When they are Sick, they are not costly, when dead, their funeral Charges are but *viz.* an old Matt, one Bottle Rum, and a lb. Sugar. The cheapness of a Commo-di-ty becomes more taking when it fully Answers the end, or T——l.

—Letter to Charleston, S.C. *Gazette,* July 17, 1736. Quoted in Winthrop Jordan, *White Over Black.*

Negroes Alone Feel the Weight

Because of the coincidence of color and class in Brazil it is easy for many whites to deny the existence of color prejudice and discrimination. Most Negroes, however, are only too well aware of the disabilities that follow color. Even the sayings of those Negroes presumably resigned to their lot betray a recognition of prejudice among whites: "The black is born to suffer"; "The Negro will never make anything of himself"; "The life of the black is ever thus." [1]

There are others who are more outspoken. "You know that in Rome slavery existed," a dark mulatto woman told an investigator. "One race enslaves the other, as happened in Brazil. But slavery disappeared and everyone became equal. No one remembered any more that some descended from masters and others from slaves. But in Brazil the contrary happened. No one forgets that

---

[1] Florestan Fernandes, *A Integração do negro na sociedade de classes* (São Paulo, 1965), II, p. 166.

the Negro was a slave and the whites have a repulsion for the Negroes because of this. They did not want to admit that the Negro, who had been their slave, was rising and became equal to him. The life of the blacks is not only different from that of the whites, they [the blacks] are even kept in a low position by the whites. . . . The Negro is accepted in many fields but in an inferior position. Only exceptionally can they achieve a position of distinction." [2] Other Negroes see a different relationship between slavery and the current position of blacks in Brazil. Among intellectual Negroes, for example, there is a widespread opinion, as one newspaper article in 1956 phrased it, that the Negro "left physical slavery only to enter moral slavery." Still others contrast the lot of the Negro under the slave regime with that since abolition, saying "in the time of slavery, when people had the luck to have a good master, the people were happier." "The monarchy was better for the Negro," remarked one Negro intellectual, "because even during the slave regime under the monarchy, various Negro personalities could rise socially. . . . In all the republican period not a single great Negro has come to the top." [3]

The assertion by Negroes that prejudice is a fact in Brazil runs the gamut from simple acknowledgement to bitter denunciation. "It is certain that prejudice exists," remarked one illustrious Negro intellectual, "and if we are received in the dominant society, it is no less certain that we are seen as colored persons, respected, but kept at a certain distance." Less gentle is the denunciation by a Negro lawyer and politician. The idea of racial democracy "cannot be palmed off on the Negro—he feels in his own flesh, the shame, the stigma, and the identification brand of 'his place'—for the myth is a fantasy composed of foolish excesses which the facts of daily life contradict every moment." A leader of the Negro rights movement referred to the concept of racial democracy as a "shop-worn cliché" that is passed off onto the less-informed foreign visitors as a way of seeing "race relations through a deliberately deformed glass. By this glass, everything here is a bed of roses. The white is white, the black is white, the yellow is white, all comprising a climate of immaculate whiteness," where all ethnic groups participate together "without conflicts, gently,

[2] Ibid., II, p. 157.
[3] Ibid., I, p. 64.

tamely, placidly." Actually, the whole is a sham, he goes on. ("A pretty suit of clothes," or "Something for the English to see," as Brazilians say.) "In truth . . . the Negro is marginal and as such discontended." [4]

Most of the foregoing remarks are from Negroes in São Paulo, but even in Bahia blacks are conscious of discrimination. One Negro in a liberal profession bitterly wrote that "a prejudice exists in which the aim is to lower again in the human scale the blacks in whom the percentage of African blood predominates." A mulatto professor at the University of Bahia pointed out that "Some affirm that the sinister racial problem does not exist among us, that the blacks enjoy the same rights, the same prerogatives as the white man. That is a sad (*triste*) utopia. The higher levels of life in the country keep their doors shut against the black." [5]

It is often said that the United States Supreme Court's decision ordering the desegregation of schools in 1954 gave Negroes "heart to fight" further against prejudice and discrimination.[6] Interestingly enough, the same thing has been said by Negroes in Brazil upon the passage of the Afonso Arinos law in 1951. Despite its weaknesses, "the law has good aspects," said one Negro, "because it gives to the Negro and mulatto an instrument to fight against prejudice. But its principal defect is how to prove it. [Prejudice] is like the dust on the hearth. No one has a clear awareness of its existence, especially among the whites. Now the law has called attention to the phenomenon. Many whites are not going to like to be compelled to accept the Negro." Another remarked, a little cynically, that the new law would be "probably more effective than a folklore monograph." Still another wondered whether the law would be enforced, for "there are many ways and devices for finding loopholes in the law." [7] (As we have seen already, his fear was well founded.)

One of the most dramatic examples of Negro response to the argument that there is no prejudice in Brazil is that reported by

[4] Ibid., II, p. 351n.; II, pp. 344, 353.

[5] Thales de Azevedo, *Les Élites de couleur dans une ville brésilienne* (Paris, 1953), pp. 94–95.

[6] Thomas F. Pettigrew, *A Profile of the Negro American* (Princeton, N.J., 1964), p. 10.

[7] Fernandes, *Integração do negro*, II, p. 331; L. A. Costa Pinto, *O Negro no Rio de Janeiro* (São Paulo, n.d.), p. 342.

Professor Costa Pinto. Significantly, in this example the assertion that there was no prejudice in Brazil came from a Negro. The scene was a session of the First Brazilian Negro Congress held in Rio in 1950. At that meeting a black member of the meeting affirmed that " 'in Brazil racial prejudice does not exist.' The wave of protests that rose from the assembly transformed the meeting into a storm. There were scoffs and protests, proposals to erase the words, shouts and whistles, which cost not a little to the presiding officer of the session to bring to a halt. . . . The statements of protest followed one another, all offered in tones running from revulsion to pity, which portrayed the author of the declaration as completely insane. The speaker, talking a second time, although he confirmed his point of view and attempted to explain it, did it in a tone of excuse, filled with emotion, and interspersed with constant appeals to unity and harmony. Such feelings, according to his thinking, ought to reign among men of color, for only in that way would they resolve their problems. 'What problem' shouted someone, 'if the speaker ends by affirming that in Brazil racial prejudice does not exist?' The question remained without an answer." [8]

As Gunner Myrdal pointed out in the preface to his classic investigation, *An American Dilemma,* all his study of the Negro in the United States led him to the conclusion that the issue was "a white man's problem. All our attempts to reach scientific explanations of why the Negroes are what they are and why they live as they do have regularly led to determinants on the white's side of the race line. In the practical and political struggles of effecting changes, the views and attitudes of the white Americans are likewise strategic. The Negro's entire life, and consequently, also his opinions on the Negro problem, are, in the main, to be considered as secondary reactions to more primary pressures from the side of the dominant white majority." In Brazil, some Negroes see the problem in a similar light. "The problem of the Negro is a problem of the white," said Sebastião Rodrigues Alves at a conference on Eighty Years of Abolition in 1968. "It is the white who created the problem of the Negro. Thus, for the solution of the Negro we must resolve the problem of the white." The heart of the matter, said one black at another time, is "to give opportu-

[8] Ibid., p. 225n.

nity to the Negro. How to provide that opportunity? Education of the white employer because it is precisely he who does not give employment to the Negro." Nor are employers the only whites who need to be reeducated. "It is necessary that the white worker understand that he is the same as the Negro and that there is no difference." A third Negro, too, advised resolving the "question by education, more of the white than the Negro, because it is the white who is badly brought up, not the Negro." Carolina Maria de Jesus, a resident of the São Paulo *favela*, whose diary was published recently, summed up the issue in her entry for May 13, the Anniversary of Abolition: "May God enlighten the whites so that the Negro may have a happier life." [9]

Eventually the Veil Falls

In *Souls of Black Folk*, W. E. Burghardt Du Bois tells a story from his own life that is familiar in its substance to all black people growing up in the United States. "It is in the early days of rollicking boyhood that the revelation first bursts upon me, all in a day, as it were. I remember well when the shadow swept across me. I was a little thing, away up in the hills of New England, where the dark Housatonic winds between Hoosac and Taghkanic to the sea. In a wee wooden schoolhouse, something put it into the boys' and girls' head to buy gorgeous visiting cards —ten cents a package—and exchange. The exchange was merry, till one girl, a tall newcomer, refused my card—refused it peremptorily, with a glance. Then it dawned upon me with a certain suddenness that I was different from the others; or like, mayhap, in heart and life and longing, but shut out from their world by a vast veil." [10]

Similar experiences are not as predictable in Brazil. In Bahia, for example, many blacks and mulattoes contend that they grew

[9] Gunnar Myrdal, *An American Dilemma* (New York, 1944), p. xlvii; *80 Anos de Abolição* (Serie Cadernos Brasileiras, Rio de Janeiro, 1968), pp. 23–25; Fernandes, *Integração do negro*, II, p. 360; Carolina Maria de Jesus, *Child of the Dark* (New York, 1963), p. 33.

[10] W. E. Burghardt Du Bois, *The Souls of Black Folk* (Fawcett Publications, Greenwich, Conn., 1961), p. 16. The book was originally published in 1903.

up without experiencing the shock of "the veil." But the experience is to be anticipated wherever prejudice and discrimination occur. "Up to ten years our children all lived together, the whites with the blacks," one mother of color reported, "but thereafter we saw our little daughter quiet and troubled, without company. She was not prepared for the treason of her best friends." Though they had played together and visited in each other's homes, "now the white children seek out the whites. They prefer the child of the bad neighbor to their former friends of color." Generally, writes Oracy Nogueira, the revelation occurs first in primary school, but it may not come until adolescence, for the absence of legal segregation makes it possible for a black Brazilian to avoid the unsettling experience for some time. In some places, white parents begin to discourage their children from having enduring friendships with Negro playmates as early as seven years. Often it is at this juncture that the Negro child comes home and reports on the strange, cool behavior of his former companions. Negro parents in Brazil, as in the United States, then have to do their best to explain the situation, hoping that they can get the child "through the crisis with the least possible psychological damage." [11]

A concrete example of how one Negro boy learned that his color could be a handicap also illustrates the ambivalence of whites toward prejudice. After visiting a circus and seeing the clowns, the boy came home to suggest to his playmates that they, too, ought to put on a circus. When the question came up as to who was to be the clown, some of his friends suggested him. Others of his playmates objected, saying that his color was a drawback. "What would be said about a circus," they wanted to know, "where the clown was a black?" (Notice that children in Brazil, like those in the United States, recognize that certain

---

[11] Azevedo, *Elites de couleur*, pp. 29–30; Oracy Nogueira, "Relações raciais no municipio de Itapetininga," in Roger Bastide, ed., *Relações raciais entre negros e brancos em São Paulo* (São Paulo, 1955), pp. 511–15; Fernandes, *Integração do negro*, II, p. 348; Bastide, ed., *Relações raciais*, p. 143. Pettigrew, *Profile of the Negro American*, p. 7 writes, "Negro parents confess to great anxiety and ambivalence over telling their preschool children what it means to be a Negro in American society. Should youngsters be shielded from the truth as long as possible? Or should they be prepared early for blows that are sure to come?"

occupations are not generally filled by Negroes.) But the denouement is almost as revealing as the objection. The supporters of the Negro boy won out and he was allowed to be the clown because he "was funny" (engraçado). Later it was also remembered that since the clown would have his face painted "no one will see his color" anyway! [12]

As these and other examples make clear, everyone in Brazil—black as well as white—recognizes the disadvantages of blackness and no one conceals the advantages that come with whiteness. Some blacks of strong mind can rise above the oppressive power of whiteness, as Carolina Maria de Jesus certainly did. When told by a publisher who had just turned down one of her plays that it was a shame she was black, she was not dismayed. In fact, she was probably used to hearing the patronizing phrase. "They were forgetting," she wrote in her diary, "that I adore my black skin and my kinky hair. If reincarnation exists I want to come back black. . . . The white man says he is superior. But what superiority does he show? . . . The sickness that hits the black hits the white. If the white feels hunger so does the Negro. Nature hasn't picked any favorites." [13] Other Negroes, however, even those of strong will and self-confidence are not so sure. Martiniano do Bonfim, whom Ruth Landes met in Bahia, was devoted to his African heritage and proud of his knowledge of African lore and magic. Yet he once told her, "If I am born again in Brazil, I want to be white and rich, and I want a white woman instead of the black one I've got." [14] A preference for white or whiteness as a measure of the impact of color prejudice in Brazil is not confined to modern blacks. Costa Pinto points out that Cruz e Sousa, the well-known mulatto poet of the nineteenth century, "came to be . . . the most Nordic poet of Brazil." The color white runs through the imagery of his poetry as if it were an obsession, suggesting that he was at once drawn and repelled by the color that counts for so much in Brazilian society.[15]

A number of studies of Negro children in the United States show that they often prefer white skin, too. "When Negro chil-

[12] Fernandes, Integração do negro, I, p. 211.
[13] De Jesus, Child of the Dark, p. 62.
[14] Ruth Landes, The City of Women (New York, 1947), p. 210.
[15] Costa Pinto, Negro do Rio de Janeiro, p. 265.

dren as young as three years old are shown white- and Negro-appearing dolls or asked to color pictures of children to look like themselves," writes Kenneth Clark, the well-known psychologist, "many of them tend to reject the dark-skinned dolls as 'dirty' and 'bad' or to color the picture of themselves a light color or a bizarre shade like purple. But the fantasy is not complete, for when asked to identify which doll is like themselves, some Negro children, particularly in the North, will refuse, burst into tears and run away. By the age of seven most Negro children have accepted the reality that they are, after all, dark-skinned. But the stigma remains; they have been forced to recognize themselves as inferior. Few if any Negroes ever fully lose that sense of shame and self-hatred." [16] In Brazil, too, the inability of the Negro to express aggression or to manipulate it constructively results in turning it against himself or other Negroes. A study of São Paulo school children first published in 1953 reported that for Negro children rejected by their colleagues "the attitudes of the Negro parents with reference to color demonstrated that they had hostility against persons of color and against themselves, having internalized the ideas of the whites. The result of such internalization is that they treat Negroes, and therefore themselves, as they see themselves treated by whites. Having repressed the hostility against the white, they displace the aggression against the Negro himself, seeing the white as a beloved and respected ideal, although also feared and hated." Not surprisingly, some Negroes declared that they preferred whites to blacks because they were easier to get along with; the same Negroes also indicated that they felt inferior to whites.[17]

Negroes easily acquire attitudes of inferiority in grade school, where whites and their values dominate. A study of attitudes among school children revealed that the white children had a strong sense of their own identity and superiority. The Negroes,

[16] Kenneth Clark, *Dark Ghetto. Dilemmas of Social Power* (New York, 1965), pp. 64–65; see also Pettigrew, *Profile of the Negro American*, p. 7, and Kenneth J. Gergen, "The Significance of Skin Color in Human Relations," in John Hope Franklin, ed., *Color and Race* (Boston, 1968), p. 122.

[17] Virginia Bicudo, "Atitudes dos alunos dos grupos escolares em relações com a côr dos seus colegas," in Bastide, ed., *Relações raciais*, pp. 269, 287; Emilio Willems, "Race Attitudes in Brazil," *American Journal of Sociology*, LIV (March, 1949), 404.

on the other hand, as might be anticipated, showed little group consciousness. They lacked even the goad of overt prejudice to create such consciousness, as would occur in the United States. In Brazil, color prejudice is frequently disguised—in the circumstances of school as bad deportment, poor academic attitudes, and so forth. Virginia Bicudo's study of school children in São Paulo found that all students, black and white, tended to associate bad qualities with Negroes and good ones with whites, as similar studies in the United States have also reported. Negro children, for example, preferred white to Negro friends. She asked white, mulatto, Negro, and Japanese school children whom they preferred for seatmates. The proportions of the choices were as follows:

| GROUP SELECTING | GROUPS SELECTED | | | |
| | Whites | Mulattoes | Negroes | Japanese |
	PER CENT	PER CENT	PER CENT	PER CENT
White children	91.72	1.67	3.86	2.75
Mulatto children	89.23	3.08	5.38	2.31
Negro children	81.55	1.94	12.95	3.56
Japanese children	75.71	0.56	2.83	20.90

Noteworthy is the fact that all children preferred white seat mates, but that all colors preferred Negroes over mulattoes, including the mulattoes themselves! Here, one can observe again one of the negative consequences of the mulatto escape hatch. Mulattoes are so insecure that they prefer Negroes over themselves. Striking also is the Japanese children's considerably higher self-esteem than the Negro children's. Over a fifth of the Japanese children, even in an environment that extols whiteness, preferred seatmates who were Japanese; barely one-eighth of the Negroes felt that confident.[18]

The Negro sense of inferiority, however, only begins in school. Arthur Ramos, a modern white student of the Negro in Brazil, writing in 1938 points out that "the inferiority complex of the Negro," despite the ending of slavery, still remained to be over-

[18] Bicudo, "Atitudes dos alunos," in Bastide, ed., Relações raciais, p. 296.

come.[19] That sense of inferiority may begin in the school, but it does not end there.

The most vicious consequence of color prejudice in Brazil, as in the United States, is that it narrows the Negro's horizons. Knowing that whites are better educated and socially more knowing, many young Negroes in Brazil are discouraged from the start. They do not bother to compete. "The best jobs are always for the whites," they say. "The Negro is left with only the remainders," with what "no one wants." Hence Negroes take the "safe" jobs— kitchen work, manual labor, and so forth. "The white race created for itself the concept of superiority and for the Negro race, the concept of inferiority," one mulatto stated. "And that concept of inferiority we feel at every step." [20] They know that certain jobs are not for them. One foreign journalist met a Negro truck driver in Rio, with whose skill he was impressed. When he asked the driver whether he did not want to train to be a mechanic or engineer, the Negro put his arm beside the journalist's and said, "Sure, if I were your color." [21]

Negro parents, internalizing the sense of inferiority, deliberately restrict their children's horizons in order, they say, to save them from disillusionment or failure. A white informant, for example, told of a Negro washer woman who discouraged her daughter from taking typing lessons because she had heard that colored typists had trouble getting jobs. She did not want her daughter to suffer disappointment. Even mulatto parents who want their children to rise, and consequently sacrifice to give them a good education, still set low occupational goals for their children. They direct the child's ambition toward being an automobile mechanic, a clerk, or a dressmaker, rather than a doctor or a lawyer.[22]

These examples have been taken from São Paulo and Rio, but a similar constriction of Negro aspiration is evident in the Northeast as well. Azevedo,[23] for example, reports on a group of the most advanced primary school children in Bahia, who were asked

[19] Artur Ramos, "Castigos de Escravos," *Revista do Arquivo municipal de São Paulo*, XLVI (May, 1938), 102–103.

[20] Fernandes, *Integração do negro*, II, p. 169; I, p. 225.

[21] Herbert Wendt, *The Red, White and Black Continent,* trans. Richard and Clara Winston (Garden City, N.Y., 1966), p. 494.

[22] Fernandes, *Integração do negro*, II, pp. 194, 236, 382–83.

[23] Azevedo, *Les Élites de couleur dans une ville brésilienne*, Paris, 1953 (*Race et Societe*), p. 84. Reproduced with the permission of Unesco.

what careers they hoped to follow later. The careers were divided into those of prestige (engineer, lawyer, doctor, dentist, teacher) and those of modest ambition (chauffeur, tailor, typist, hairdresser, printer). Despite the early age of the children, the difference between the aspirations of the white and the colored was already evident, as shown by the following table.

TYPE OF JOB	WHITES		MULATTOES		BLACKS	
	Males	*Females*	*Males*	*Females*	*Males*	*Females*
	PER CENT		PER CENT		PER CENT	
Prestige	80	62.5	33	46.8	44	15.7
Modest	20	37.5	67	53.2	56	84.3

It will be recalled, too, that in Bahia, as in the rest of Brazil, the so-called prestige jobs are virtually all held by whites.

The restraint that colored people place upon their ambitions has a further effect. In failing to extend themselves, out of fear of rejection or failure, Negroes reinforce the whites' stereotype of the unambitious or incompetent black. As Thomas Pettigrew has observed, in the United States compliant Negroes can "prove" racists right. "A vicious circle can thus be established: the deeper the scars from discrimination, the more in keeping with the discrimination is the Negro's behavior, the greater the reinforcement of the discriminatory pattern, and thus the deeper the scars." Costa Pinto makes a similar point for Brazilian blacks. "The Negro, historically placed in an economically and socially inferior position, has that social position explained and justified by the purveyors of prejudice as being a product of *racial* inferiority. That opinion, on the other hand, generates and maintains stereotypes which function as barriers, whether of an objective or subjective order, which impede or make difficult the social ascension of the Negro. Thus these products of prejudice and inequality of opportunity are used as their own justification." More recently, in 1968, Luiz Luna, the Brazilian writer, made the same connection between slavery and the low opinion of the Negro. "The truth is that no one at the time of slavery, like many still today, has confidence in the Negro as a free man and master of his destiny. Even today it is common to read newspaper ads for domestic servants giving preference to employees of light color. There is also the hygienic aspect. Few believe in the cleanliness of the Negro, probably reminiscent of the promiscuity of the slave quarters. When one wants to offend someone one hurls the epithet *Negro* and when one insults a black, one does not forget to add: *dirty Negro!*" [24]

Even those who do not interpret the Negro's lack of competitiveness pejoratively, often conclude that the Negro lacks confidence in himself, retreating even from fields in which no white would contest his presence. One white informant from a traditional family in São Paulo said he considered blacks equal to whites, but that "color prejudice though presently attentuated, still is a very great obstacle to be surmounted. Almost a majority of the blacks themselves accept it as an inevitable condition, limiting their aspirations and placing themselves, by their own actions, in an inferior position." [25]

One measure of this attitude is that both whites and blacks in São Paulo often express surprise at seeing a Negro in a position of responsibility. To blacks it means he has overcome prejudice, as in the statement of a black *paulista* that "a Negro competing under equal conditions with a white has to be better in order to win." A black girl in the city of Bahia told a reporter in 1967, "The Negro in order to win cannot be ordinary. In order to get ahead as a doctor, engineer, artist, student, or simple mechanic, he has to be exceptional. Any slip that he makes is thrown in his face with the comment: "Don't you want to be anything but a Negro?" To whites, however, the meaning is simply that Negroes are not expected to achieve. "If he, as a Negro, achieved such a position, it is because he must truly be competent," is a characteristic white statement. "If he, being a Negro, attained that position, think if he were white!" "Think how he must have struggled as a Negro to achieve that position." [26]

[24] Pettigrew, *Profile of the Negro American*, p. 24; Costa Pinto, *Negro do Rio de Janeiro*, pp. 197–98; Luiz Luna, *O Negro na luta contra a Escravidão* (Rio de Janeiro, 1968), p. 225.

[25] Fernandes, *Integração do negro*, II, p. 187.

[26] Ibid., II, pp. 220–22; Narciso Kalili and Odacir de Mattas, "Existe preconceito de côr no Brasil," *Realidade*, II (October, 1967), 46; Nogueira, *Relações raciais . . . Itapetininga*," in Bastide, ed., *Relações raciais*, p. 514n.

The Flight from Blackness

One of the consequences of the Brazilian style of prejudice is that Negroes receive much greater inducement to reject their racial origins. Even in Bahia, blacks who "make it" often cut themselves off from their racial brothers. One of the milder forms this rejection takes is to refuse to recognize, or even to talk about, the problem of race or color. Thales Azevedo, for example, despite his experience in the complicated color and class patterns of Bahia, had very great difficulty approaching such people to discuss questions of race.[27] Some socially mobile blacks sever relations with friends, neighbors and even families, because such connections may reveal the Negro background that is being escaped. A Bahian quatrain sums up the problem and advances at least one possible solution:

> Of his white father, whom he never saw,
> He has a picture in the parlor;
> But of the Negro woman who gave him birth
> He has no picture, nor does he even speak of her.[28]

It is not uncommon even in the Northeast for a mulatto, though clearly of Negro ancestry, to assert seriously and insistently that all his ancestors were Indians, for Indian blood does not carry the taint that Negro blood does. As in the United States, Indian blood can be a source of pride or at least of jocular admission, but Negro blood is never boasted about and rarely admitted unless necessary. The difference in attitude is neatly summed up by Vianna Moog: "When Brazilian mulattoes, instead of falsely claiming to be *caboclos* [mixture of Indian and white], lying and aggravating with the lie their inner anguish and anxieties, can speak serenely, without shame and without subterfuge, of their Negro ancestors, as the *caboclos* speak of their Indian ancestors, there will no longer be a racial problem in Brazil."[29] Cardoso

[27] Thales Azevedo, *Cultura e Situação racial no Brasil* (Rio de Janeiro, 1966), p. 38.

[28] Donald Pierson, *Negroes in Brazil* (Chicago, 1942), p. 227.

[29] René Ribeiro, *Religião e relações raciais* (n.p., n.d.), p. 119; T. Lynn Smith, *Brazil, People and Institutions* (Baton Rouge, 1963), p. 69n.; Vianna Moog, *Bandeirantes and Pioneers*, trans. L. L. Barrett (New York, 1964), p. 237.

and Ianni point out that in Florianopolis a woman mulatto never wants to be confused with a Negro. She wants to be called *morena* not *preta*, and certainly not *negra*. One mulatto recollected that in the course of his social rise he would have preferred to be called "the son of a whore" rather than "Negro." One way that mulattoes emphasize their identification is to court women "whiter in color than in reputation," as Thales Azevedo put it.[30]

In other respects, however, as Roger Bastide has written, a middle-class Negro "is occupied before all with respectability and honorableness. He will be, as in the United States, a Puritan. He will justify his rise in the eyes of the whites by separating himself as much as possible from the lower class, refusing any contact which might compromise him or make him lose the dignity so laboriously won."[31] The Brazilian middle-class Negro as described here reminds one of E. Franklin Frazier's denunciatory description of an equivalent class in the United States, those Negroes of the middle class whom Frazier called the *Black Bourgeoisie,* in a book of the same name. Or those blacks whom Kenneth Clark described more recently in *Dark Ghetto.* "The fantasy of *accommodation* or *acceptance,* which used to be the primary pretense of Negroes, still affects some, particularly certain successful Negroes who surround their lives with typical middle-class daydreams. Just as the white of threatened status may trace his lineage to the *Mayflower* and seek refuge in the Daughters or Sons of the American Revolution, so the Negro may boast that his family were freed Negroes earlier than others were, or that his parents 'had money.' Or, as one successful Negro professional, who lives in a beautiful home, is wont to say: 'All Negroes need to do is prepare themselves, save money, invest properly, buy decent homes, and then there would be no more prejudice.'" Some North American Negroes, Clark goes on (like some blacks in Brazil), deny their "own identification with the racial dilemmas: 'I have no racial problem; I get along with all whites.' So, too, a single Negro or a few Negroes on a prestige campus or

[30] Fernando Henrique Cardoso and Octavio Ianni, *Côr e mobilidade social em Florianópolis* (São Paulo, 1960), pp. 211–12; Azevedo, *Les Élites de couleur,* p. 32.
[31] Bastide, ed., *Relações raciais,* p. 163.

in a church or a profession may 'fit in beautifully.'"[32] In the United States, however, because of the definition of the Negro and the rigidity of the caste system, no middle-class Negro can actually escape from his color. That is why Clark calls such attempts "fantasy." But in Brazil there is a real possibility of such an escape, thereby making the dissociation even more appealing —and often psychically corrosive.

One of the consequences of the effort to dissociate from other blacks in Brazil is the arousal of resentment among "those—and they are numerous—who remain in the lower levels of society." Often such socially mobile mulattoes are censured even in the Northeast "for wanting to be white or appearing as if they do not want to be colored."[33] A revealing version of this reaction is reported from São Paulo. A woman who worked in a home at which Negro and mulatto intellectuals gathered, resented their better position. "Who do they think they are?" she asked. "They are no more than I am. They are even less than I am for I am lighter than they."[34] Significantly, she used color to denigrate other Negroes because their class position was better than hers. No better example could be given of how light color is invoked, even in Brazil, in an effort to enhance status.

As Thales Azevedo has pointed out, the position of Brazilian mulattoes who rise is in some ways like that of the Negro in the United States who "passes." For in addition to experiencing the resentment of other blacks, they also feel "the doubts and the difficulties resulting from their situation."[35] For like the Negro who tries to pass in the United States, they may not be accepted. The status to which they aspire may be denied, as happened to a well-educated secondary school teacher in Rio de Janeiro who was treated by a club as if he were a Negro, though in fact he was a mulatto. "Club X refused me entrance as a member," he complained, "but I refuse to dance in a common dive [where Negroes gathered]. Where must I then seek company and diversion? With those who are my equals. But who is equal to me: those who have the same color or those who have

[32] See E. Franklin Frazier, *Black Bourgeoisie* (Glencoe, Ill., 1957) in general, and Clark, *Dark Ghetto*, pp. 225–26.
[33] Azevedo, *Cultura e situação racial*, p. 38.
[34] Fernandes, *Integração do negro*, II, pp. 212–13.
[35] Azevedo, *Cultura e situação racial*, p. 38.

the same education?"[36] As his comment makes evident, the lot of the mulatto in Brazil can be anxiety-producing. Not white, yet often wanting to be so, the mulatto nevertheless can be classed as a black at any time a room clerk or maitre d'hotel chooses to treat him as such. This, too, is the negative side of the mulatto escape hatch.

The mulatto's position can produce pathological manifestations, too. Gilberto Freyre ascribes to the mulatto background of the Brazilian poet Antonio Goncalves Dias the fact that he was always "a sad misfit." Dias' classmate at Coimbra said that the knowledge he was the offspring of a colored woman resulted in "sleepless nights" and covered Dias' "heart with clouds." Florestan Fernandes reports in his study of colored alcoholics in São Paulo, most of whom were mulattoes, that they suffered from the social maladjustment and self-hatred typical of people caught between two worlds. Another study of racial attitudes in São Paulo concluded that "during the interviews it became obvious that the dark *mestiço* [mulatto] identifies himself with the white, but he lives in permanent fear of being confused with Negroes." On the basis of his interviews and conversations with Negroes and mulattoes in São Paulo, Fernandes estimated that about half of them were torn between the acceptance of their own inferiority and the desire to assert their equality with whites.[37] This inner turmoil is also a consequence of the mulatto escape hatch.

The Black Mother on Two Continents

Daniel Patrick Moynihan in his now famous "report" on *The Negro Family*, which was issued as a government document in 1965, was not the first person to point out that one of the long-

[36] Costa Pinto, *Negro no Rio de Janeiro*, pp. 222–23n.; Raymond Sayers, *The Negro in Brazilian Literature* (New York, 1956), p. 52 says that the earliest defense of the mulatto was made in a sermon delivered in Recife in 1745. The priest told the listening mulattoes that they should be proud of their color, arguing that mixed color was superior to either white or black. That such a defense was necessary is, of course, significantly revealing of the attitudes of whites at that time.

[37] Gilberto Freyre, *The Mansions and the Shanties,* trans. Harriet de Onis (New York, 1963), p. 371; Willems, "Race Attitudes," *American Journal of Sociology* (1949), 404; Fernandes, *Integração do negro*, II, p. 184.

range consequences of slavery and racial discrimination in the United States was the disorganization of a large proportion of lower-class Negro families.[38] In fact, a generation earlier, E. Franklin Frazier had identified the essential feature, namely the absence of the father. The 1940 census "showed a larger proportion of families with women heads among Negroes than among whites in both rural and urban areas of the South," Frazier wrote. "Moreover, it also appeared that in the Southern cities a larger proportion of Negro families were under the authority of women than in the rural areas." In another place he said, "In Northern cities with a total population of 100,000 or more, from 10 to 30 per cent of the Negro families have female heads. This is higher than the proportion among either the native whites or foreign-born whites." This pattern of family disorganization he discerned "in its purest and most primitive form in the rural South." And the causes he traced back to what he called "a natural maternal family organization that flourished during slavery."[39] Moynihan, however, went farther than Frazier. Following Nathan Glazer, Moynihan attributed the incomplete character of the lower-class Negro family to the peculiar nature of North American slavery, implying that other forms of slavery did not have the same effect. Indeed, Moynihan asserted quite specifically that the protections for the family under slavery in Brazil provided black people in that country with a quite different history and sociology than had United States slavery. As we have seen in Chapter II, however, the historical evidence does not support that interpretation.

Now is the occasion to mention another reason for doubting that the slave family in Brazil was any more protected than the slave family in the United States. The reason is that the incomplete or disorganized family is at least as common among lower-class black families in Brazil as it is in the United States. (It is

[38] The official title of the so-called Moynihan Report is *The Negro Family. The Case for National Action,* Office of Policy Planning and Research, U. S. Department of Labor (Washington, D.C., 1965). See Chapter III especially.

[39] E. Franklin Frazier, *The Negro Family in the United States,* rev. and abridged ed. (Chicago, 1966), pp. 103, 246. The original edition was published in 1939. See also E. Franklin Frazier, "The Impact of Urban Civilization upon Negro Family Life," in G. Franklin Edwards, ed., *E. Franklin Frazier on Race Relations* (Chicago, 1968), pp. 162–63 and Pettigrew, *Profile of the Negro American,* p. 16.

not uncommon, incidentally, among poor white families in both Brazil and the United States, as well, but that comparison is not at issue here.) Indeed, remarks Florestan Fernandes, it was just this lack of a developed or complete family under slavery that so handicapped the Negro once slavery was ended. In the competitive, individualistic environment of the city, to which the freedman moved, the family was a basic necessity. His lack of it was "truly catastrophic." "Only a minority of the 'Negro population,'" Fernandes writes, "viewed marriage as a social value and followed a style of life at all compatible with the stability of the integrated family." Negro men did not want to assume responsibility for the children they fathered and Negro women did not want to hold men against their wills. "Many 'single mothers' possessed and maintained children of two, three, or more successive affairs," Fernandes notes. On the other hand, the life of the Negro provided no "mechanisms of solidarity or of understanding, to reform or to compensate for, at least, or to aid effectively the woman and children on either the material or the moral level. Loneliness, penury, and humiliation marked the path followed by the woman who had the indomitable courage to remain with 'the fruit of her weakness' and to battle for her survival." Considering the poverty of the Negroes, parents and relatives could not help much. "The 'Negro family' as it manifests itself in São Paulo during the first three decades of this century," Fernandes concludes, "could be defined as an *incomplete* family. It is impossible, in our day, to determine the frequency with which the various structural arrangements occurred. But it appears beyond a doubt that the most frequent arrangement consisted of . . . the unmarried mother, or her eventual substitute, almost always the grandmother, and her child or children." The "incomplete family" may have assumed several forms, he points out, but all of them revealed "if they indicated anything, that the woman and not the man—constituted the dominant figure where any sort of disintegration in family or conjugal ties persisted. Without her cooperation and her possibilities for remunerative work, provided by domestic employment, a good part of the 'colored population' would have succumbed or removed to other areas." [40]

After surveying the hard lot of the black woman of the incom-

[40] Fernandes, *Integração do negro,* I, pp. 152–54, 156, 158–59, 162.

plete family among São Paulo's poor blacks in the first third of the twentieth century, Fernandes sums up her achievement in this moving apostrophe: "Mute and silent heroine; she could no more than protect the fruits of her body: to maintain with her life that to which she had given life! Abandoned, uncomprehending, and defamed, she carried, almost alone, the hard battle for the right to be a mother, and paid more than the others, truly with 'blood, sweat and tears'—the price for the disorganization of the Negro family. In the worst times she was the 'bread' and the 'spirit,' consoling; she furnished the warmth of charity and the light of hope. No one can look at that phase of our past, without being moved by the immense human greatness of the humble 'colored domestics,' agents at the same time of the propagation and the salvation of their people." [41]

Fernandes' tribute is echoed, less eloquently, but no less accurately in the United States by Jessie Bernard in the introduction to her *Marriage and Family Among Negroes* which was published in 1966: "This book is dedicated to Negro women, one of the most remarkable phenomena in American history. With a minimum of preparation against all but insuperable odds, these women have borne the major burden of pulling up the Negro population by its bootstraps. They have been spirited and independent, as well as self-sacrificing." [42]

Yet, Fernandes makes clear, even in the early years of the twentieth century, there was a minority of Negro families in São Paulo, which could be described as "integrated," that is, with mother, father, and children. The parents were not always married, it is true, often living in what Brazilians call the *amasiado* relationship, but these common-law unions could be as stable and enduring as church or civil marriages. The integrated Negro family, regardless of the character of its bond, however, was a union of the elite, the members of which often assumed a superior attitude toward the acknowledged promiscuity practiced in the black tenements. And though these integrated families suffered great strains, they did demonstrate the ability of some blacks, newly out of slavery, to form stable relationships. In the United

[41] Ibid., I, p. 262.
[42] Jessie Bernard, *Marriage and Family Among Negroes* (Englewood Cliffs, N.J., 1966), p. x.

States, too, as Joel Williamson has documented, some Negroes were able to emerge from slavery and immediately establish complete and stable families.[43] Indeed, the recent, and as yet unpublished research of Herbert Gutman of the University of Rochester shows that the complete family, with the father present, was characteristic of the black family even immediately after emancipation. In his investigations of census and other documentary evidence, Gutman has found that complete families constituted 80 to 90 per cent of the families he examined.

Fernandes suggests that a particular Negro union in São Paulo would be strong if at least one of two conditions were true: that there had been a stable relationship prior to the couple's arrival in the city and that the pair came into contact with immigrants once they settled in the city. It was from the example of immigrant families, Fernandes believes, particularly Italians, many of whom migrated to São Paulo at the end of the nineteenth century, that the Negro learned about the family. One Negro recalled going to live with an Italian family in 1911 at age ten. Then he saw, he later said, "what it was to live in the midst of a family. . . . I liked it because I ate from a table"; he suddenly appreciated what is meant "to live like people." [44] (If this contact with immigrant models was important, it would help to explain the greater incidence of incomplete families in Bahia, where there were few immigrants. In the United States South, which also did not attract European immigrants, Negroes also had little chance after slavery to encounter potential immigrant models. But on balance, it is not likely, despite Fernandes' evidence, that mere emulation was a major source for family construction among blacks. The social and historic causes of the disorganized family would seem to be too powerful to be overcome simply by a desire to copy a model.)

Even the integrated Negro family in São Paulo offered testimony to the burdens of prejudice and discrimination. Though more stable than the disorganized family, "it was a long way from creating the integrative, and socializing means for control that would meet the standards of the going society. . . . Even the 'disorganized family' among the Italians," Fernandes asserts, "pos-

[43] Fernandes, *Integração do negro,* I, p. 154–57, 163; Joel Williamson, *After Slavery* (Chapel Hill, N.C., 1965), pp. 306–12.

[44] Fernandes, *Integração do negro,* I, pp. 155, 132–33.

sessed decided advantages over the 'Negro family' in that respect." The black integrated family was undermined by the fear that the young girls would be seduced, or that the boys would bring scandal upon the family, or that income would be inadequate or simply fail entirely.[45]

Fernandes' evidence and conclusions pertain to the Negroes of São Paulo, but the lower-class Negro family in other parts of Brazil has also been incomplete or disorganized. E. Franklin Frazier, the American sociologist, who, before his death, was the leading expert on the Negro family in the United States, concluded after a reseach trip to Bahia just before World War II that "because of the weakness of institutional controls, the family among the majority of our informants tended to assume the character of a natural organization," that is, without a father permanently present. It was, he noted, similar to "the family among many Negroes . . . in the Southern United States."[46]

More recently, Thales Azevedo has noted that the state of Bahia has the highest proportion of unmarried mothers of any state in Brazil. Azevedo is not writing about illegitimacy or delinquency, but about the incomplete or disorganized family and he relates this high proportion of women heads of families to the high concentrations of descendants of slaves and to the many indices of low economic and educational achievement in the state. For each one thousand women in 1950 in the state of Bahia, 455 were unmarried mothers, as compared with a rate of 342 in Minas Gerais and 299 in São Paulo. "The highest proportions of unmarried mothers, according to physical type, are encountered among the blacks in Bahia, in Pernambuco, and in Rio de Janeiro," he writes. As Fernandes noted for São Paulo, Azevedo observes in Bahia the "taboo of virginity" is weak among the lower class because of illiteracy, "the enduring effects of the slave regime," and "the precarious economic conditions." Under such circumstances, "it is not rare for the women to have known two or three men and to have had children by all of them." The children of previous men are accepted by subsequent lovers without discrimination, except that "only the mother is really responsible for the children by other unions." Generally the women in these

[45] Ibid., II, pp. 166–67.
[46] Frazier, *Negro Family*, pp. 477, 470.

amasiado unions spurn marriage or any formal ties, often on the grounds that such compulsion destroys love and true affection.[47]

What Fernandes called the *incomplete family* in São Paulo, and Carmelita Hutchinson called the *partial family* in Bahia, North American sociologists refer to as the *matrifocal family*. All are family relationships in which the husband is conspicuous by his absence or for his lack of economic or moral authority. It is the mother who raises the children, educates them, and starts them on the road of life. Whether in Bahia, in São Paulo, or in the United States, the matrifocal family is especially noticeable among lower class Negroes. Harry Hutchinson, in his study of a small Bahian community, notes that ninety of the 290 households counted in the census of 1950 reported a female head of household. Although some reported that they were widows, Hutchinson doubted that most of those who claimed to be were so in fact. In any event, he makes it clear that all of these women were either mulatto or black.[48]

The widespread incidence of the matrifocal family in Brazil and the United States is not surprising when one recollects that the institution of slavery in both places did little to preserve the family and in the case of Brazil, because of the imbalance of the sexes, actually made it difficult for the family to be established at all. In both countries, too, it is evident that prejudice, discrimination, and poverty have been the great perpetuators of the matrifocal family.

Black Panthers Not Allowed

If the fatherless family is as much a part of black experience in Brazil as in the United States, the history of Negro rights organizations is not. In this fact, too, is mirrored another difference

[47] Azevedo, *Cultura e situação racial,* pp. 121–23; Nogueira, "Relações raciais . . . de Itapetininga," in Bastide, ed., *Relações raciais,* p. 467n. notes that in 1940 the proportion of unmarried mothers was the highest in the states with large numbers of Negroes and mulattoes, with Maranhão first, Bahia fifth, and São Paulo last. In Bahia 20 per cent of women over twelve years of age with children were unmarried; in Maranhão the proportion was 32 per cent whereas in São Paulo state it was 2.5 per cent. It is worth adding that São Paulo was then, as today, the wealthiest of the states, too.

[48] Harry William Hutchinson, *Village and Plantation Life in Northeastern Brazil* (Seattle, 1957), p. 117.

in the nature of race relations in the two countries and a further burden of color.

Negro rights organizations of one form or another have punctuated the history of the United States. The National Association for the Advancement of Colored People, founded in 1910, is not only the longest-lived, but the most powerful of such groups. Today the NAACP, it is true, is viewed by many so-called militant blacks and other Negro organizations like CORE and SNCC as a moderate, if not accommodationist organization. But in Brazil the NAACP would be considered a highly militant, if not racist organization. Indeed, in Brazil today there are no Negro rights organizations that can be even remotely compared in prominence, power, or age to the NAACP. In fact, in all of Brazilian history there have never been Negro rights organizations of any significance. Many Brazilians like to believe that the absence of such organizations measures the lack of racial tension and prejudice in their society. To a certain extent that is true, for without such organizations the tension undeniably is less. But absence of racial tension is not equivalent to lack of prejudice. As we have seen already, too much prejudice and discrimination against Negroes and mulattoes exist in Brazilian society to account for the absence of Negro protest organizations on that ground. The weakness of Negro rights organizations in Brazil is rather a function of the special character of Brazilian race relations. It is for that reason that an examination of the nature of Negro organizations and the efforts to form them is worth our attention.[49]

First of all, the fact that Negro rights organizations have been founded in the 1920's down into the 1960's, weak and short-lived as they may have been, offers further testimony that black men have not been satisfied with their status as the slogan of racial democracy would imply. The motto of the best known of these organizations, *Frente Negra Brasileiro* (Brazilian Negro Front), founded in 1931, was, significantly enough, "We, the Negroes, alone feel color prejudice in Brazil."[50]

It is a second point, however, that is worth emphasizing here. The weakness of Negro rights organizations in Brazil is directly

[49] Only organizations primarily concerned with Negro rights and equality of opportunity are discussed here. Cultural or fraternal organizations of Negroes have existed for a long time in Brazil, but they have not been interested in asserting Negro equality.

[50] Fernandes, *Integração do negro*, II, p. 29.

related to the nature of prejudice in that country. As we have seen already, by making a distinction between mulattoes and Negroes, Brazilian society provides an escape from the disabilities of blackness for some colored people. This fact alone diminishes significantly that sense of solidarity that is indispensable if a Negro rights organization is to succeed. "Look at my children," a woman of color said to an investigator. "They're white already. What's the use of fighting, forming Leagues for the defense of the Negro, and all that?" [51] Her children could escape by whitening. Moreover, because of the close correspondence between class and color lines, many Negroes either deny the existence of color prejudice or are confused as to whether it is color or class. Those who deny it are usually either traditional blacks newly arrived from the countryside or Negroes who have successfully risen into the middle class. One who could not make up his mind said, "I am not certain if what exists in São Paulo is prejudice or something else by another name. . . . The white does not trust the Negro. That is true. The black does not know how to do things. He has not had the time to prepare himself like the white. From that stems the attitude of the whites against the blacks. But if the blacks prepared themselves and made themselves equal to the whites, they would be accepted and treated by them in a different manner. I do not know if prejudice even exists or if it is some other thing, owing to the distrust of the white and the inability of the black to behave as the white expects." Indeed, Florestan Fernandes reports from his research among Negroes that one of the three most common explanations for color prejudice offered by Negroes themselves is that they do not know how to behave in public. (The other two are that the Negro is not aggressive enough and that color prejudice holds the Negro back.) [52]

Because Negroes, even in São Paulo, cannot be sure that any discrimination they may suffer is a result of color rather than class, they do not automatically assume, as in the United States, that they suffer from prejudice or discrimination. The indecision or confusion is enhanced by the social ideology that proclaims

[51] Roger Bastide, "Dusky Venus, Black Apollo," *Race*, III (November, 1961), 12.

[52] Fernandes, *Integração do negro*, II, pp. 330, 362.

"We are all Brazilians." Consequently, it is not unusual to have Negroes assert that "it does not happen to me"; "some people have a persecution mania"; "it is necessary to distinguish between selection and prejudice"; and so forth. The very dominance of an ideology that proclaims the absence of prejudice in Brazil prevents many Negroes from asserting their blackness in organization. Azevedo, in accounting for the weakness of the movement for Negro rights organizations in Bahia quotes a leader of the tiny movement there as saying, "the Black of Bahia is not convinced that he is black." [53]

And it is not accidental that in the Northeast, Negro organizations have been weakest. In that region, as we have seen, discrimination and prejudice are least defined and consistent. In the Northeast, one might say, the Brazilian approach to race relations is at its purest, an observation that is quite consistent with the proposition that the weakness of Negro organizations is a function of the Brazilian attitude toward race and color. Historically, Negro organizations in the Northeast have been anthropological or historical in concern; they have not been what North Americans consider Negro rights organizations. Their purpose has been to study and publicize Negro and African cultural achievement. Sometimes they have run afoul of the law or the police because of their encouragement to non-Christian African religious rites, but their goals and programs have not included the equalization of economic or social opportunities.

It is farther south, in Rio de Janeiro and especially in São Paulo, that such organizations have gained whatever success these groups have achieved in Brazil. It is, in short, in the areas where Negroes and mulattoes are in the minority and acceptance by whites is less easy than in the North that Negro rights organizations have been strongest. Some signs of such organization were discernible in the 1920's, when there was an ephemeral movement to have the word *Negro* used in place of *homen de côr* (colored man). Also, in 1924, the Negro newspaper *O Clarim da Alvorada* (Trumpet of the Dawn) was founded in São Paulo. The high point of the movement, however, came in the 1930's and 1940's, probably as part of the reaction against

[53] Azevedo, *Les Élites de couleur*, p. 102.

the racism of the German Nazis. The best known organization was the *Frente Negra Brasileira* (Brazilian Negro Front), which was founded in São Paulo at a meeting of some two thousand in 1931. It lasted until 1937, when the Vargas government banned it on the grounds that it was a self-proclaimed political party. In its literature the *Frente* declared itself to be a "political and social union of the black national people, to affirm the historic rights of the same, by virtue of their material and moral activity in the past and to proclaim their social and political rights in the Brazilian community in the present." [54]

In 1942, after a research trip to Brazil, E. Franklin Frazier published a message to American Negroes from another Negro organization, The National Union of Men of Color of São Paulo. The message called for "closer cultural community with our North American brothers" and complained that "the Negro struggles in Brazil with disadvantages; although the text of the law established equality, inequality is apparent and real." At its conclusion, the message painted a pessimistic picture of the Brazilian Negro's social condition: "Completely neglected, disunited, uncared for

[54] Artur Ramos, "O Epiríto associative do negro Brasileiro," *Revista do Archivo Municipio de São Paulo,* XLVII (May, 1938), 125; Thomas Blair, "Mouvements afro–brésiliens de liberation, de la période esclavigiste à nos jours," *Presence africaine* (1965), p. 100, offers the following list of Negro organizations, with date and place of founding: *O Movimento Brasileiro contra o preconceito racial,* founded in Rio de Janeiro in 1935; *Associação dos Brasileiros de Côr,* founded at Santos, 1938; *Congresso Brasileiro do Negro,* Rio de Janeiro, 1940, organized by Abdias do Nascimento, Edison Carneiro, and Guerreiro Ramos; *Cruzada social e cultural do Preto Brasileiro,* founded at São Paulo in 1948; *O Teatro experimental do negro,* Rio de Janeiro, 1944; *União dos Homens de Côr,* Rio de Janeiro, 1948; *Justicia Social cristiana,* Rio de Janeiro, 1950. Costa Pinto, *Negro no Rio de Janeiro,* p. 305n. quotes the pledge taken by members of the *União dos Homens de Côr:* "I enlist in the Union of Colored Men of the federal district, a society of the black family with social and civic ends. That family continues to be treated officially with social injustice, without consideration of the rights of men, because of color prejudice inherited from slavery even though the Imperial law 3353 of the 13th of May, 1888 assured the equality and the rights of all Brazilians without distinction of color. The black family is relegated to the margin of politics in the upper levels of administration of the country, thereby continuing its moral and civil slavery. I enlist in the Union in order to combat color prejudice, and in order faithfully to carry out the commandment of Jesus Christ—'Love one another.' "

by public authorities, without instruction, debilitated by the scourge of syphilis, alcohol and debasing dances; without a strong family organization upon a solid base, the Negro is degenerating." [55]

During World War II, in 1944, the Negro Experimental Theater was founded in Rio de Janeiro in behalf of the Negro connected with the Brazilian stage. As in Bahia, Negroes in the Rio theater were generally confined to stereotypic or comic roles. When a play called for a Negro in an important part, a white was given the role and then colored black. Indeed, there was such a dearth of vehicles for blacks on the stage that Abdias do Nascimento, the founder of the theater, wrote to Eugene O'Neill asking for permission to put on *The Emperor Jones*. Given the Brazilian conception of relations between the races, no plays would be written explicitly for Negroes, for that implies a special concern that the ideology rejects as unnecessary. O'Neill's answer to Nascimento, in a letter dated December 6, 1944, was at once a commentary on Brazil and the United States. "I herewith give you permission to stage *The Emperor Jones* without any payment to me," O'Neill began, "and wish you all the success in the world for the Negro Experimental Theater. I am familiar with the conditions you describe in regard to the Brazilian Theater. We had similar conditions in our own theater before *The Emperor Jones* was staged [in] New York in 1920—serious roles would always be played by white actors in black face, with the exception of musical comedy and vaudeville, where a few Negroes had achieved success. After the great success of *The Emperor Jones*, played originally by Charles Gilpin and later by Paul Robeson, the way was open for the Negro as a serious actor. Now the great difficulty is the lack of suitable plays. But I am expecting Negro dramatists of real merit to meet this need. In whatever situation you find yourself you may count on my cooperation." [56]

The Negro Experimental Theater did put on O'Neill's play, along with others of his. It also spurred interest in the worth of blackness by various devices, including a contest for the Queen

[55] Printed and translated in *Phylon*, III (1942), 284–86.
[56] Quoted in Abdias do Nascimento et al., *Relações de Raça no Brasil* (Rio de Janeiro, 1950), pp. 18n., 19.

of the Mulattoes. The purpose, as Professor Costa Pinto has elegantly put it, was that the black man may say "without fear or shame: niger sum!" [57]

Even more vigorous in its opposition to discrimination of all kinds, not simply in the arts, was the *União dos Homens de Côr*, founded in 1949 in Rio. Calling for the raising of funds to overcome Negro deprivation, it advocated the establishment of schools and cooperatives and the provision of medical care in the *favelas* of Rio de Janeiro and in the backcountry. One of its goals was "to increase and expand literacy among children, adolescents, and adults of the Afro-Brazilian ethnic group." In 1951 it publicly thanked the President of the Republic for accepting the Afonso Arinos law, but then called on him to name a Negro State Minister in order to demonstrate that his government was not racist. It also protested against the fact that there was no Negro among the career diplomats in the Brazilian foreign service. Most ironic was the fact, the Union pointed out, that the Brazilian delegation to a recent Assembly of the United Nations contained no Negroes, for at that meeting a white Brazilian had spoken out vigorously against the oppression of the Negro in South Africa, "forgetting that the black suffers here in Brazil itself." [58]

One important reason for the weakness of Negro rights organizations in Brazil, both in the North and in the South, is that the nature of race relations there tends to inhibit the development of the natural leaders of such organizations. In Brazil, as in the United States, the better educated, the more skillful, and the wealthier portion of the colored population are mulattoes. Thanks to the mulatto escape hatch, however, these natural, potential leaders are encouraged to see themselves as different—indeed better—than Negroes. They are not included in the Brazilian definition of *Negro* and so they go their own way, withholding their skills, money, and prestige from the development of Negro rights organization. (This is not intended as a criticism of such individuals, incidentally; simply a description of what undoubtedly has happened.) In the United States, on the other hand, the inclusion of the mulatto in the definition of *Negro* forces light-skinned Negroes to identify, willy-nilly, with the whole black population.

[57] Ibid., pp. 9–12; Costa Pinto, *Negro no Rio de Janeiro*, pp. 286–93.
[58] Ibid., pp. 300–302, 304–305.

Potential leadership for organization is retained and indeed goaded into action because it is the mulattoes in the United States who feel most keenly their deprivation because they are the better educated and socially mobile. It is not accidental that many of the great leaders of Negro organizations in the United States have been mulattoes, men like Frederick Douglass, Booker T. Washington, W. E. B. DuBois, Whitney Young, Walter White, John Hope, Adam Clayton Powell, and Roy Wilkins. In Brazil such men would have been sorely tempted to ignore their connection with other blacks and use the mulatto escape hatch for their individual advancement. Indeed one might say that the great potential leaders of blacks in Brazil have all escaped through the hatch, to their own improvement, but to the loss of Negroes in general.

Negro organizations in Brazil are affected in another way by the nature of race relations in the country. The hostility to any racial or genetic definition of the Negro and the national commitment to the ideal of racial democracy makes Brazilians suspicious of any organization that makes appeals to race or color. A measure of that attitude and its effects upon Negro organizations was provided by the response to a suggestion at a meeting of the First Brazilian Congress of the Negro held at Rio de Janeiro in 1950. A participant suggested the creation of a National Confederation of Negro Groups, presumably to coordinate the rising interest in Negro organizations across the country. But the suggestion was put off as premature and dangerous because whites would oppose such a body "as racist." [59]

All through the history of Negro organizations in Brazil runs the fear that the whites will accuse the organizers of fomenting racism or of drawing the color line. "We repel completely those countrymen, who, erroneously [want to bring to Brazil] the Yankee Negro problem of hateful struggle against the white," read a statement of the *Frente Negra Brasileira* in 1937. "That is not our temper. We reject the North American conception, the basically anti-Christian fruit of the mentality of that people. We do not want segregation in national life, but a national affirmation of the Negro, a real and true integration." As recently as 1968, the veteran Negro leader from São Paul, José Correia

[59] Ibid., p. 299.

Leite, recalled the 1930's as a time when "The Negro could not open his mouth but that he was denounced as a racist. There was then the fear, and even today we are in our statements, protests, and so forth powerless to take a position, a road that would let the Negro make himself known." At the same meeting in Rio de Janeiro at which Correia Leite spoke, Souza Dantas, also a Negro, pointed out that "we know that the Negro is relegated to a situation of social inferiority and every time that he rises up against the state of things he is taken as subversive, as forward, and particularly as a black racist." The occasion for the meeting, incidentally, was the eightieth anniversary of the abolition of slavery in Brazil. (Significant for the future of race relations in Brazil, as will be noticed in more detail in the last chapter of this book, was the disagreement over whether Negroes ought to organize as blacks or simply as poor people. Abdias do Nascimento, the founder of the Negro Experimental Theater, argued for black organizations—"Negritude"—while Edison Carneiro, an equally respected student of the Negro, though a mulatto himself, contended that to organize on the basis of race would exacerbate tensions and animosities.) [60]

Even white scholars, like Arthur Ramos, who have been interested in the cause of the Negro have found it necessary to defend the creation of Negro organizations, even when those organizations are not political. At one point, for example, Ramos described such organizations as designed to awaken interest and pride among blacks, who were ashamed of "the color of their epidermis. . . . There is no hostility. There are no extreme positions. There is no social separation. There is no color line as in North America." After quoting from the purposes of one Negro organi-

[60] Fernandes, *Integração do negro*, II, p. 30; Bastide, *Relações raciais*, p. 167 reported that when Negroes in Brazil were asked what they thought of the Negro's position in the United States, "Those who knew the facts, felt a certain attraction for it; they were proud to know that Negroes could be capitalists, own automobiles, and private homes, become bankers or businessmen, but they also understood the price that was necessary to pay for all of this. No one wanted to lose any of the much freer and friendlier atmosphere of Brazil." See also "80 Anos de Abolição," *Cadernos Brasileiros*, X (May–June, 1968), 21; "80 Anos de Abolição," pp. 23–25. The main lines of the argument between Edison Carneiro and Abdias do Nascimento as to the proper approach for the Brazilian Negro to take in advancing his position are set forth in Ibid., pp. 84–88.

zation, Ramos assured his white readers, "They are legitimate anxieties to which no one of good will will refuse cooperation." [61] Even the *União dos Homens de Côr,* a militant group by Brazilian standards, chose as its symbol two interlaced hands, one black, one white, "representing the fraternal association of the two races" and which one of its leaders wryly interpreted as 'my mother the washerwoman and my father the greengrocer,' " that is, the Negro woman and the Portuguese man. [62]

Sex, But Not Marriage

As that ironic comment suggests, miscegenation in Brazil is at once more widespread and more accepted than it is in the United States. Mixing of the races in the United States, it is true, has been taking place throughout its history and certainly has been more common than many white North Americans often recognize. It has been estimated, for example, that between three-quarters and four-fifths of all so-called Negroes in the United States have some white ancestry. [63] How many so-called whites in the United States have Negro blood is unknown, but it must run into the hundreds of thousands, if not millions. It is the historic emphasis upon "purity" of race that bars the public acceptance and admission of race mixing in the United States. Lacking that emphasis on purity, Brazilians are freer to acknowledge the mixing, at least in general terms.

Despite this difference, it is important to recognize that in Brazil most mixing of ancestry today, as in the past, takes place outside of marriage, especially among the middle and upper classes. For as we have seen in examining studies of social distance scales, marriage with blacks or mulattoes is not acceptable to the overwhelming majority of whites in any region of the country or among any class, though there are some regional and class variations. Also, it is worth remembering that in a society

[61] Ramos, "Espirito associativo," *Revista do Archivo municipal* (1938), p. 125.

[62] Costa Pinto, *Negro no Rio de Janeiro,* p. 305.

[63] Pettigrew, *Profile of the Negro American,* p. 68 notes that the estimates of the proportion of United States Negroes with white ancestry varies from 72 to 83 per cent.

like Brazil, in which prejudice is officially denied not only by law, but more important, by general culture, attitudinal studies are probably skewed in favor of nondiscrimination as compared with actual behavior. In short, those whites who actually marry Negroes are likely to be fewer even than the social distance studies suggest.

One measure of white Brazilians' strong feelings against marriage across color lines is the way they justify refusal to marry a Negro. On this subject, even in Bahia, where a racial basis for aversion to Negroes is difficult to find, the argument comes close to being racist. White Bahians will refer quite openly to organic differences between the races, and say for example, that Negroes smell bad. Significantly, the odor is said to be not only disagreeable, but irremediable, "the disagreeable odor of the Portuguese and other immigrants being attributed only to the absence of bodily care." [64] On the other hand, Brazilians do not object to the mixing of blood from Negroes and whites in blood banks, as North Americans did until the time of World War II.

Interracial couples, if the contrast in colors is great enough, arouse astonishment and resentment. In 1967 reporters for the magazine *Realidade* (October, 1967) arranged for the photographing in the streets of Rio de Janeiro of the reactions of passerby upon seeing a Negro man and a white, blonde-haired girl holding hands and generally acting as if they were attracted to one another. The stares and frowns were pronounced and unconcealed, as the published photos make clear.

Actual figures on marriages between the races reflect the resistance to it. Pierson found for Bahia even, that official records for 1933–34 listed only 3.3 per cent of marriages as taking place between blacks and whites. Almost two decades later Azevedo checked out some 222 unions in the same city to ascertain the extent to which lines of color had been crossed in marriage. He found that 34 per cent of the couples were of the same color, 43 per cent were composed of dark males and lighter females, and 22 per cent were unions in which the females were darker than the males. Because the "crossings," however, were measured by color, many of the unions of different colors were probably of mulattoes of different shades rather than of whites' marrying

[64] Azevedo, *Cultura e Situação raciais*, p. 45.

blacks. Hutchinson remarks that in his Bahian community no one liked to see wide divergences in the color of married couples; the phrase used to describe such marriages is strikingly Brazilian in its attitude toward the black—*mosca no leite* (literally, a fly in the milk).

Farther south, as one would anticipate, the crossing of the color line in marriage is no more likely. An examination of some 42,000 marriages in Rio de Janeiro in 1890 found that only 5.9 per cent of them were between whites and colored, that is, Negroes or mulattoes. Florestan Fernandes' study of marriages in São Paulo in 1961 revealed that most blacks married other blacks (only 11 per cent of Negroes married white women), but about 25 per cent of mulatto males married white women. Nogueira calculated that in 1948, in the town of Itapetininga in the State of São Paulo, over 96 per cent of marriages were within color lines.[65]

Although it is frequently asserted that in Brazil lower-class whites marry blacks and mulattoes more frequently than middle-class or upper-class whites, the claim is not easily substantiated. It will be recalled, for instance, that the social distance studies did not reveal very great differences in the attitudes for classes toward marriage across color lines. When Cardoso and Ianni tried to test the point more closely they still did not find any sharp differences in attitude on the part of the classes, as shown in the table on p. 188.[66]

Taking together all of these examples of attitudes and practices toward marriage between white and colored people, it is evident that as one moves south, resistance to intermarriage strengthens, but that in all areas of Brazil intermarriage between races is not considered desirable by the whites. There is less objection to marriage with a mulatto, as is to be expected. Differences in attitude toward marriage between white and black exist among classes, but they are not great. The middle class, at least on the

[65] Pierson, *Negroes in Brazil*, p. 147; Azevedo, *Cultura e Situação raciais*, p. 39; Harry W. Hutchinson, "Race Relations in a Rural Community of the Bahian Reconcavo," in Charles Wagley, ed., *Race and Class in Rural Brazil*, 2nd ed. (New York, 1963), p. 125; Herbert S. Klein, "The Colored Freedmen in Brazilian Slave Society," *Journal of Social History*, III (Fall, 1969), p. 45; Fernandes, *Integração do negro*, II, p. 133; Nogueira, "Relações raciais . . . Itapetininga," in Bastide, ed., *Relações raciais*, p. 544.

[66] Cardoso and Ianni, *Côr e mobilidade*, pp. 184–85.

	NEGRO			MULATTO		
	Low Class	Middle Class	High Class	Low Class	Middle Class	High Class
Would not like friend to marry:	30	39	34	25	33	29
Would not like my brother to marry:	63	76	80	60	71	76
Would not like my sister to marry:	64	78	82	61	73	77
Would not like to marry	86	91	89	80	90	88

basis of the Ianni and Cardoso study at Florianopolis, has the highest resistance to intermarriage, but the other two classes are not far behind. Yet, in comparison with the practices and attitudes in the United States, the amount of intermarriage as well as the acceptability of it in Brazil can be described only as extraordinary. In such differences, we once again see the difference between a society with color prejudice and one with race prejudice.

Also considerably more common in Brazil than in the United States is the acceptance of, even encouragement to interracial sexual relations outside of marriage. The virtual apotheosis of the dark-skinned woman as a lover in Brazil is widely recognized. In the nineteenth century, for example, one traveler quoted an old aphorism:

> White women are for marrying
> Mulatto women are for fornicating
> Black women are for service.

The delights of black or brown love were much less publicly praised in the United States though Winthrop Jordan points out, significantly, that in eighteenth century South Carolina, where blacks out numbered whites, the public prints did discuss the relative merits of love with a black woman to a degree that was unheard of in the rest of continental English America. To the Brazilian male, the dusky Venus, as Roger Bastide has called the myth of the beautiful, erotic *mulata,* is the height of sexual attractiveness. René Ribeiro quotes a white sugar planter who lived for years with a mulatto woman: "Man, I believe that she was the best woman that I ever knew." But significantly when he himself was ready to marry a white woman, he married the *mulata* off to his stable hand—also a mulatto. The practice is an old one, as Ribeiro observes in mentioning an example of a similar incident from the Brazilian past.[67]

Brazilians like to cite this long history and obviously widespread practice of miscegenation as proof of their lack of prejudice. And in comparison with the compulsive concern with racial purity in the United States, the Brazilian experience is at once refreshing and enlightening. But as Professor Costa Pinto caustically observes, "all the legendary and folklore materials which can be collected in regard to the asserted extraordinary qualities of the woman of color—especially the *mulata*, as sexual companion—are no more than pure rationalizations of the accessibility of the *mulata* to seduction by the white." The test that he suggests in order to clinch his point has a surprisingly familiar ring to North American ears. He advises asking any Brazilian who asserts that interest in dark-skinned women is a sign of lack of prejudice, the question, "Would you want to marry a Negro or would you want to see your sister or daughter marry a Negro?" (Costa Pinto goes on to say that "in a discussion on racial equality" there is "no question more Brazilian than that." It is considered, he declares, capable of immediately silencing all those who argue in behalf of racial equality.[68] A North American might well answer that there is no question more North American than that same one.)

The very emphasis upon a *mulata* and not a Negro as the ideal sexual companion, even outside of marriage, carries strong racial implications, for the choice is of a woman who has the accessibility of a Negro, but in appearance is more like a white than a black woman. Furthermore, simply because black or mulatto women are sexual objects of white men does not necessarily im-

[67] Hermann Burmeister, *Viagem ao Brasil* (São Paulo, n.d.), p. 247; Winthrop D. Jordan, *White Over Black* (Chapel Hill, N.C., 1968), pp. 144–51 discusses the belief among Englishmen in North America that Negro women were more passionate than white; Ribeiro, *Religião e relações raciais*, p. 115.

[68] Costa Pinto, *Negro no Rio de Janeiro*, p. 214.

prove the status of blacks, as the sexual exploitation of black women by white men in the United States South under slavery and after ought to remind us. Indeed, it is germane to recall here that the "yaller" girl or light-skinned Negro woman is also a favorite sexual object in the United States, renowned for her ardor and beauty. The so-called octoroon balls of antebellum New Orleans testify in a concrete way to this interest. The light-skinned black woman unites in her person in the United States, as she does in Brazil, the accessibility of the Negro with the appearance of the white woman.[69]

Roger Bastide is probably excessive, but certainly suggestive when he asserts that extramarital sexuality between the races "effectively reduces a whole race to the level of prostitutes. . . . Behind miscegenation is exactly what is behind the institution of prostitution in the West: the defense of one group considered as superior, and therefore untouchable, to the detriment of another racial or social group."[70] The assertion that black women are the "protectors" of white women against white masculine lust recalls to mind a piece of testimony reported by John Dollard in *Caste and Class in a Southern Town.* A white informant told how a boy she loved brought her home one night "and she kissed him warmly at the door. An older woman saw her and warned her never to kiss a boy like that; she said he might go 'to nigger town' afterward." Dollard observed that "This seems again to emphasize the displacement of direct sexual feeling from white to Negro woman." It was only a half-joke in the town, Dollard further reported, that white men "until they were married . . . did not know that white women were capable of sexual intercourse."[71] Although in both the United States and Brazil there are and have been many examples of true affection as well as sexual exploitation in the liaisons between the races, the conclusion to be drawn from that history is not "that love breaks down barriers and unites human beings," but "that racial ideologies extend their conflicts even into love's embrace."[72]

One of the obvious consequences of miscegenation, whether in

[69] John Dollard, *Caste and Class in a Southern Town,* 3rd ed. (Anchor Books, Garden City, N.Y., 1957), pp. 140–41.
[70] Bastide, "Dusky Venus," *Race* (1961), p. 11.
[71] Dollard, *Caste and Class,* pp. 139–40.
[72] Bastide, "Dusky Venus," *Race* (1961), p. 18.

or outside of marriage, is offspring of mixed bloods. As we have noticed already, in Brazil the children of a white and black couple are neither black nor white. This fact in itself encourages "whitening" by racial mixture. Indeed, it has been argued that a national policy of Brazil is to have everyone eventually white, through the mixing of blood. This expectation has been called "the progressive Aryanization of Brazil." [73] "The problem of racial assimilation and absorption between whites and blacks is a solved problem in Brazil," one Brazilian expert on the Negro optimistically wrote in 1930.[74] Certainly many blacks are interested in racial mixing, given the advantages to be gained by whiteness. Even in the Northeast it is popularly believed that Negroes "are crazy for a white woman." A Negro man there has been known to marry a poor white woman who has been seduced and deserted by a white youth,[75] for in that way his own children by the woman will "whiten." Lightness of color in itself is not sufficient to place a person in the upper class, but it always improves one's position over that of a darker person. For the poor, lightening of skin may be more easily obtainable for one's children than money or education. (Of course, since both partners cannot be satisfied in such a competition, men more often marry lighter than women. As one informant put it, "The woman does not marry whom she wants, but with him who wants her." [76])

When he is poor, the Negro usually accepts marriage with one of his color, but "when he is a doctor, he wants a white for his wife." This comment also means that when a Negro is educated he has sufficient status to make him acceptable to a white wife and her parents. As a Brazilian novelist observed in 1968, "it is not easy to meet a white man married to a black woman. Generally, the opposite occurs, for society understands that marriage causes the position of the white to fall while at the same time it elevates the Negro." [77] When a black or mulatto succeeds in marrying lighter, he speaks of "purging his blood"—a phrase that

[73] Ibid., p. 12.

[74] Nelson de Senna, *Africanos no Brasil* (Belo Horizonte, Brazil, 1938), p. 48.

[75] Ribeiro, *Religião e relações raciais,* p. 110.

[76] Ibid., pp. 111–12.

[77] Cardoso and Ianni, *Côr e mobilidade,* pp. 211–12; Luna, *Negro contra escravidão,* p. 211.

in itself is revealing of what the process connotes in the minds of Brazilians. Now his children, at least, will have a better chance of moving upward socially. Hutchinson tells of a former fisherman in a community in the Northeast who was black and who married a woman who was poor, but almost white (*branca de terra*). He then went on to become a well-to-do merchant. Although his wife's poverty brought him no economic advantages, she did "whiten" his children, who were sent to the city to be educated. In that way their own social mobility and ability to marry lighter were enhanced.[78] Ribeiro reports on a Negro musician in Recife who married a beautiful Portuguese woman as part of his effort to rise. Later he told his mulatto sons never to marry a person of color: "If I had married a Negro you would be so ugly that no one would look at you." When one of his sons fell in love with a Negro girl the father promptly broke off the relationship. "I did everything in order to put you in the living room," he told his son, "and you run for the kitchen." All but one of the sons married lighter than himself. But the one daughter, who was the darkest of the children, married a Negro despite the parents' opposition. When her first child was born and it was very dark, and the grandfather was disconsolate, saying "all my work is lost." Then there is the anecdote of the mulatto who refused to consent to the marriage of his children to darker-skinned persons. "Aren't you ashamed to think of marrying Negroes?" he sternly inquired.[79]

To a North American such remarks by a mulatto are almost incredible, but they are quite understandable in the Brazilian context. They are a reflection of what amounts to the national belief in whitening. That is, such remarks and behavior patterns in marriage frankly assume that whiteness is desirable and blackness is to be escaped from. Both Negroes and white have been brought up to believe that to be white is to be best and to be black is to be last. When a child is born in Brazil to parents of different colors, it is said that the color of the child is the first thing examined, even before the fingers and toes are counted or

[78] Hutchinson, "Race Relations . . . Reconcavo," in Wagley, ed., *Race and Class*, p. 125.

[79] Ribeiro, *Religião e relações raciais*, pp. 120–21; Bastide, "Dusky Venus," *Race* (1961), p. 12.

the body scrutinized for defects. If the child is lighter than the parents, people consider it lucky; if the child is darker, then people are sorry for it.[80]

Because it is possible for a person to improve his children's status by "whitening," the Brazilian system clearly encourages both miscegenation and integration. Yet, even as Brazilians talk of racial democracy and acceptance, they look forward to the eventual disappearance of Negroes! The irony of this "solution" to the problem of race has not been lost on some Negroes. "We are not against miscegenation," asserted one black in 1951. "But we are against a policy of imposed miscegenation, with the aim of making the Negro race disappear. The whites' policy actually is to make the Negro race disappear. First, by miscegenation. Second, by submerging it in a torrent of white immigrants. This, associated with a police policy of degrading the Negro, to the end of also seeing him disappear by tuberculosis, syphilis, and prostitution. What we want is that it be recognized that we are citizens like everyone else and that we have a right to education, to integrate ourselves into society and not be freely abandoned to the hope that we will disappear." [81]

A further paradox in Brazilian policy is that the hope for eventual whitening of the population must confront the large amount of impressionistic and systematic evidence, which has already been discussed, showing that few whites actually want or intend to marry Negroes. One of the consequences of that paradox is that the whitening has been taking place at a glacial pace. In 1870 Negroes—under the Brazilian definition—constituted slightly less than 20 per cent of the population, in 1890 they were a little less than 15 per cent, but in the census of 1940 the ratio was the same as in 1890. The proportion of whites rose from 38 per cent in 1870 to 63 per cent in 1940, the upsurge being a result of massive white immigration from Europe and the "passing" of

[80] Oracy Nogueira, "Preconceito de marca e preconceita racial de origem," *Anais do XXXI Congresso Internacional de Americanistas* (São Paulo, 1954), p. 423. An English version of Nogueira's important article is "Skin Color and Social Class," *Plantation Systems of the New World* (Washington, D.C., 1959).

[81] Fernandes, *Integração do negro*, I, pp. 82–83; "It is significant," writes Ronald Hilton, "that Brazilian immigration laws exclude Negroes," H. V. Livermore, ed., *Portugal and Brazil* (Oxford, 1953), p. 337.

many mixed bloods into the white category. In 1968 a newspaper reported the decline of Negroes from 10 per cent of the population in 1950 in the Rio de Janeiro area to an estimated 7 per cent in 1960. Mulattoes, on the other hand, rose from 30 per cent in 1950 to almost 40 per cent in 1960, a rise explained by the shift of blacks into the category of mulattoes.[82] Although these figures from Rio suggest a more rapid lightening than the earlier figures, they still show that the process is a lengthy one, especially if complete whitening rather than mere lightening is the goal. If complete "bleaching" of the population is the Brazilian solution to the so-called racial problem, then it is at best a very long-range solution. On a rather basic and practical level it offers no improvement in the lots of blacks already born and perhaps not much more to their *future* offspring because even mulattoes are still treated differently from whites.

Yet miscegenation in Brazil does offer a theoretical possibility that in some distant future differences in physical appearance, on which social discriminations have been based in the past, will disappear. In the United States no such possibility, even theoretically, can exist. The very definition of a Negro as anyone with African ancestry decrees that miscegenation actually *increases* rather than decreases the Negro population. Every white person in the United States who marries or mates with a black automatically produces as offspring only Negroes. The system neither encourages integration nor brings it about. In practice, of course, hundreds, if not thousands, of so-called Negroes pass into the white world each year and in that way whitening does occur, in spite of the system. But the period of time that would be required for complete whitening would be very much longer than in Brazil. One measure of the slowness of such whitening is that in the United States Negroes have consistently constituted about 10 per cent of the total population for the last hundred years.

Indeed, given the fear of being overwhelmed by blacks, which whites in the United States historically have had and still exhibit,

[82] The census is reported in Nogueira, "Relações raciais . . . Itapetininga," in Bastide, ed. *Relações raciais,* p. 462n.; the more recent figures are by Eduardo Pinto, "Preconceito de class atinge negros 80 anos apos abolicao," *Jornal do Brasil,* May 12, 1968. I am indebted for this last reference to Rebecca Bergstresser of Stanford University.

miscegenation becomes a singularly dangerous act and therefore reprehensible in the eyes of whites. By outlawing miscegenation, a practice that has been common in the United States until very recently, whites assuage that fear, but at the same time they inhibit the creation of mixed offspring that would help to break down the fear and lessen the hostility between black and white. Thus the fear of blacks has resulted in policies and laws that have only perpetuated and institutionalized the very fears against which the policies were at least in part directed. It seems unlikely, therefore, even with the recent judicial rejection of laws against miscegenation, that interracial marriage can be a "solution" to the problem of the races in the United States. It would require the repudiation of the nation's experience out of which the peculiar United States definition of the Negro emerged. The nature of that experience will be the substance of the next chapter.

The Brazilian acceptance of whitening—which is really another way of saying they have reserved a place for the mulatto—has still another social consequence. It reduces social discontent among blacks, for the barriers that hold back mulattoes in the United States, regardless of class or education, are much less rigid in Brazil. Thus a Negro in Brazil can expect that his children will be able to breach the barriers that have held him back if only he can marry lighter than himself. His children, in short, may advance socially and occupationally even though he has not. Such a real possibility acts as a safety valve on discontent and frustration among Negroes and mulattoes. As we have noticed already in discussing Negro organizations, it is undoubtedly a major reason why Negroes in Brazil have not been driven to form protest organizations as have Negroes in the United States. It is also possible to interpret this situation in a less favorable light for the future of the Negro in Brazil, but that consideration is more properly a matter of the future of race relations in the two countries and so it will be put off until the concluding chapter.

"A Negro with a White Soul"

Simply because there are innumerable gradations between black and white in Brazil, the definition of who is white is less sharp than it is in the United States. Some persons who are considered white in Brazil are denominated Negroes in the United States. Oracy Nogueira, for example, tells of a Brazilian intellectual, accepted as white in his native country, who was discriminated against in a Chicago hotel on the grounds that he was a Negro. Gilberto Freyre has ascribed the anti-Americanism of Brazilian writer Eduardo Prado to the fact that he was denied service in an elegant barber shop in the United States because he was a Negro, though he thought of himself as a white.[83] On the other hand, sometimes Negroes go to Brazil and find that their overtures to people they view as blood brothers are repulsed on the ground that the so-called "blood brother" does not consider himself a fellow Negro.

Indeed, one of the difficulties in arriving at an accurate picture of the historical extent of acceptance of blacks in Brazilian society, particularly from travel accounts, is that the traveler, especially if he comes from the United States or England, may misread the significance or meaning of what he observes. To North Americans all people with some African ancestry are Negroes, but this is not, of course, the case with Brazilians. Brazilians, for instance, are surprised to learn that some of their historical personages like Castro Alves or Floriano Peixoto are viewed by North American Negroes as Negroes; they are not so regarded in Brazil. They are not even thought of as mulattoes because they are so light-skinned.[84] The North American white or black will return home from a visit to Brazil talking of the easy acceptance of "Negroes." What he has witnessed, however, is the acceptance of mulattoes, a quite different thing in the eyes of Brazilians, as we have seen. Gilberto Freyre, for instance, has caught at least one instance of this misreading of the Brazilian racial pattern in the past by a traveler who imported the North American definition of a Negro. René Ribeiro noticed it in Perdigão Malheiro, who wrote about the social mobility of former slaves in nineteenth century Brazil. "Evidently there was confusion here," comments Ribeiro, "in that social ascent is referred to . . . among the mulattoes, for whom in that period such opportunities were open, and the blacks, for

[83] Gilberto Freyre, *Ordem e Progresso,* 2nd ed. (Rio de Janeiro, 1962), p. clix.

[84] Nogueira, "Preconceito de marca . . . de origem," *Anais do XXXI Congresso* (1954), p. 427n.

whom they were very much restricted." On the other hand, Brazilians interested in showing off the racial democracy of their country, especially to foreigners, will talk about blacks in a given situation of successful advancement, when in fact the people in question are mulattoes or even *mulato claros*.[85]

In Brazil, in contrast with the situation in the United States, it is possible to believe in the inferiority of Negroes without thinking that all Negroes are so in fact. (This disjunction between general and individual perceptions occurs to a limited extent in the United States, too. Ralph McGill, the well-known southern liberal, for example, tells of the deep and moving friendship between himself and a Negro roofer for whom he worked as a young college boy. It is not without significance, however, that McGill's parents apparently did not believe in segregation or racial prejudice and so he had a freedom to enter into such a relationship vouchsafed to few white Southerners of his generation. For rarely are such relationships permitted to be public or to exceed the narrow norms set by a society of white supremacy.) [86] In Brazil exceptions can be and are made, as witness this remarkable statement by a member of an old, traditional family in São Paulo: "Putting aside all the sentimentalism of sympathy and piety that the Negro always arouses in our country, we see that this race has had conferred upon it sentiments which it never possessed. It is important nevertheless not to confuse the cultural value of a race with the virtues of particular persons. History indicates in various countries, blacks who have exercised with complete success in various times, the most varied professional activities such as journalists, lawyer, engineer, doctor, etc. But on the other hand, the science that observes the facts coldly, free of any passion, has proved that, even today, the Negroes have not made themselves into a civilized people. . . . From it I can

---

[85] Freyre, *Ordem e Progresso*, p. 3; Ribeiro, *Religião e Relações raciais*, p. 95; Fernandes, *Integraçã do negro*, II, p. 225. Harry Hoetink, *The Two Variants in Caribbean Race Relations* (New York, 1967), p. 34 observes correctly that Frank Tannenbaum confuses Negro and mulatto in his study of the Negro in the Americas (*Slave and Citizen*) so that the social mobility he discerns is really that of the mulatto and not of the Negro.

[86] Ralph McGill, *The South and the Southerner* (Boston, 1963), Chapter V.

only conclude that some Negroes are capable of exercising some professional activity, but that the majority of the race is, as daily facts show, totally incapable." [87]

Less hostile, though no less indicative of the individual exception to a general dislike of blacks by whites, is the incident reported by Ribeiro from Recife. Two friends, white and black, but of the same social class, went to a lecture, in the course of which the Italian conquest of Ethiopia was discussed. The white person turned to her black friend and said, "It is good they took Ethiopia, for it will give education to those Negroes! I do not like blacks." The remark was said naturally and without application to the black friend beside her. Sometimes, after such a comment a white will explicitly exclude the black who is present, with the patronizing remark, "You are not a Negro," or "You are a Negro with a white soul." For some colored persons such condescension is intolerable, but for those seeking acceptance it is precisely what they want to hear.[88]

If the Brazilian emphasis upon individual exception permits some blacks to rise above their fellows, despite their color, it has also two other effects. It does not alter the white's impression of Negroes in general and it does not help to advance the status of blacks in general. To whites the black who gets into the best club or succeeds in a liberal profession is truly an exception; his success is the result of individual talent, whereas defects and failures "are attributed to the universal negative characteristics of the Negro." Fernandes illustrates this point in the story of a white man who had been drinking in a bar with a Negro. When the Negro left, the white complained to other whites about "bold" Negroes. He said he did not think Negroes were worth much; they seemed always to be in lowly occupations. When he was reminded that he knew a Negro lawyer, he declared him to be "one in a thousand. All the others are illiterates." When pressed to explain the contradiction between his apparently egalitarian behavior and his prejudice he simply said, "I do not like them. A person has to accept them. Otherwise they say you are proud. But I do not like them. What is one to do? A person has to live

[87] Fernandes, *Integração do negro,* II, p. 307.
[88] Ribeiro, *Religião e Relações raciais,* p. 133; Fernandes, *Integração do negro,* II, pp. 218–19.

in accord with the custom of the country." [89] In short, even his experience with individual blacks had not altered his opinion of them as a group. (It is worth noticing, too, that this man's prejudice in this instance did not result in discriminatory behavior.)

The same observation can be made about whites in general, for whenever a black is accepted it has no effect on the acceptability of other blacks. Since each is admitted to the club on his "individual merits" no general acceptance has been made. In the United States, on the other hand, if one Negro is admitted to a heretofore exclusively white club or hotel, it is understood by all that the racial barrier is down for all. This difference can be a source of misunderstanding on the part of North Americans when they visit Brazil. For when they see Negroes or mulattoes in certain places they erroneously assume, from their own home experience, that it means all Negroes or mulattoes are therefore acceptable. In fact, all that it means is that particular blacks have been accepted, and no more.

The Brazilian accent upon individual exception also has the effect of permitting the white man to talk of racial democracy while maintaining control over the social mobility of blacks. There is just enough upward movement for Negroes and especially mulattoes to sustain the argument that failure to rise is a consequence of individual inadequacy and not discrimination. Negroes themselves sometimes indicate their disbelief in the existence of prejudice. Thus in 1968 the *Jornal do Brasil* wrote, "Erlon Chaves does not believe in racial prejudice and he cites his own case: 'I was never segregated for being a Negro.' . . . He is married to a white woman, 'like Pelé' [a well-known Negro soccer star] and finds that when the Negroes attain a higher status, the problems that are today reported will cease to exist." [90] Thus the burden of proof of discrimination is put on the black, for the correspondence between color and class and the mulatto escape hatch permit the white society to deny discrimination. Yet the gates of social mobility are actually only half open, carefully guarded by tests of color, financial means, profession, education, and moral upbringing. At any moment the white can shut the gate through the application of the tests.

[89] Ibid., II, pp. 271, 299–300.
[90] Pinto, "Preconceito de classes," *Jornal do Brasil*, May 12, 1968.

Finally, there is one other contrast in the race relations in the two countries. There is an explicitness, even harshness, about the relations between blacks and whites in the United States that is absent in Brazil. In the days of legal segregation in the United States, for example, signs pointed out special drinking fountains, rest rooms, waiting rooms, and ticket booths for blacks; Negroes were openly excluded from certain hospitals, cemeteries, theaters, and so forth. Blatant assertions of Negro inferiority were to be heard in Congress and read in the press. Fear of the Negro, coupled with hatred, are commonplace in the race relations of the United States. Indeed, fear and hatred are taken as a fact of life on both sides of the color line. John Griffin in his book *Black Like Me*, in which he traveled around the Deep South disguised as a Negro, delineates one example of that hatred, which manifested itself when he inadvertently sat at a table in a restaurant from which Negroes were excluded. "Once again a 'hate stare' drew my attention like a magnet. It came from a middle-aged, heavy-set, well-dressed white man. He sat a few yards away, fixing his eyes on me. Nothing can describe the withering horror of this. You feel lost, sick at heart before such unmasked hatred, not so much because it threatens you but because it shows humans in such an inhuman light." James Baldwin, the well-known black writer, powerfully set forth the other side of the equation. "And there is, I should think," he wrote, "no Negro living in America who has not felt, briefly or for long periods, with anguish sharp or dull, in varying degrees and to varying effect, simple, naked, and unanswerable hatred; who has not wanted to smash any white face he may encounter in a day, to violate, out of motives of the cruelest vengeance, their women, to break the bodies of all white people and bring them low, as low as that dust into which he has been and is being trampled." [91] Such hatred is extremely rare on both sides of the color barrier in Brazil. Even during slavery, as we saw in Chapter II, Brazilians might fear the rage of rebellious slaves, but they did not fear and therefore did not hate blacks as whites often have and still do in the United States. Consequently, the mirror image of that hatred, which

[91] John Howard Griffin, *Black Like Me* (Signet, New York, 1961), p. 53; the statement from James Baldwin is quoted in John Hope Franklin, ed., *Color and Race* (Boston, 1968), p. 58.

Baldwin gives voice to is also absent in Brazil. The kind of almost automatic lining up behind one's color in a dispute between black and white, which has been characteristic of whites in the South and frequently outside the South in the United States is not at all common in Brazil.

Today in Brazil, as in the past, it is the practice to dissemble prejudice, or, as the Brazilians say, "to save the appearances." Employers do not deny a job to a black as such; they say it is filled already. When speaking of Negroes people lower their voices, "in order not to offend." When a person is thought to have some Negro ancestry he is said to have a foot or an ear "in the kitchen." Equally common is the picturesque phrase, "In the house of a hanging, do not speak of rope." Indeed, the very word *Negro* is avoided by most whites, in southern Brazil as well as in the Northeast, for though it does not have the extremely insulting connotation of "nigger" in the United States, it has taken on pejorative overtones that most people seek to avoid. (It is used in anger by a white person who wants to put down resoundingly a Negro or mulatto opponent. It is especially crushing, of course, when used against a mulatto.) Brazilians prefer *preto*, which also means black, but it lacks any bad connotation. In a situation calling for deference a white Brazilian will use *moreno* (light-skinned Negro), regardless of the actual shade of skin of the person being spoken to. Such euphemisms are yet another sign of the low esteem in which blackness and Negroes are held. They also have the effect of directing opposition against the manifestation of prejudice or discrimination rather than against the thing itself. The white Brazilian accepts the prejudice unchallenged, in effect, and even helps thereby to perpetuate it. Sometimes the Negro himself is inveigled into doing the same thing. For when a Negro is not wanted at a meeting or party to which he might think he is invited, he is warned away in a similarly covert way, with a phrase like "It is enough to hit the harness for the burro to understand." [92] Perhaps the most accurate way of describing color prejudice among Brazilians is to compare it to the attitudes

[92] Ribeiro, *Religião e Relações raciais,* pp. 142–43; Nogueira, "Skin Color and Social Class," *Plantation Systems,* p. 177; Pierson, *Negroes in Brazil,* p. 138; Fernandes, *Integração do negro,* II, pp. 364–65; Bicudo, "Attitudes dos alunos," in Bastide, ed., *Relações raciais,* p. 270; Nogueira, "Relações raciais . . . Itapetininga," Ibid., p. 511.

North Americans take toward a physical disability, like a withered arm or club foot. It is something to be taken into consideration or allowed for, but not to be noticed publicly. One may well have a strong affection for an *individual* with the deformity and others can understand why, but obviously one does not want to have many of his friends or members of his family suffering from the same handicap.

In the United States, on the other hand, as we have seen, prejudice and discrimination against blacks is commonly suffused with feelings of distaste, fear, and often hatred. Moreover, because all blacks are inferior in the North American conception, many whites cannot accept with equanimity an intimate relationship between individuals of the two races. All such liaisons or friendships are condemned as evil and unnatural. In other words, because there is no sharp line between the races in Brazil, whites do not feel it necessary to "police" the line, as North Americans do. In Brazil individual blacks who may cross the line threaten neither the system nor any white. Though if large numbers of blacks should cross the line, that would be another matter.

Perhaps the easiest way to illustrate the Brazilian's relative absence of fear or hatred of blacks is to call attention to another marked difference in attitudes in Brazil and in the United States. It is an axiom of popular psychology of race relations in the United States that when Negroes approach a majority of the population in a given area, tension rises proportionately, impelling the whites to take stricter measures to "control" the Negroes. Hence in North American eyes it is quite understandable that historically the legal and other limitations on Negroes have been most numerous and strictest in the Deep South, where the Negroes have constituted large proportions, in some places reaching a majority of the population. Yet in Brazil it is in the Northeast, where the Negro and mulattoes have always comprised a majority of the population, that the acceptability of Negroes and mulattoes has been greatest.[93] It will also be recalled from Chapter III that it is in the Northeast that intermarriage with blacks was more acceptable to whites than marriage with Jews, a distinction that is usually explained by the greater familiarity of

[93] Nogueira, "Preconceito de marca e . . . de origem," *Anais do Congresso* (1954), p. 430.

nordestinos with blacks than with Jews. Conversely, in those areas of Brazil—particularly in the South—where Negroes have been very few, prejudice has been traditionally most severe. Whatever the source of greater white prejudice and discrimination against blacks in southern Brazil, it clearly is not fear of numbers or of being overwhelmed by them as it is said to be in the United States.

The Heart of the Matter

Although it has been the intention of this and the preceding chapters to set forth in some detail the nuances of the relations between whites and blacks in Brazil and compare them with those in the United States, the many details ought not to obscure the fact that the differences between the two societies are reducible to two principal ones.

The first is that in the United States, virtually from the beginning of the colonial period, some kind of discrimination was made between blacks and whites, whether slave or free, and that this differentiation was embedded in the law. Colonial Brazil also made a distinction between whites and blacks in the law, as we have had occasion to notice, but as time wore on, unlike the development in the United States, these laws either fell into disuse or were abandoned. Thus in the late nineteenth century Brazil was virtually without any discriminatory laws for blacks. Meanwhile, North Americans not only retained in practice the discriminatory legislation they inherited from the colonial period, they added to it, building up, by the opening of the twentieth century, at least in the South, a great body of legislation separating the races in a large number of activities.

The second difference that calls for explanation is that in the United States the definition of a Negro became anyone with African ancestry, and this definition is unqualified by criteria of class. On the other hand, in Brazil, as in Latin America in general, this simple, biological definition of the Negro never developed. Instead, a special place was reserved for the mixed blood—the mulatto—a development that opened up much wider possibilities for social mobility.

The fact is, as has already been implied in this chapter, the man who was neither black nor white can be taken as the symbol of the differences between the race relations of the two countries. Virtually all of the particular differences pointed out in Chapters III and IV are really manifestations of this single underlying difference in the social definition of the mulatto. When we have found an answer to the question of why the mulatto escape hatch developed in Brazil, we will be well on our way also to finding an answer to why Brazil did not retain its discriminatory legislation of the colonial period. Let us now turn to an examination of the history and inherited culture of the two societies, for it is there that the explanations are to be sought.

The Roots of Difference

V

What could one expect . . . from a society founded on adventure, and not on labor, on hunting the Indian, on the enslavement of the Negro, on the degradation of women, on general concubinage, on injustice, on ignorance, on superstition, on injustice and fear? What could one expect of a country whose lands were given away free and in immense tracts, to nobles incapable of cultivating them while denying a corner of land to those who wanted to plant and grow?
—Abelardo Romero, *Origem da Imoralidade no Brasil,* 1967.

. . . among the moderns the abstract and transient fact of slavery is fatally united with the physical and permanent fact of color. The traditions of slavery dishonors the race, and the peculiarity of the race perpetuates the tradition of slavery. . . . You may set the Negro free, but you cannot make him otherwise than an alien to the European. . . . Whoever has inhabited the United States must have perceived that in those parts of the Union in which the Negroes are no longer slaves they have in no wise drawn nearer to the whites. On the contrary, the prejudice of race appears to be stronger in the states that have abolished slavery than in those where it still exists; and nowhere is it so intolerant as in those states where servitude has never been known.
—Alexis de Tocqueville, *Democracy in America,* 1835.

Perhaps the quickest way to cut into the knotty problem of origins of differences is to look at those historical experiences that Brazil and the United States have had in common. For it is the similarity in the history of the black man in the two countries that defines the problem and complicates the explanation.

Consciousness of Color

Both Brazilians and North Americans today, as in the past, are conscious of differences in appearances between whites and blacks. Neither people is color blind. In fact, as we have seen, the Brazilians might be said to be the more color conscious of the two if the comparison is based on their attention to shades of color. An awareness of color, however, ought not to be surprising. There are good scientific and historical grounds for believing that all people, not simply so-called racists, draw social distinctions when they perceive differences in appearances. Gordon Allport, the social psychologist, has suggested that there is no need to postulate a "consciousness of kind," to explain a person's awareness of others. When a person makes such a mental distinction he is taking the easiest intellectual path; *not* to make distinctions requires an effort, Allport notes. Moreover, when such distinctions are made they express pride in one's own appearance and culture,[1] that is, they are reinforced by simple narcissism. One can observe further that to categorize people on the basis of how they look undoubtedly aids in understanding the world—and perhaps of controlling it a little. For without such quick and constant categorizing of impressions, the world appears to the beholder as little more than a mass of unrelated, disparate things, animals, persons, and ideas. Whether in science or in popular thought, it is a property of thought to group and to distinguish at the same time. To refer to a well-known scientific example, take the instance of Linneaus, the Swedish botanist, who set forth the classification and nomenclature for the animal and plant worlds. His great contribution to science was his ability to perceive distinctions among the myriad living things of the earth, thereby dividing them into categories, while at the same time taking account of similarities so that he could group as well as divide the world of living things. Finally, in suggesting that awareness of racial differences is inherent in man, it is relevant to observe that the sense of sight is the most highly developed and acute of all human senses, unlike the situation among all other animals, except birds and primates. Moreover, man is probably alone among animals, again with the exception of the anthropoids, in being able to distinguish colors.[2]

[1] Kenneth J. Gergen, "The Significance of Skin Color in Human Relations," in John Hope Franklin, ed., *Color and Race* (Boston, 1968), p. 114; Gordon W. Allport, *The Nature of Prejudice* (abridged Anchor ed., Garden City, N.Y., 1958), pp. 18, 127.

[2] Weston La Barre, *The Human Animal* (Chicago, 1954), pp. 34–38, and p. 279, where it is said: "Now the eye has almost fantastic powers of accommodation and can see objects illuminated with a brightness all the way from that of a noon-day coral beach to that of a jungle path on a moonless night–a ratio of a billion to one."

Considering these human endowments, it is not surprising that the visual perception of differences in other men is at once acute, close, and intense. Winthrop Jordan, in *White Over Black*, points out how shocked white Englishmen were when first they encountered black men in Africa; [3] significantly, it was their color—something *seen*—that attracted most attention, not their speech or their smell. It is not without significance, for example, that in all western languages, beginning with the Portuguese and Spanish, who were the first modern Europeans to encounter Africans, the name assigned to these newly discovered people was *Negro* or black, not *African* or some version of a tribal designation. It was what Europeans *saw* that evoked the lasting response.

To perceive physical distinctions is the first step toward making social distinctions. Social psychologists today tell us that their research confirms the idea that similarities between people arouse positive feelings, whereas perceived differences evoke uneasiness and even fear. To meet people who differ in a striking way from oneself is to have called into question long-standing ways of perceiving and relating to others. As one social psychologist has said, such an experience shakes a person's security "in knowing how to act adaptively." Allport, too, points out that experiments with children show that strangeness in appearance is quickly perceived and can easily carry over into feelings of fear. Moreover, he goes on, visible differences are generally taken to imply "real," that is, internal or mental differences, as well as physical ones. [4]

---

[3] Winthrop Jordan, *White Over Black* (Chapel Hill, N.C., 1968), pp. 4–7.

[4] Gergen, "Significance of Skin Color," Franklin, ed., *Color and Race*, pp. 115–16; Allport, *The Nature of Prejudice*, pp. 128–29. The conclusions of Mary Ellen Goodman, *Race Awareness in Young Children*, new, revised edition (New York, 1964), p. 245, are pertinent here. "Getting acquainted with our 103 children [four years of age] has taught us . . . that 'little children' sometimes pay a startling amount of attention to race, that they are ready to pay attention to race just as soon as they pay attention to other physical—and socially significant—attributes (like age and sex), and that the amount and kind of attention paid by different children vary as a function of certain interrelated factors. The high degree of race awareness we have seen in many of these children is startling, and not only because it does not fit our adult expectations. The fact is that mere intellectual awareness of the physical signs of race is not all of the story. There is another part which is not merely startling but quite shocking to liberal-humanitarian sensibilities. It is shocking to find that four-year-olds, particularly white ones, show unmistakable signs of the onset of racial bigotry."

Nor should it be thought that only white Europeans are aware of differences of color. Harold Isaacs, observes that throughout Asia sharp distinctions are drawn by Filipinos, Indians, and Malays between themselves and people of different appearance. Recent conflicts based on differences in color between Chinese and Malays in Singapore further remind us how color is used as a basis of difference. Frantz Fanon, the black psychiatrist–writer, when he went to North Africa to help the Algerians in their fight against French overlords was shocked to discover what he called racism between the Algerians and the Arabs on the one hand, and against the black Africans on the other.[5]

Among Chinese and Japanese, as among westerners, white color has high social and aesthetic value. As late as the 1940's, that is before attacks on western imperialism became a matter of policy, Chinese writers extolled the "snow-white" skin of their beloved ones.[6] Long before there was any contact with either white-skinned Caucasians or dark-skinned Africans or Indians, the Japanese valued white skin as beautiful and denominated black skin as ugly. Some Japanese samurai who visited the United States soon after the opening of their country in the mid-nineteenth century commented in their private diaries on the beauty of the white skin of the United States women they met, though they did not like the "large" eyes or light-colored hair of the western women. On the same trip, when the samurai stopped in Africa, they were repelled by the black faces of the native peoples, whom they likened in appearance to monkeys.[7]

Even in Africa, where the population is dark-skinned, a tendency to value white or light color and to disprize dark color or black is evident. Victor Turner found that among certain African groups black has evil connotations. Among the Mandja, for example, black means death. "Black is the symbol of impurity. The colour white is that of rebirth." Even human beings, among the Ndembu of central Africa, who are Negroes themselves, "are classified as 'white' or 'black' in terms of nuances of pigmentation.

[5] Harold R. Isaacs, "Group Identity and Political Change: The Role of Color and Physical Characteristics," in Franklin, ed., Color and Race, pp. 84–86.

[6] Ibid., p. 92.

[7] Hiroshi Wagatsuma, "The Social Perception of Skin Color in Japan," in Franklin, ed., Color and Race, pp. 129, 136–37.

There is here an implied moral difference and most people object to being classified as 'black.'"[8]

If the culture of peoples with pigmented skin as well as that of white Europeans is permeated with a preference for white as a color and in skin, then perhaps we are in the presence of an attitude that is universal and not simply the consequence of mere history. It is surely more than a coincidence that in Africa and Asia as well as in Europe, black is associated with unpleasantness, disaster, or evil. Black undoubtedly evokes recollections of the night—that time when men, with their heavy dependence upon sight, are most helpless and in greatest danger. White, on the other hand, is the color of light, which emanates principally from the sun, which in turn is the source of warmth and the other conditions that support life. Night is not only dark, but cold and therefore a threat to life.[9] Is it any wonder that white is seen everywhere as the symbol of success, virtue, purity, goodness, whereas black is associated with evil, dirt, fear, disaster, and sin? (In Christian iconography, too, the devil is invariably black, whereas God and the angels are dressed in white and surrounded by light; to be free of sin is to be washed as white as the lamb, and so forth.)

For our purposes the conclusion to be drawn from this brief excursion into color symbolism is that perceptions of dark color are not only universally made, but that dark color is generally denigrated. It would seem that color prejudice is a universal phenomenon, not simply North American or Brazilian. But to

[8] Gergen, "The Significance of Skin Color," in Franklin, ed., *Color and Race*, pp. 119–20; Victor W. Turner, "Colour Classification in Ndembu Ritual," in Michael Banton, ed., *Anthropological Approaches to the Study of Religion* (London, 1966), pp. 55–58. I am indebted to Kennell Jackson of Stanford University for bringing the Turner reference to my attention.

[9] Ibid., pp. 73–74. Turner suggests the following explanation for the African denigration of black: "My own hypothesis is that black tends to become an auspicious colour in regions where water is short, for the black clouds bring fertility and growth (apparently of hair, as well as plants!). In regions where water is plentiful and food more or less abundant, black may well be inauspicious. Thus it is not only among the Forest Bantu and Malagasy peoples that we find black to be inauspicious." He then goes on to quote from a study of the Yoruba, published in 1962, in which it is said that "Black is associated with the night and the night is associated . . . with evil. It is at night that sorcery and witchcraft are abroad and men are most vulnerable."

draw that conclusion is only the beginning in accounting for the low position of the Negro in North America and Brazil. Prejudice, as we have had occasion to notice already, is merely a reaction to perception; it is not behavior. The making of a mental note of differences between the self and others, even when the other is a darker color, is only a first step in making social distinctions. It may be the only step taken, in which case there are no measurable social consequences, for what goes on in a human head without affecting behavior is not socially important. It is here that the conception of power has to be introduced, for upon power depends the ability to put into practice the perception. Dark-skinned people, after all, also perceive white-skinned persons as different from themselves. For example, James Pope-Hennessy, in a recent book, tells of the reaction of a Gold Coast King when he first saw a European (a Dane) in 1661. The Dane had actually been sent because the king had expressed doubts that white men were really human beings like himself. Even though the interpreter explained that the Dane's queue was not a tail growing out of his neck, the King was not convinced of his human character; he asked the European to strip off his clothes. The Dane refused to do so in public. After he had eaten a meal, one of the king's wives remarked, "He eats like a man, really he *is* a human being." After he had removed his clothes in private for the king, the monarch concluded, "Ah, you really are a human being, but only too white, like a devil." [10]

Usually, however, black or colored peoples have not been in a position to enforce their sense of difference upon the white man, as the Gold Coast King was able to do with the Dane. But even when they have possessed the power, they may have lacked the incentive, the third element in accounting for active discrimination based upon color. This third element might be called competition for resources, that is, to obtain something that the weaker group has.[11]

This threefold explanation for discrimination puts in schematic form a particular event like the enslavement of Indians and Ne-

[10] James Pope-Hennessey, *Sins of the Fathers* (Capricorn Books, New York, 1969), p. 33.

[11] The original formulation of this scheme was made by Donald L. Noel, "A Theory of the Origin of Ethnic Stratification," *Social Problems*, XVI (Fall, 1968), 157–72, to which I am much indebted.

groes in the New World by Europeans. What these colored peoples possessed and what white Europeans wanted was the labor that was necessary to realize the potentialities of wealth in a region where land and other resources were abundant but where labor was lacking. The explanation also accounts in general terms for the close—almost perfect—correspondence or association between slavery and Negroes, whether in Brazil or in the United States. (Both societies, incidentally, experimented with enslaving Indians, also a dark-skinned people, but both the Portuguese and the English found the largely hunting and food-gathering culture of the Indians in their respective colonial areas unsuited to sedentary agriculture. Negroes, on the other hand, were well acquainted in African society with organized agriculture, the use of the hoe, cattle raising, iron manufacture, and settled communities. Neither the English in North America nor the Portuguese in Brazil encountered the kind of advanced Indian cultures that the Spanish met and exploited in Peru and Mexico.)

The Historical Dimension

The historical association between Negroes and slavery, coinciding with an awareness of differences in color, resulted in distinctions in law between Negroes and whites in both Brazil and North America during the colonial periods. Contrary to the conclusions of some recent historians, Negroes and mulattoes as free men in Brazil were clearly discriminated against in the laws of the colony and the Crown. During most of the colonial period, for example, Portuguese law forbade marriage between whites and Negroes or Indians. In 1775 a law attempted to encourage marriage between whites and *caboclos* (the offspring of an Indian and a white), but Negroes and mulattoes were still excluded. In fact, as Charles Boxer, an authority on colonial Brazil has written, "Colonial legislation discriminated against [mulattoes] much more than it did against mamelucos or caboclos. . . . Even free mulattoes were often coupled with enslaved Negroes in the laws, which either forbade them to carry weapons or to wear costly clothes, etc." The Crown seemed to go out of its way to differentiate Indians from Negroes, perhaps as part of a policy to divide and conquer. Thus it was ordered that Indians were not to be called "Negroes because of the offense and affront this implied," as Gilberto Freyre has pointed out. The law also denied to free Negroes and mulattoes the opportunity to carry weapons.[12]

Church law, too, excluded Negroes and mulattoes from the priesthood and other positions in the church. Convents, for example, refused to admit any but white girls and as late as 1754 three daughters of a sergeant major petitioned to return to Portugal because none of the three convents in Bahia would accept them because they were "pardos to the second degree." Lay orders often did not permit nonwhites to join, insisting upon purity of blood. Even marriage with a black or someone of dubious racial origin was grounds for expulsion from the order. Jews converted to Christianity and colored people were considered persons with "infected blood" (*pessoa de sangue infecta*) and as a consequence were looked upon as "persons of the basest condition" (*pessoa de infima*).[13]

Both the law in general and the Crown in specific instances made clear that blacks and mulattoes were considered beneath whites. Thus in the frontier settlements in Mato Grosso in the course of the eighteenth century gold searches, the law denied free Negroes and slaves the opportunities to carry weapons. In the provinces of Maranhão and Pará mulattoes and *mamelucos* and other mixed bloods were forbidden by law to participate in expeditions into the backcountry. In 1621 the Crown ordered that no Negro, mulatto, or Indian was to be trained in or to practice the art of goldsmithing. When four persons were to be appointed to jobs in Bahia in 1715, the Crown specified that the appointees should be "all white men free of infected blood." In 1712 the Crown asked for a report on the *limpeza de sangue,* or cleanness of blood, of an applicant for a job in the Treasury at Bahia, saying that no "stain" could be accepted. The post of Crown procurator in Bahia was denied to a lawyer in 1730 "for being a pardo." All

[12] Thales Azevedo, *Cultura e Situação racial no Brasil* (Rio de Janeiro, 1966), p. 87; Charles R. Boxer, *Golden Age of Brazil, 1695–1750* (Berkeley, 1962), pp. 17–18; Gilberto Freyre, *The Mansions and the Shanties,* trans. Harriet de Onis (New York, 1963), p. 240; Magnus Mörner, *Race Mixture in the History of Latin America* (Boston, 1967), p. 52.

[13] José H. Rodrigues, *Brazil and Africa* (Berkeley, 1965), p. 60; A. J. R. Russell-Wood, *Fidalgos and Philanthropists* (Berkeley, 1968), pp. 143, 329.

through the colonial period Negroes were enlisted only in black companies. All-black lay brotherhoods extended this division by color to the church, too. Indeed, as early as the seventeenth century, Antonio Vieira, the great Jesuit preacher, complained that Brazil was divided into three parts; white, black, and brown, suggesting that the law was not the only source of discrimination. And as late as the early nineteenth century, the tendency of the Portuguese Crown to seek to separate the colors by law was reflected in the guidelines set forth by the Prince Regent, Dom João, for reorganizing the militia in Rio Grande do Sul. It was provided that the soldiers should be white, which was carefully defined as "those whose grandparents were not black, and whose parents were born free." This definition of a black comes close to what is today the definition of a Negro in North America.[14]

The reason for listing these examples of legal discrimination against Negroes and mulattoes is not to suggest that the practice was the same in Brazil as in the English colonies of North America. Rather the point is to show that the Portuguese government attempted to draw distinctions between the colors in Brazil. It is, therefore, no more permissible to see in the laws of Portugal the sources of Negro acceptance in the twentieth century than it is to see the origin in the special character of Brazilian slavery. If Portuguese law is all that one examines, as Henry Koster pointed out at the beginning of the nineteenth century, then there can be no doubt that the Portuguese legally differentiated between blacks and whites, to the disadvantage of the former.[15]

The truly significant conclusion to be drawn from these colonial

[14] Boxer, *Golden Age*, pp. 142, 260, 300; Rodrigues, *Brazil and Africa*, pp. 56–69; Russell-Wood, *Fidalgos and Philanthropists*, p. 140n.; Azevedo, *Cultura e Situação racial*, pp. 89–90.

[15] Henry Koster, *Travels in Brazil*, 2nd ed. (London, 1817), II, pp. 198–200. In contrasting Spanish and Portuguese America Koster writes, "In the Portuguese South American dominions, circumstances have directed that there should be no division of casts [*sic:* the Spanish legal division between the colors], and very few of those degrading and galling distinctions which have been made by all other nations in the management of their colonies. That this was not intended by the mother-country, but was rather submitted to from necessity, is to be discovered in some few regulations, which plainly show, that if Portugal could have preserved the superiority of the whites, she would, as well as her neighbors, have established laws for this purpose."

laws is that they were not enforced or were rendered unenforceable by local conditions. Unlike the Spanish, as the Brazilian historian Sergio Buarque Holanda has pointed out, the Portuguese were not legalistically minded nor even well organized. Their laws have mirrored their intentions, but their administration was not always able to make them stick. For example, although the law forbade marriage between Negroes and whites, long before the legal ban was lifted, in the middle of the eighteenth century, the church and the society accepted such unions informally. (Principally, one suspects, because of the shortage of white women.) Moreover, although the law barred anyone with Negro blood from civil office, including sitting on the local municipal council, the prohibition was often and easily surmounted. In 1725 the Overseas Councillors asked the Crown to forbid colored men from holding municipal posts or to permit only the husband or widower of a white woman to do so. The purpose was to offer encouragement to white men to marry white women or to stop having children by Negroes or mulattoes. But that effort through the law proved futile, too, for it was not obeyed.[16]

Nor should one think that all the efforts of the Crown were uniformly in the direction of separation of the races. But significantly, even when they were not, they were still susceptible to nullification by local sentiment. Thus, when the Crown accepted a suggestion from the Viceroy in 1732 that distinctions according to color in the regiments of the army be abolished, local people simply did not follow out the order. The separation of whites and mulattoes, on the one hand, from Negroes, on the other, persisted in the army until the advent of the Republic at the end of the nineteenth century. Although in Portuguese law a Negro was either a slave or a free man, in practice in Brazil the distinction was apparently ignored when it suited the local whites. This tendency was sufficiently well known that one free Negro, who was preparing to leave Lisbon for Brazil, reported his intention to the king in order to safeguard his freedom when he got to the colony. Although in 1773 the Crown ordered that color would no longer be a disqualification for holding office, a few years later a

16 Rodrigues, *Brazil and Africa*, p. 60; Azevedo, *Cultura e Situação racial*, p. 112; Boxer, *Golden Age*, p. 166.

governor of Bahia was still forbidding mulattoes from practicing in the courts.[17]

In the English colonies of North America, contrary to the situation in Brazil under the more centralized empire of Portugal, the Crown played virtually no role in specifying relations between the races. But local laws in all of the British colonies spelled out those relations, usually to the disadvantage of blacks. Negroes, for example, were prohibited from marrying or mating with whites in virtually all of the mainland colonies and though not every one of the colonies denied arms or the vote to free blacks, most did.[18] The law in the British colonies, in short, like that in Brazil, was not yet consistent or uniform, but there was no question that it discriminated against Negroes in a variety of ways. As in Brazil, local prejudices and attitudes shaped the practices as well as the law. The principal difference in the law in the two places was that in North America, thanks to the English principle and practice of local government, the attitudes of the colonists were more directly and clearly embodied in law. To the extent that the Portuguese Crown took a different line from that of the local people, the legal regulation of relations between the races

---

[17] Azevedo, *Cultura e Situação racial*, pp. 87–88; Russell-Wood, *Fidalgos and Philanthropists*, p. 139; Charles Ralph Boxer, *Race Relations in the Portuguese Colonial Empire, 1415–1825* (Oxford, 1963), p. 74 observes that Pombal's decree of 1761, in which the King's first minister noted that color was not to be the basis of discrimination among royal officials if they were baptized, was not actually promulgated until 1774, though few other of Pombal's decrees were acted upon as slowly. In 1759 the Viceroy of Portuguese Goa denounced "the contempt with which the natives of this state are treated by the Europeans who call them Niggers, Curs, and other insulting names, for no other reason than the difference of colour." Ibid., pp. 74–75. Professor Stuart Schwartz of the University of Minnesota has kindly supplied me with a reference to illustrate the reason for the fear felt by the free black mentioned in the text who was migrating from Portugal to Brazil. The reference is an *alvara de Perdão* (decree of pardon), April 17, 1677 found in the *Livro de Perdão*, p. 495, in the Arquivo Publico de Estado da Bahia (Salvador). The case concerns a man arrested for illegally using as a slave a mulatto who was actually free. The accused was pardoned without explanation.

[18] On the origins of slavery see Carl N. Degler, "Slavery and the Genesis of American Race Prejudice," *Comparative Studies in Society and History*, II (October, 1959), 49–66, and Jordan, *White Over Black*, Chapter II. This question will be canvassed more fully later in this chapter.

in Brazil was probably more inconsistent than in the English colonies. But in neither place was the law uniform or consistent in this regard, though in both places it clearly discriminated against Negroes and mulattoes.

Hence, as the future United States and Brazil emerged into independent nationhood, the law in each defined the Negro as an inferior. In the case of the United States, however, the law and practice persisted and intensified as time passed. Eventually the segregation of free Negroes in schools, public transportation, theaters, restaurants, hotels and other public places would be embodied in law, but long before that happened social practice decreed it in both the northern and southern states. Denial of the ballot to free blacks was also characteristic of all sections of the country prior to the Civil War. Even later, after the enactment of the Fourteenth Amendment and the passage of civil rights acts by some northern states, segregation and discrimination against Negroes persisted despite the Constitution and the laws. The constitutional commitment to equality that issued from the Civil War was rendered a dead letter in both the North and the South. In the southern states after 1895, at about the same time that the Negro was being deprived of the ballot by state law, a whole body of additional legislation was placed on the statute books separating blacks from whites in almost all aspects of social life, running from public schools to telephone booths. Jim Crow became legal as well as respectable. By the time of World War I, even United States government offices were segregated, despite the commitment to equality that was written into the national constitution. In the United States, in short, the practice of segregation generally outran or preceded the law.[19]

In Brazil, on the other hand, the discriminatory laws were overrun or overturned by the practice of integration. As the history of race relations and the law during the colonial period foreshadowed, during the early nineteenth century, Brazilian society repudiated or repealed the discriminatory laws left over from the colonial years. As one foreign traveler wrote in 1835, "Some time ago in Brazil, the laws which excluded mulattoes from all

[19] Leon Litwack, *North of Slavery. The Negro in the Free States, 1790–1860* (Chicago, 1961); Paul Lewinson, *Race, Class, and Party* (New York, 1965) on disfranchisement after 1877, and C. Vann Woodward, *The Strange Career of Jim Crow*, 2nd rev. ed. (New York, 1966), pp. 83–86.

civil and ecclesiastical offices have fallen into disuse. One finds colored men in all branches of administration in the holy offices, in the army, and there are many of excellent family." The law, he continued, may restrict jobs for colored men, but "nothing is easier than to disobey the law." The law persisted, but the society neither heeded nor enforced it. One French visitor phrased it this way in 1862: "It is true that the law does not confer upon Negroes the right to vote or to hold office; but the more or less dark-skinned officials make no difficulty about recognizing as whites all those who wish to so style themselves, and provide them with the necessary documentation legally and indisputably to establish the purity of their origins." [20] Here the mulatto escape hatch can be observed in operation.

To North Americans who visited Brazil in the nineteenth century, the position of free people of color appeared to be a different world from that of the Negro in the United States. "In Brazil everything is in favor of freedom," D. P. Kidder wrote extravagantly in 1857 after a visit to Brazil. "If a man has freedom, money, and merit, no matter how black may be his skin, no place in society is refused him." Thomas Ewbank was no less struck with the contrast. "Here are many wealthy people of color. I have passed black ladies in silks and jewelry, with male slaves in livery behind them. . . . Several have white husbands. The first doctor in the city [Rio] is a colored man, so is the President of the province. The Viscountess C——a, and scores of the first families are tinged." [21]

Actually, the opportunities for and acceptance of Negroes was not as open as Kidder, Ewbank, and other North American visitors thought. For one thing, they usually failed to make a distinction between mulattoes and Negroes, a distinction that is crucial, as we have seen, in the race patterns of Brazil. For another, color was not as neutrally perceived as their North American-accus-

[20] João Maurício Rugendas, Viagem pitoresca através do Brazil, 3rd ed. trans. S. Milliet (São Paulo, 1941), pp. 94, 193; Gilberto Freyre, O Escravo nos anúncios de jornais brasileiros do Seculo XIX (Recife, Brazil, 1965), p. 399; René Ribeiro, Religião e Relações raciais (Rio de Janeiro, n.d.), p. 76.

[21] D. P. Kidder and J. C. Fletcher, Brazil and the Brazilians (Philadelphia, 1857), p. 133; Thomas Ewbank, Life in Brazil (New York, 1856), pp. 78, 267.

tomed eyes led them to believe. Negroes (though not mulattoes) and whites continued to be separated in the army and the denial of the suffrage to Negroes and their exclusion from certain offices in church and state by the Imperial Constitution itself, certainly limited their participation in society. In certain parts of the country Negroes were not allowed to worship in church with whites; separate masses were held for blacks and whites or the blacks listened outside the church door. In 1835 a law in a town in São Paulo required all Negroes, free and slave, to worship under the choir, on pain of prison and fine.[22] In the province of Paraná in 1885 the law stipulated that free Negroes could be held as vagabonds and compelled to work at public projects if they were absent from their established domicile within five years after receiving their freedom. And if they were without work they could be forced to work by the police. (Such a restriction, incidentally, is reminiscent of the so-called Black Codes enacted in the southern states of the United States immediately after the Civil War in order to provide a halfway house between slavery and freedom for the recently emancipated Negroes.) In Florianapolis, in southern Brazil, slaves and free Negroes, too, were prohibited by law from participating in carnival as well as from dancing in the African style. Police even stopped Negroes from celebrating Emancipation Day (May 13, 1888) in a rural part of São Paulo state. In the province of Rio de Janeiro, freed Negroes were known to be taken into custody by police when they could not clearly establish their freedom or had committed a suspicious act.[23]

[22] Koster, *Travels in Brazil*, II, p. 210; Rugendas, *Viagem pitoresca*, p. 195; Emília Viotti da Costa, *Da Senzala à Colônia* (São Paulo, 1966), pp. 278–79; Octavio Ianni, *Os Metamorfoses do Escravo* (São Paulo, 1962), p. 261; Azevedo, *Cultura e Situação racial*, p. 173 refers to Freyre's observation that though blacks and whites attended the same churches they did not always sit together, and at times blacks stood outside to listen to mass. A similar point is made for São Paulo in Roger Bastide, ed., *Relações raciais entre negros e brancos em São Paulo* (São Paulo, 1955), p. 178 and by Nogueira in his study in *Ibid.*, p. 400.

[23] Ianni, *Metamorfoses*, p. 180; Fernando Henrique Cardoso and Octavio Ianni, *Côr e mobilidade social em florianopolis* (São Paulo, 1960), pp. 126–27; Florestan Fernandes, *A Integração do negro na sociedade de classes* (São Paulo, 1965), I, p. 55n.; Viotti da Costa, *Da Senzala*, p. 313.

Discriminatory social practices continued as well. "One never sees blacks dancing with mulattoes or whites," wrote the German traveler Burmeister about a trip to Minas Gerais in 1850, "but mulattoes do dance with whites. However, the whites of a certain category maintains his reserve, dancing only with whites of both sexes." The Frenchman Charles Expilly, who seems to have devoted himself to "exposing" the racial prejudice of Brazilians, nevertheless admitted that men of color could become barons, deputies, and commanders of the Empire. "But prejudice declares them unworthy of allegiance with the white families," he hastened to add. "They marry among themselves. Blacks and mulattoes cross only with difficulty, the threshold of individual houses."

Burmeister, too, noticed that color and class tended to coincide. "Latifundias in the hands of people of color are exceptional cases. The proprietors of lands and mines are almost entirely whites. It is hard to see a white married to a woman of color for each tries to keep in the family the purity of his race, avoiding any relationships with the people of the other." Below the top of the social pyramid, however, Burmeister conceded, Negroes with some property are met with. "In the places where there are whites and colored people, the former are always the elite. Among the government employees, the clergy, and the businessmen, as a rule, we find whites; only the small shops belong sometimes to people of color." There may not be any differences under the law between the colors, Burmeister observed, "but well established habits cause such differences in fact. In the annals of Brazil it would be difficult to find a case in which a poor person won out over a rich or in which justice had been done by a mulatto against a white." [24]

Yet even when the evidence of the law and the social practices of whites towards blacks are canvassed, one cannot help but be struck by the sharp contrast with the situation in the United States. The laws of discrimination of the colonial period have either been repealed or fallen into disuse. Moreover, the new discriminatory laws that may have been enacted to control the freed-

[24] Herman Burmeister, *Viagem ao Brasil* (São Paulo, n.d.), pp. 244–45, 252; Charles Expilly, *Mulheres e Costumes do Brasil*, trans. Gastão Penalva (São Paulo, 1935), pp. 280–81.

man immediately after emancipation were remarkably few in number and even then often not lived up to. Socially the Negro is disprized, it is true; but the mulatto is clearly recognized as capable of occupying high positions and at times he achieves them. All recognize, of course, that white skin is always better, other things being equal, than dark skin.

One further difference in the position of the free Negro in the two countries is worth noting. The very fact that a large number of slaves were freed, all through the nineteenth century, as we have seen earlier, meant that sharply defined social categories for mulattoes, whites, and Negroes could be worked out gradually and peacefully. "It can be said," writes Roger Bastide, "that throughout the nineteenth century a highly refined etiquette became elaborated; a way of knowing how to mark out distances according to colour of skin, kind of work, social situation or education. This opened the kitchen door to the Negroes and dark-skinned half-castes—slaves—the bedroom door to mulatto women, the anteroom of the drawing room to freed mulattoes. By degrees it allowed these latter to approach closer and closer to integration with whites, without, naturally, going as far as admitting the possibility of their entering the bosom of white families."[25] Bastide writes, properly enough, from the standpoint of absolute equality between the races, but viewed from the United States, the actual situation in Brazil during and after slavery in the nineteenth century was, nevertheless, remarkably different. In the United States the colonial restrictions did not evaporate and the mulatto escape hatch did not develop. Instead, the line between the races hardened, the laws of separation multiplied, and the exclusion of the Negro was defended and justified. In this contrast lies the problem. Given the remarkably similar beginnings—a common human tendency to perceive differences, a common desire to exploit the labor of blacks through slavery, and a common prevalence of discriminatory laws all through the colonial period —how does one account for the quite different attitude and behavior toward blacks by whites in Brazil in the nineteenth century from those in the United States?

[25] Roger Bastide, "The Development of Race Relations in Brazil," in Guy Hunter, ed., *Industrialization and Race Relations: A Symposium* (London, 1965), p. 13.

The Mulatto Is the Key

Before plunging into what is a rather complicated explanation, it is worth clearing the decks by a brief examination of a commonly advanced explanation. It is often said that the much longer experience of the Portuguese with dark-skinned people is an important part of any explanation. It is true that the Portuguese confronted Africans two centuries or more before Englishmen first faced them in any numbers in North America. For the Portuguese expansion into Africa began in 1415, whereas the first Negroes did not come to Jamestown until 1619, and then in very small numbers. Indeed, the disparity in years is even greater because black slaves entered Portugal even before the expansion in to Africa; slavery persisted in Portugal, as it did not in England, right through the Middle Ages into modern times and black slaves entered Portugal occasionally through Arab traders even before the Portuguese themselves confronted Africa.

Despite the suggestiveness of the argument from time, however, it is misleading. Time in itself does nothing. What counts is what goes on during the passage of time. For example, there may be some minor differences in the attitude and behavior of white Georgians or South Carolinians toward blacks in 1790 as compared with 1940, but they are unimportant; in both periods whites consistently treated blacks as inferiors. Yet during that century and a half, whites and blacks lived, loved, worked, and died, side by side. Mere proximity over four or five generations did almost nothing to alter the relationship between the races and the reason is that during that time the full weight of the society was directed toward maintaining white supremacy. On the other hand, in a mere fifteen years since 1950, integrational events and circumstances have done more to weaken the idea and the practices of white supremacy than ten times that number of years, even if the idea and practice have still not been totally eliminated. In short, it is what happens during any given period of time that is important in historical explanation rather than the mere passage of time, regardless of how long or how short that period may be. Time is neutral, but events are not.

Put in such concrete terms, the proposition that the passage of time brings change is obviously inadequate. Usually when time is advanced as an argument there is the unstated premise that events or circumstances were operating to bring about change. Under such circumstances, of course, change in attitudes and practices may well be anticipated. It is, therefore, to the identification of those events, circumstances, and conditions that we address ourselves. For it is in the history and the culture of the English and Portuguese people in both the Old and the New World that we must look for the explanation of the differences in their behavior toward black men. The role of time in all of this is to provide the arena in which these circumstances, events, and social forces work themselves out.

The key that unlocks the puzzle of the differences in race relations in Brazil and the United States is the mulatto escape hatch. Complex and varied as the race relations in the two countries have been and are today, the presence of a separate place for the mulatto in Brazil and its absence in the United States nevertheless define remarkably well the heart of the difference. Let us look for a moment at some of the ways in which the mulatto escape hatch distinguishes race patterns in Brazil and the United States.

The existence of the mulatto, for example, makes most difficult, if not impossible, the kind of segregation patterns that have been so characteristic of the United States. With many shades of skin color, segregating people on the basis of color would incur both enormous expense and great inconvenience. Facilities, for instance, would have to be duplicated several times, beyond reason and financial feasibility. Furthermore, in a society in which distinctions are made among a variety of colors, rather than by race as in the United States, families would be split by the color line. Children of mulattoes, after all, vary noticeably in color. In view of the high value that western society places upon the nuclear family it would be neither practical nor likely that a system of segregation that would disrupt families would be permitted to develop. Moreover, in a society in which the mulatto has a special place, a racist defense of slavery or of Negro inferiority cannot easily develop, for how can one think consistently of a white "race" or a Negro "race" when the lines are blurred by the mulatto? The search for purity of race is thus frustrated before it begins. Similarly, the existence of the mulatto escape hatch helps to explain why relations between the races in Brazil have been less rigid and less prone to hostility than in the United States. The presence of the mulatto not only spreads people of color through the society, but it literally blurs and thereby softens the line between black and white. To seek out the origins of the mulatto as a socially accepted type in Brazil, then, is to be on the trail of the origins of significant differences in the race relations of Brazil and the United States.

The point should not be misunderstood. I am not contending that the mulatto escape hatch in itself "prevented" the development of racist thought, or segregation laws, or somehow "caused" a system of race relations in which it occurred to be milder than one in which it did not develop. Such an argument would reify a social abstraction and turn it falsely into a so-called historical "factor." It is men, after all, not abstractions, who act and thereby make history. Yet even that statement, true as it is, needs qualification. It should not be construed to mean that the mulatto escape hatch was the conscious or intentional act of men. It was not that either. It was the result of many men's actions, none of which was *intended* to create the mulatto escape hatch. As Karl Marx wrote, "Men make their own history, but they do not know that they are making it." It is the historian, looking at the events later who discerns, if he can, the pattern of actions that quite unconsciously resulted in the development of an institution like the mulatto escape hatch.

Put another way, I am contending that when a society develops a place for the mulatto, as occurred in Brazil, then certain other responses to the presence of black men in a white-dominated society, such as those that were worked out in the United States, for example, are foreclosed. The mulatto escape hatch serves as a symbol, actually a condensation of a range of relationships between blacks and whites and of attitudes toward one another. If we focus attention upon that symbol and seek to explain its historical development, then an explanation for the whole range of social attitudes and behavioral patterns for which that symbol stands is also accounted for.

It is in that sense that I call the mulatto escape hatch the key to the difference between race relations in the United States and Brazil. It does not encompass all that we want explained, but it is a crucial part of the answer.

The Beginnings of the Mulatto Escape Hatch

The search for the origins of the mulatto escape hatch must begin with the mulatto, the product of sexual relations between white and black. No extensive evidence is needed to prove the prevalence of interracial sex in colonial Brazil. The large number of mulattoes provide ample testimony. The principal question is, why was interracial sex so common? Gilberto Freyre was so impressed by the great amount of sexual congress between Portuguese men and their black slaves that he concluded that the Portuguese males were not only exceptionally lascivious but also had a special passion for dark-skinned women, which he ascribed to their familiarity with Moorish women in Iberia. And there is some evidence to support that view. One chronicler in the early seventeenth century, for example, told of upper-class Brazilian planters fleeing from the Dutch invaders in Pernambuco with their mulatto mistresses riding behind them on their horses while the white wife stumbled along on foot. Charles Boxer writes that in Minas Gerais in the eighteenth century even though white women were available, some Portuguese men apparently preferred *mulatas* for mistresses. One foreign visitor to Bahia in 1718, who was obviously repelled by the Brazilian habit, wrote, "Frequently I asked them how they had come by a taste so bizarre, that induced them to ignore their own kind." He concluded that the appetite came from the fact that many white Brazilians had been raised at the breast of black slaves.[26]

Yet there is also good reason to doubt that Freyre's combination of the Portuguese male's highly developed sexuality and preference for dark-skinned women is the entire story. In Angola, Africa and in Portuguese India (Goa), the alleged preference for dark women seems to have been expressed only weakly, for the inevitable half-caste products of such unions are remarkably few today. In 1956 in Portuguese India, for example, there were only about one thousand mixed-bloods among 500,000 people, while at the same time over a third of the population in Brazil was mulatto.

Obviously other forces were at work. Among them was the

---

[26] Boxer, *Golden Age*, pp. 16, 165–66; Rodrigues, *Brazil and Africa*, pp. 55–56.

small number of Portuguese men in both the African and Indian outposts, which were essentially military establishments. As such they produced fewer offspring than those Portuguese males who settled in substantial numbers on plantations in Brazil. A seventeenth century estimate placed the proportion of whites to colored as 1 to 3 in Bahia, but at 1 to 10 in Luanda, Angola. Moreover, for all of its proneness to tropical diseases, Brazil was a healthier place than Africa for white men and their offspring; more mulattoes survived there. The cultures of Africa and India were also more resistant to Portuguese penetration than that of the primitive and thinly settled Indians of Brazil with whom the womenless Portuguese males mated from the beginning.[27] Negro slave women in Brazil, of course, were even less able to resist the need of Portuguese males for mates. Slavery made black women available not only to Portuguese men in Brazil but to white masters and their sons on the plantations of the United States South as well. Processes of settlement and the state of the native culture were, in short, more important than the libido of the Portuguese male. Although probably not too much reliance ought to be placed upon the accuracy of nineteenth century Brazilian census figures, they probably are in general sufficiently accurate to provide some comparative evidence of the role of slavery in promoting miscegenation. The first national census of 1872 showed Negroes making up a little less than 20 per cent of the population. The census of 1890, the first after complete emancipation, reported that Negroes constituted a little less than 15 per cent of the population, a decline of about five percentage points. Fifty years later, the census of 1940 found Negroes comprising almost precisely the same percentage of the population as in 1890. The suggestion is that once slavery was ended the rate of miscegenation also fell off.[28]

Undoubtedly, however, the most important reason for the large amount of miscegenation in Brazil was the shortage of Portuguese or white women, particularly during the first century of settle-

[27] Boxer, *Race Relations in the Portuguese . . . Empire,* pp. 37–39.

[28] Figures are given in Rodrigues, *Brazil and Africa,* p. 73. The figures for 1940 and 1950, however, suggest that the Negro population is once again declining. In 1950 Negroes were cited as making up 10.96 per cent of the total population, whereas *mestizos* or mixed bloods were listed as constituting 26.54 per cent of the population.

ment. Certainly such was the explanation offered by contemporaries for the mixing of the races that they observed. The first superior of the Jesuits in Brazil, like some Crown officials, was horrified at the extent of sexual relations between white and black; the Jesuit suggested to the king that "wayward women" be sent to Brazil to be wives for the settlers. None was sent at the time, but later the queen dispatched some orphans, though the number was far from adequate for the demand. During the gold rush into Minas Gerais in the eighteenth century the lack of women was felt so keenly that the government in 1732 prohibited white women from leaving Brazil for Portugal. In the backcountry white women were almost nonexistent even in the eighteenth century, so that liaisons of varying duration occurred between Portuguese men and Indian and Negro women. Even at the beginning of the nineteenth century the shortage of white women was the chief explanation offered by the English planter Koster in accounting for the large number of mixed bloods in Brazil. It is also worth recalling that the deficiency of white women lasted longer in the less organized and more sparsely settled Portuguese colonies than in the Spanish colonies, which also were settled largely by men.[29]

Sexual relations between white men and native and Negro women also occurred in the English colonies in the seventeenth century and after, but the proportion of the population that engaged in mixing the colors was strikingly less. The explanation for the difference is clear: the English colonies, almost from the beginning of settlement, emigrated by families, that is, with many white women present. Because America in the early seventeenth century was a rough and dangerous frontier, the men emigrating from England always exceeded the women in number. In some ten thousand emigrants from Bristol between 1654–86, for example, there were 3.3 males for each female. Yet this figure represented something like a 50 per cent drop in the ratio since the earliest days of settlement. It is also important to remember that until the last quarter of the seventeenth century, Negro slaves constituted a tiny minority of the population of the southern colonies and an insignificant proportion of the people in the

[29] Azevedo, *Cultura e Situação racial,* pp. 111–12; Boxer, *Golden Age,* pp. 165, 269; Koster, *Travels in Brazil,* II, pp. 199–200; Mörner, *Race Mixture,* p. 73.

Middle Atlantic and New England colonies. Negro women simply were not available in the English colonies, as they were almost from the outset of settlement in Brazil. By the eighteenth century in the English colonies, when the number of Negroes in Virginia, Maryland, and the Carolinas grew appreciably, the balance between the sexes among the whites was almost even.[30]

Consequently, the prohibitions that Virginia and Maryland enacted against black–white unions were supported by social practice. Similar laws in Brazil, however, as we have seen, were evaded, for there the sex ratio among whites was not only far out of balance, but the number of black women available as wives, concubines, or mistresses probably exceeded the number of white men. In Brazil the basic conditions for widespread miscegenation were present. Under such circumstances, whatever special preference Portuguese man may have felt for dark-skinned women would have ample opportunity to be exercised. Even that positive force, however, was probably not necessary, if one can judge from the experience of white Englishmen in similar demographic circumstances. In the British West Indies, where white women were scarce and black women slaves numerous, miscegenation was widely practiced. Similarly in Rhodesia "during the pioneer days," write.the historians of white men in Africa, "affairs between white men and black women were admittedly quite common." The paucity of white women lasted for only a brief period and when white women came into Rhodesia in numbers, miscegenation fell off. Moreover, although the Dutch, with their northern origins, were not as used to dark-skinned women for mates as the Portuguese, soon after the Dutch occupation of northeastern Brazil in the early seventeenth century, liaisons between Dutch men and Negro women became sufficiently common for the local Dutch church to speak out against them.[31]

[30] Herbert Moller, "Sex Composition and Correlated Culture Patterns of Colonial America," *William and Mary Quarterly,* 3rd Series, II (April, 1945), 118–22.

[31] Winthrop D. Jordan, "American Chiaroscuro: The Status and Definition of Mulattoes in the British Colonies," *William and Mary Quarterly,* 3rd Series, XIX (April, 1962), 193–98; Lewis H. Gann and Peter Duignan, *White Settlers in Tropical Africa* (Penguin Books, Baltimore, 1962), pp. 71–72; J. A. Gonsalves de Mello, Neto, "A Situação do negro sob o dominio Hollandez," in Gilberto Freyre, et al., ed., *Novas Estudos Afro-brasileiros* (Rio de Janeiro, 1937), pp. 210–11.

Finally, there is the reverse situation that proves the rule. Although the general pattern of Brazilian settlement in the first century or so was single men seeking wealth, adventure, or fame, there was a small part of Brazil that was settled by families, generally from the Azores. On the Portuguese Atlantic islands, unlike the situation in Portugal proper, the population outran the availability of land, causing whole families to leave. During the eighteenth century the Crown, for military reasons, encouraged the settlement of the southernmost part of Brazil, in what is now Rio Grande do Sul and Santa Catarina, through small land grants to families. Several thousand families from the Portuguese Atlantic islands settled there to give the region its very special social cast in the Brazilian regional pattern. These settlements, writes the Brazilian economic historian Caio Prado, are "almost unique in the colonization of Brazil. . . . The ownership of land is very much divided, slavery is rare, almost non-existent, the population is ethnically homogeneous." A parallel, he goes on, "is met in America only in the temperate regions," that is, in the United States.[32]

One of the consequences of extensive sexual relations between Portuguese men and Negro women was not only offspring, about which more will be said in a moment, but subtle changes in relations and attitudes. Sexual relations do not necessarily result in a softening of attitudes of racial animosity, but they may, especially when white men *marry* Negro women, as some did in Brazil, or when they establish less formal but no less affectionate bonds. In such circumstances white men begin to see Negroes as less different and strange, a perception, incidentally, that is not confined only to men who marry or mate with Negro women. Other whites cannot help but be influenced positively by the sight of and knowledge that Negro women are wives or lovers of other white men. In the evolution of racial attitudes in Brazil, widespread miscegenation contributed more than simply offspring.

Yet, on balance, it is the offspring that seem to exert the principal influence. It was not unknown in either Brazil or the United

[32] Boxer, *Golden Age*, p. 254; Caio Prado, Junior, *Formação do Brasil Contemporaneo Colonia*, 7th ed. (n.p., n.d.), pp. 102–103, 109, 290; Caio Prado, Junior, *História Economica do Brasil*, 10th ed. (n.d.), pp. 95–96; Fernando Henrique Cardoso, *Capitalismo e escravidão no Brasil meridional* (São Paulo, 1962), pp. 272, 272n.

States for white men to be careless of the fruit of their sexual encounters with slave women. Luiz Gama, the Brazilian abolitionist, as has already been pointed out, was sold into slavery by his own white father; undoubtedly there are similar examples to be found in the history of United States slavery. But the significant point is that such instances were not typical of either society. Mulattoes were much more numerous among free blacks in the United States than Negroes, presumably because white masters were sufficiently concerned about their offspring to free them. In Mississippi in 1860, for example, 77 per cent of the free Negroes were mixed bloods, whereas only 8 per cent of the slaves were mulattoes. A similar pattern is discernible in Louisiana at the same date. Apparently the same high proportion of mulattoes among free Negroes occurred in Brazil, if we can judge from the impressions of travelers and from what statistical evidence we have. "The number of free blacks is not great," commented Burmeister in the middle of the nineteenth century, "being very much less than that of mulattoes." In the town of Itapetininga in the state of São Paulo in 1799 only 4 per cent of the mulattoes were slaves, whereas 95.6 per cent of the blacks were slaves. Most recently Herbert Klein has calculated from several local censuses in five Brazilian provinces in the nineteenth century that mulattoes made up more than 75 per cent of freedmen, but less than 20 per cent of the slaves in four provinces and only 26 per cent in the fifth. Even as late as 1872, Klein points out, mulattoes constituted 32 per cent of slaves, but 78 per cent of freedmen in all Brazil.[33]

[33] Charles S. Sydnor, "Free Negroes in Mississippi," *American Historical Review*, XXXII (July, 1927), 787; Joe Gray Taylor, *Negro Slavery in Louisiana* (Baton Rouge, 1963), p. 162; Oracy Nogueira, "Relações raciais no município de Itapetininga," in Bastide, ed., *Relações raciais*, p. 390n. for proportions of colors; Herbert S. Klein, "The Colored Freedmen in Brazilian Slave Society," *Journal of Social History* III (Fall, 1969), 39; Burmeister, *Viagem ao Brasil*, p. 54 notes that the "number of free blacks is not great, being very much less than that of mulattoes." In the United States it is occasionally possible to document instances of individual white masters seeking to free and provide for their offspring from slave women. See the cases quoted in Helen T. Catterall, ed., *Judicial Cases Concerning Slavery and the Negro*, 5 vols. (Washington, 1926), I, 231–32 (Virginia, 1854); III, 92 (Georgia, 1866); 286 (Mississippi, 1858); 342–43 (Mississippi, 1871); 540 (Louisiana, 1841); 572 (Louisiana, 1848); 640 (Louisiana, 1855); 656 (Louisiana, 1857); 658 (Louisiana, 1857) and the examples in Orville W. Taylor, *Negro Slavery in Arkansas* (Durham, N.C., 1958), pp. 200–201.

In neither society, then, was it uncommon or unnatural for a white man to show some concern for his offspring. The difference is that in Brazil this concern, because of the greater amount of miscegenation, had a larger field in which to express itself. "The marriage, and even more, the concubinage of land owners and Negro and mulatto women," read a report from Minas Gerais in 1805, "have made a third of the population free, without providing means for their maintenance, without teaching them good habits, and they have the crazy idea that free people don't have to work." The report then went on to suggest controls that ought to be placed over the proliferating number of mulattoes in the province.[34] Few white men who fathered mulattoes in the United States acknowledged their offspring as frankly. What was it that prevented the natural concern of men for their offspring from expressing itself in the United States to the same degree as in Brazil?

White Wife Against White Man

Part of the answer, as has been said, is simply numbers; only a tiny fraction of white men in English America produced mulatto offspring. But why were even those few usually produced only extramaritally and clandestinely? The answer lies in large part in the different cultural patterns the two peoples brought with them to the New World. When Englishmen came to North America they arrived not only in families, as we know, but with Englishwomen, who were a quite different breed from the women of Portugal. Even today in Brazil, Emilio Willems, a modern sociologist, reports that the family is still dominated by the father, who is in complete and independent control of his own sexual activities; his wife simply ignores his mistress or extramarital escapades. He, in turn, is careful not to neglect the welfare of his family. Middle- and upper-class women, of course, are expected to be faithful after marriage, as they were expected to be virgins

[34] Quoted in Freyre, *The Mansions and the Shanties,* pp. 395–96; "Although the whites procreate with the Negroes and mulattoes and they do not disdain to recognize publicly these children, they do not want their children to marry with those races," Johann Baptist Emanuel Pohl, *Viagem no interior do Brasil,* 2 vols. (Rio de Janeiro, 1951), I, p. 329.

before. The civil code still permits a marriage to be dissolved if it is discovered that the wife was not a virgin. No wonder that some women seek to have their virginity "restored" by surgical operation! Young men, on the other hand, are known to pride themselves on the contraction of venereal disease, which they interpret as a measure of their manhood. Adultery is defined legally different for men and women. For a man it is permanent extramarital relations; for a woman it is occasional. In such an atmosphere of *machismo,* wives in middle- and upper-class families do not expect faithfulness on the part of their husbands; the procreation of children and adequate financial support are their chief expectations. Significantly enough, Willems discovered that this highly patriarchal character of the family, which he took to be a consequence of the plantation and partiarchal society of colonial Brazil, was in fact closely paralelled in Portugal today. The plantation, to be sure, did nothing to break down the patriarchal conception of the family, but the Portuguese inheritance is also an important source.[35]

If today the Brazilian family is one in which the wife has little independence and certainly no control over the actions or behavior of her husband, the pattern was even more deeply etched in the colonial and independence periods. In the eighteenth century, for example, the Portuguese were well known for the seclusion of their women, a fact that was attributed to their contact with the Moors. Even the Spanish, certainly no open-handed people with their women, made fun of the Portuguese' hiding of theirs. In the early nineteenth century the Englishman Walsh reported that in the residential sections of Rio "the windows were barred up like those of the Turks." At one time, he went on, all houses displayed similar protective barriers for the women. Even churchmen were heard to complain about the seclusion of women, saying it was keeping the women from attending mass. In the cities of early nineteenth century Brazil some upper class women did not even leave the house to shop; peddlers brought samples and wares to the door for their inspection and purchasing. A French visitor in the nineteenth century wrote that the old Portuguese

[35] Emilio Willems, "The Structure of the Brazilian Family," *Social Forces,* XXXI (May, 1953), 340–44; Azevedo, *Cultura e Situação raciais,* pp. 117–18, 135.

proverb still ruled in Brazil: "A woman is well enough educated when she can read correctly her prayers and can write her recipe for *goiabada* [a kind of guava jelly]. More than that would be a danger to the household." A visitor from the United States sympathized with Brazilian women. "Owing to the prevailing opinion that ladies ought not to appear in the streets unless under the protection of a male relative," he wrote, "the lives of the Brazilian women are dull and monotonous to a degree that would render melancholic a European or an American lady." [36]

Women kept under such physical and psychological restraint were in no position to object to liaisons with slave women, even when those connections might be as public as they in fact were in Brazil. During both the colonial and imperial periods Brazilians and foreigners alike acknowledged that the offspring of unions of masters with slave women were accepted as part of the family. Men did not seek to conceal their black mistresses, either; it was not unusual for them to parade about with their Negro bedmates even though their wives were present. One planter was more discreet—or less tolerant of having a wife underfoot—for he sent his wife to a convent while a black slave mistress moved in the house with him, "The wife does not resist," drily commented one foreign visitor, "the man orders and she obeys." A modern Brazilian political scientist has summed up the attitude toward women historically as follows: "The woman, among us, during the economic and social predominance of masculine superiority, suffered true degradation in the house, in the street, even where she did not go except rarely, at the table, in the domestic circle, in conversation, in which she almost never participated. From all of that she acquired a character of sullenness and timidity that

---

[36] Boxer, *Golden Age,* pp. 137–38; R. Walsh, *Notices of Brazil in 1828 and 1829* (London, 1830), p. 143; Gilberto Freyre, "Social Life in Brazil in the Middle of the Nineteenth Century," *Hispanic-American Historical Review,* V (November, 1922), 609–10; Kidder and Fletcher, *Brazil and the Brazilians,* 164–66. "Portuguese women were the most jealously guarded in Europe. . . . In the Portuguese overseas empire the seclusion of the white women was, if anything, more severe. Travellers of other European nations to the Orient or to Brazil never failed to comment on the seclusion of the Portuguese female, be she wife or daughter," writes Russell-Wood, *Fidalgos and Philanthropists,* p. 320.

disfigured her like a slave, in the midst of every repression and prohibition." [37]

In the English colonies and the slave states of the later United States the situation was in sharp contrast. For one thing, women in England in the sixteenth and seventeenth centuries enjoyed a freer and much more independent position within the family and in society generally than they did in Portugal. Moreover, there is some reason to believe that in the early seventeenth century, just as the North American colonies were being settled, the position of English women within the family and in society improved appreciably. Signs of this change, Wallace Notestein has shown, appeared in letters between husbands and wives beginning around 1620. "Husbands addressed their wives with affection and informality," Notestein tells us, "sometimes with pet names and indicated in many ways their confidence in the understanding, and judgment of their helpmates. As for the women, they seemed less afraid of their husbands and behaved more nearly as equals." [38] Another authority offers evidence to sustain a similar point in the rather sharp controversy in the pamphlet literature on the position of women. Some seventeenth-century English women writers asserted equality for women, whereas other writers —generally male—became very indignant over the practice of some women to dress and act like men in public. Even King James I was alarmed by what he took to be a new and undesirable forwardness among women.[39] Particularly noted for their independence and social competence were the wives of tradesmen, whose degree of freedom was unheard of among Iberian women. "Middle-class women were frequently admitted to guilds on equal footing with men," writes one historian, "and were permitted to engage themselves as shop managers and assistants."

[37] Expilly, *Mulheres e Costumes,* pp. 412–13; Stanley J. Stein, *Vassouras A Brazilian Coffee County 1850–1900* (Cambridge, Mass., 1957), p. 158; Burmeister, *Viagem ao Brasil,* p. 246; the quotation on the historic position of women is from Nestor Duarte, *A Ordem privada e a organização politica nacional,* 2nd ed. (São Paulo, 1966), pp. 78–79.

[38] Wallace Notestein, "The English Woman, 1580–1650," in J. H. Plumb, ed., *Studies in Social History* (London, 1955), pp. 96–105.

[39] Carroll Camden, *The Elizabethan Woman* (Houston and New York, 1952), pp. 255, 263–64, 270–71. I am indebted for this and the succeeding reference to John Evans of Stanford University.

Whether this relatively independent position for women was a consequence of the growing influence of Puritans in English life, as some authorities have suggested,[40] or of the peculiarly English experience of having lived under two queens, one of whom, at least, was among the great rulers of all times, need not concern us here.

The significant point is that an English heritage of such a character helps to explain the high position that most commentators acknowledged women occupied in the English colonies of the New World. Gottlieb Mittelberger, a rather hostile witness on things American, nonetheless commented in 1750 (after a visit to Pennsylvania) that "the women enjoy . . . great liberties and privileges." He was shocked, too, to find that a Pennsylvania court would uphold a mere servant girl who sued her master for getting her with child. The English practice of permitting widows to follow their husbands' calling of merchant flourished in America. A group of such women placed an advertisement in the New York *Weekly Journal* in 1733 that clearly showed their independence: "We are House Keepers, Pay our Taxes, carry on Trade and most of us are she Merchants. . . . We have the Vanity to think we can be full as Entertaining, and make as brave a Defense in Case of Invasion and perhaps not turn Taile as soon as" some of the men. In the southern colonies, too, women filled a variety of jobs outside the home, as teachers, shopkeepers, artisans, tavern keepers, and even planters. Eliza Lucas of South Carolina is credited with not only managing her father's plantation in his absence, but developing the indigo seed that made the commercial growing of that crop feasible in Carolina. Margaret Brent of Maryland was the executrix of Lord Calvert's estate, in which capacity she was one of the leading political and legal figures in the seventeenth century colony. Richard Morris has shown that the legal rights of women were actually greater in the English colonies of North America than in England itself, for by the end of the colonial period women could make contracts and exercise some control over their property after marriage. In some colonial courts a woman could testify against her husband in

[40] Lu Emily Pearson, *Elizabethans at Home* (Stanford, Calif., 1957), pp. 397–99.

civil and criminal proceedings, though even in England it had been held by Blackstone that inasmuch as the husband and wife were one, they could not have divergent interests, it being understood that the husband's interest was hers.[41] Thus the experience of women in the New World probably enhanced the freedom and independence that they carried with them from Old England.

That women in fact occupied a position of some consequence in social life is shown by an episode from the history of colonial Georgia. When the colony was established in 1732, a concern for the defense of the exposed colony dictated the requirement that land was to be inherited only by males or revert to the founding corporation. From the outset, however, this restriction was resisted, suggesting that Englishmen as well as women believed that women ought to be able to inherit land. Within two years the prohibition was being flagrantly disobeyed and so the corporation began to make a series of amendments, each one of which made it easier for an additional class of women to inherit land. Finally, in 1750, the last restriction was dropped.[42] Whether one interprets these changes as simply a means to attract settlers (which they were) or a response to the wish that women be able

[41] For a general statement on the position of women in the English colonies, see Carl N. Degler, *Out of Our Past*, rev. ed. (New York, 1970), pp. 54–58; for a fuller picture see Julia Cherry Spruill, *Women's Life and Work in the Southern Colonies* (Chapel Hill, N.C., 1938), especially Chapters 11–14, on the occupations of women, and Chapter 16 on their legal status. The work of the remarkable Eliza Lucas is detailed on pp. 308–11 and that of Margaret Brent on pp. 236–41. In a recent study of the family in seventeenth century Plymouth, Massachusetts, John Demos has called attention to the high position of women. "In some societies and indeed in many parts of Europe at this time, a wife was quite literally at the mercy of her husband—his prerogatives extended even to the random use of physical violence. But clearly this was not the situation at Plymouth. . . . There is no evidence at all of habitual patterns of deference in the relations between the sexes." John Demos, *A Little Commonwealth. Family Life in Plymouth Colony* (New York, 1970), pp. 94–95.

[42] Trevor Richard Reese, *Colonial Georgia* (Athens, Ga., 1963), pp. 41–44; Spruill, *Women's Life and Work*, Chapter I provides numerous examples of the seventeenth century colonial interest in attracting women to the southern colonies, including the offer of land grants to them. "Women heads of families," writes Spruill, "were offered lands on the same terms as men," Ibid., pp. 14–15.

to inherit land, the point is the same. Women were of sufficient importance that if settlers were to be attracted to the colony women could not be denied the opportunity to inherit land.

Given the relatively strong social and familial position of women, a wife was in a good position to compel liaisons between white husbands and black slaves to be at least kept out of public notice. If that was not sufficient, there was the ultimate sanction of divorce. The several cases cited by James Hugo Johnston show that white wives did not hesitate to name black rivals as the basis of their petitions for divorce. Occasionally wives went beyond the courts. In the 1820's, for example, the white women of New Orleans mounted a campaign to end the famous Quadroon Balls, at which white men sought the sexual favors of beautiful, light-colored Negro women. The fight for the prohibition was successful, but the enforcement of the ban was not.[43] Nevertheless, such an action on the part of Brazilian women was unthinkable.

Most important, however, was the fact that in the United States the wife was sufficiently secure in her position in the family to refuse to accept the offspring of master–slave liaisons, as the Brazilian wife was not. For in the United States as in Brazil, as we have noted already, white men favored their mulatto offspring at least to the extent of freeing them more frequently than they did blacks. Despite this left-handed recognition, it was a rare white man in the slave states of the United States who forthrightly acknowledged his Negro offspring or his slave paramour. The reason such acknowledgements were few, one suspects, is that their wives and the feminine influence throughout the society would not countenance it. In this difference between Brazilian (Portuguese) and North American (English) social practices and values that we come to an important part of the explanation for the development of the mulatto escape hatch.

Several elements coalesce to account for the failure of the United States to develop a mulatto escape hatch. Let us review them briefly. The first is that in North America, when the ratio between the sexes was heavily weighted in favor of men—that is,

[43] James Hugo Johnston, *Race Relations in Virginia & Miscegenation in the South 1776–1860* (Amherst, Mass., 1970), pp. 237–49; Roger A. Fischer, "Racial Segregation in Ante-Bellum New Orleans," *American Historical Review*, LXXIV (February, 1969), 931.

in the early years of settlement—Negroes were few, and hence informal liaisons or marriages similarly were rare. Then, long before the number of Negro women increased significantly, settlers came in families, bringing their own women with them. Thanks to the rough balance between the sexes among whites, there was little demographic pressure for black–white matings. The third element is the comparatively high position of women in society and in the family, which prevented men from acknowledging what mulatto offspring they may have had under the opportunities provided by slavery. In short, the conditions for widespread miscegenation that prevailed in Portuguese America were simply lacking in English America.

A Path Not Taken

If we look beyond Brazil and the United States for a moment we can catch a glimpse, so to speak, of these factors in actual historical operation. The scene is the British West Indies, where English social attitudes were introduced into a physical and demographic pattern quite different from that prevailing in continental English America, but similar to that characteristic of Brazil. Negroes constituted considerably more than a majority of the population in all of the British West Indian islands in the early eighteenth century, while at the same time the white population in some of the islands, at least, was made up largely of single males. Winthrop Jordan has calculated that the ratio between blacks and whites ran from a low of 75 per cent black (in the island of Barbados) to over 90 per cent (in Jamaica). The highest proportion of blacks in the mainland English colonies was 60 per cent (in South Carolina); the second highest (in Georgia), was only 40 per cent black. Furthermore, as we have seen, on all of the mainland colonies the sex ratios among the whites in the eighteenth century was almost balanced; in Jamaica, however, there were two white men for each white woman.

Given this special character of Jamaica—a very high ratio of blacks and a very low ratio of women among the whites—it is revealing, if not entirely surprising, that a special place for the mulatto was worked out in the law. Unlike the situation in Virginia, Maryland, South Carolina, and the other southern mainland colonies, in Jamaica there was no legal prohibition against sexual relations between whites and blacks. Moreover, the Jamaica legislature passed a number of private acts giving mulatto offspring and sometimes Negro mistresses of planters the right to inherit property as if he or she were a white person. Most interesting of all is that the mulatto escape hatch was actually written into law in Jamaica. A law of 1733 stated that after the third generation, mulattoes "shall have all the Privileges and Immunities of his Majesty's Subjects of this Island, provided they are brought up in the Christian Religion." In short, they would be legally white. Strikingly enough, at about the same time, in neighboring Barbados, where the sex ratio among whites was about equal and the proportion of blacks considerably less than in Jamaica, the law barred anyone who was shown to be descended from a Negro—that is, a mulatto—from voting or testifying against whites.[44] The Jamaican example strongly suggests that under certain circumstances even the quite different cultural attitudes of Englishmen could be changed, and in a direction remarkably like that taken by the Portuguese in Brazil.

It also suggests that the idea of defining a Negro by ancestry was not a foregone conclusion among Englishmen. This suggestion is reinforced by an event in the history of a mainland English colony. In 1765 the Georgia legislature actively encouraged the immigration of free mulattoes, probably as a way of building up the free population for defense against possible attack from the neighboring Spanish colony of Florida. As an inducement for such immigration, the legislature provided that free mulattoes and mustees (offspring of a Negro and an Indian) might be naturalized as white men by the legislature with "all the Rights,

[44] Jordan, "American Chiaroscuro," *William and Mary Quarterly*, (1962), pp. 195–98. In his book *White Over Black*, p. 147, Jordan notes that "only in Charleston was it possible to debate publicly, 'Is sex with Negroes right?' In other colonies [on the mainland] the topic was not looked upon as being open." It was only in South Carolina, of course, of all the mainland colonies, that blacks outnumbered whites in the early eighteenth century. Samuel J. and Edith F. Hurwitz, "A Token of Freedom: Private Bill Legislation for Free Negroes in Eighteenth century Jamaica," *William and Mary Quarterly*, 3rd Series, XXIV (July, 1967), 424–25 notes that not all mulattoes who profitted from the law bestowing "the same rights as a white man" actually gained complete equality, as Jordan had assumed.

Priviledges [*sic*], Powers and Immunities whatsoever which any person born of British parents" except the right to vote and sit in the Assembly. As it turned out, the Legislature never naturalized a mulatto or anyone else under the law.[45] Yet in this instance a mainland English colony came close to legalizing the mulatto escape hatch just as was done in Jamaica.

Even in the nineteenth century there were hints that under different circumstances the English mainland colonies might have developed the mulatto escape hatch. In 1802, for example, a dark-complected man held as a slave sued in the North Carolina courts for his freedom, arguing that he had been raised as a slave after having been found as an infant in a barn. Although admittedly not a white, he claimed he had not been born a slave. The appeal court agreed that *Negroes* must establish their freedom by documents or witnesses, because they were slaves upon arrival. "But I am not aware," the judge contended, "that the doctrine of presuming against liberty has been urged in relation to persons of mixed blood, or to those of any colour between the two extremes of black and white; and I do not think it reasonable that such a doctrine should receive the least countenance." People of mixed ancestry might well be descended from free mulattoes or Indians, the court asserted. "Considering how many probabilities there are in favour of the liberty of these persons, they ought not to be deprived of it upon mere presumption; more especially as the right to hold them in slavery, if it exists, is in most instances capable of being satisfactorily proved." Since there was neither documentation nor witnesses to prove the plaintiff had been born a slave, he was declared to be free.

Three years later, in Louisiana, an appeal court reached a similar conclusion in the case of Adelle v. Beauregard. Interestingly enough, the Louisiana court used some of the precise phrases of the North Carolina court, suggesting a borrowing of idea as well as language. Thirty-five years later, in 1845, it was held that "Ever since the case of Adelle v. Beauregard . . . it has been the settled doctrine here, that persons of color are presumed to be free . . . except as to Africans in the slave-holding States, the presumption

[45] Jordan, "American Chiaroscuro," *William and Mary Quarterly*, 1962, p. 186–87.

is in favor of freedom, and the burden of proof is on him who claims the colored person as a slave." [46]

In 1831 a South Carolina court also rejected the argument that "every admixture of African blood" is enough to make one a Negro. "It would be dangerous and cruel," the court contended, "to subject to this disqualification, persons bearing all the features of a white, on account of some remote admixture of Negro blood." Nor has society, the court continued, taken blood as the only basis of judgment; the admixture must be "visible" and the degree is something to be decided by a jury. With a certain amount of approval, the court noted that in Louisiana's Black Code a descendant of a white and a quadroon is a white. "Perhaps it would be desirable that the Legislature should adopt some such uniform rule here. The rule may be of use to juries in their decisions—not as a rule of law, which we have no authority to declare it, but as being founded on experience, and conformable to nature." The legislature, of course, did not choose to upset the traditional view that anyone with Negro blood was a Negro.

Four years later, also in South Carolina, a court once again took up the question of what constituted a Negro, when witnesses were impugned on the ground that they were part Negro in ancestry. "If we should say," the court argued, "that such an one is to be regarded as a person of color, on account of *any* mixture of negro blood, however remote, we should be making, instead of declaring the law, and making a very cruel and mischievous law. . . . We cannot say what admixture . . . will make a colored person. . . . The condition . . . is not to be determined solely by . . . visible mixture . . . but by reputation . . . and it may be . . . proper, that a man of worth . . . should have the rank of a white man, while a vagabond of the same degree of blood should be confined to the inferior caste." This interpretation, if adopted, would have eliminated the whole idea of color caste

[46] Gobu v. Gobu, 1 North Carolina Reports (1802) 100–101. The words in Adelle v. Beauregard, (1810) Catterall, *Judicial Cases* III, 447 are, "Considering how much probability there is in favor of the liberty of those persons [mulattoes and Indians], they ought not to be deprived of it upon mere presumption." The words in Gobu v. Gobu are, "Considering how many probabilities there are in favour of the liberty of these persons, they ought not to be deprived of it upon mere presumption." The 1845 Louisiana case is in Ibid., III, 571.

in America. It was not adopted, of course, but it did suggest that the possibility was at least present as late as the early nineteenth century.

Finally, one last case might be cited to suggest that the mulatto escape hatch was incipient in English America. The case originated in Alabama in 1859. A citizen challenged a constable's authority on the ground that the constable's great-grandparents were mulattoes, making him, thereby, legally incapable of holding his position. The court, however, refused to accept the evidence, saying that pedigree could not be looked into every time someone disliked an official's action. By this date, it was evident that the court was more concerned with protecting the judiciary's time and the constabulary's integrity rather than with the freedom of the mixed blood.[47]

These cases adumbrating a tendency to see a distinction between mulattoes and Negroes, it is worth emphasizing, were not only few in number but they were accompanied by other judicial interpretations that advanced the opposite and prevailing view. Thus in 1857, when a lower court in Alabama freed from slavery two plaintiffs on the ground that they had less than one-quarter Negro ancestry, the appeals court overturned the decision. The legislature, the court noted, has "manifestly used the word [mulatto] in a more latitudinarian sense, and in a sense in which it is generally understood, we presume, by the people of the state. That is, they meant to embrace in the term mulatto, persons belonging to the *negro race*, who are of an intermixture of white and negro blood, without regard to grades." Then, too, a series of cases in South Carolina shows that throughout even the earliest years of the nineteenth century Negroes and mulattoes were generally lumped together. Thus in 1791, 1818, and again in 1821 the court held that to call a person a mulatto constituted a slander, for it could deprive him of his civil rights because as a mulatto he would come under "the negro act." [48]

The principal exception to the conclusion that Negroes and mulattoes were to be treated in the same way was the law of

[47] State v. Davis; State v. Hanna 2 Bailey (South Carolina) 558–60 (1831); Catterall, *Judicial Cases,* II, 359; III, 129, 232, 241; See also 36 Alabama Reports 276–77 (1860).

[48] Daniel v. Guy, et al., 19 Arkansas Reports 133–34; Catterall, *Judicial Cases,* II, 274, 307, 317.

Louisiana, which did draw a distinction between Negroes and free persons of color, as mulattoes were called in that state. But even that distinction came under attack in the middle of the nineteenth century by a defendant who contested the legality of the testimony of a free mulatto against a white man. The lower court's ruling was upheld by the court of appeals. In the course of his opinion, the judge admitted that the practice in Louisiana differed from that in the other slave states. Significantly enough, he traced the development of that difference to demography. "This difference has no doubt arisen from the different condition of that class," for from the beginning of the state "free persons of color constituted a numerous class. In some districts they are respectable from their intelligence, industry, and habits of good order. Many . . . are enlightened by education and the instances are by no means rare in which they are large property holders . . . such persons as courts and juries would not hesitate to believe under oath." In short, in that white man's mind, at least, experience with large numbers of free mulattoes who had proved themselves, had established a distinction between them and Negroes.[49] Was this, perhaps, an example of the way it happened in Brazil, where free blacks were much more numerous than in North America?

Inconsequential as these few cases may have been in the United States, they make it clear that the definition of the Negro that was finally worked out was neither foreordained nor implicit. It was, rather, the consequence of the interaction of English mores in the special circumstances of settlement in North America, just as the Brazilian definition evolved from the confrontation of Portuguese culture with the particular environment of Brazil and the resulting settlement processes.

Until now the origins of the mulatto escape hatch have been discussed in analytical categories, which means that each causal factor has been taken up separately, for only in that way could an orderly exposition be made. But that procedure necessarily abstracts causes from their settings, and more important, ignores

[49] Catterall, *Judicial Cases*, III, 601. Three South Carolina cases, in 1835, 1843, and 1846 also reveal the struggles of the courts with the problem of the mulatto in a strictly biracial society; see Ibid., II, 358–59, 385–86, and 400–401.

the significant interaction among them. Thus when demographic factors encourage miscegenation, the resulting mixing of the races in itself becomes a cause, weakening the sense of difference between people of different color and encouraging additional miscegenation as well as diluting interracial hostilities. Similarly, when a variety of objective circumstances requires Negro slaves to be armed, as we have seen in Chapter II, the effect is equally self-perpetuating, not only in regard to arming slaves in the future, but also in respect to whites' attitudes toward Negroes. It conditions white men to perceive Negroes as more worthy than mere slaves or menials. It also resulted in large numbers being manumitted in recognition of their service as armed fighters, thus further enhancing the willingness of whites to accept large numbers of free blacks.

Cultural and Social Values Make a Difference

As we have seen in Chapter II, one of the significant differences between slavery in the United States and in Brazil was the greater ease of manumission in the latter. Part of this willingness to free blacks in Brazil is attributable to the mulatto escape hatch, that is, the recognition of a special place for mixed bloods. Another part of the explanation, as noted earlier, is certainly the simple need for any kind of labor, slave or free, as compared with the United States where the white population was large, rapidly growing and quite adequate for virtually all tasks.

Demography, however, is only a part of the explanation for the greater willingness of Brazilians to manumit. It is true that white people were few in number in Brazil, but it was equally important that even those who were there often did not consider work, especially manual labor, worthy of them. Iberian culture placed low social value upon work and the very existence of slavery reinforced it. For as Fernando de Azevedo has observed, elaborating upon a Brazilian statement from colonial times, Negro slaves were "'the hands and feet' not only of the master of the sugar mill, but of the urban bourgeoisie, for they performed all or almost all of the activities, of the manual and mechanical base, in agriculture, and in the shops, in the field and in the cities." In 1772 the Governor of Pernambuco wrote to the Overseas Council, "it is the custom in Brazil to send one's slaves to learn all types of skills, the result of which is that white artisans give up their trades and lead lazy and libertine lives." One governor of Rio de Janeiro complained that "The whites and the natives of Portugal even though they be reared with hoe in hand, in setting foot in Brazil not one of them wants to work."[50] Maria Graham, visiting the Northeast in the early part of the nineteenth century, told of a superintendent of a mill who said "that the creole negroes and mulattoes are far superior in industry to the Portuguese and Brazilians, who, from causes not difficult to be imagined, are far the most indolent and ignorant." Other foreign travelers also noticed the tendency of white Brazilians to avoid socially degrading jobs. As one wrote, Brazilians would "starve rather than become mechanics." And it was true, Maria Graham reported, that the slaves and free mulattoes "are the best artificers and artists. . . . All decorative painting, carving, and inlaying is done by them; in short, they excel in all ingenious mechanical arts."[51] Like Portugal, the mother country, Brazil lacked that conception of the moral value of work, which goes under the name of the *Protestant ethic*. It was not that Brazilians did not work, for of course circumstances compelled most of them to labor. The point is rather that work conferred no dignity; it earned no status. Being something associated with the lower classes and slaves, it was shunned when possible. It was readily left, therefore, to free Negroes and mulattoes.

In the society of the United States, even in the South, work was not viewed and could not be viewed as principally a function of black slaves. For one thing, slaves were a majority of the working population in only limited regions of the South, much less throughout the nation. Furthermore, Englishmen brought with them to the New World a belief in the virtue of work that contrasted with the *hidalgo* (*fidalgo* in Portugal) tradition of Iberia

---

[50] Fernando de Azevedo, *Canaviais e Engenhos na Vida política do Brasil*, 2nd ed. (São Paulo, 1958), p. 39; Quoted in Klein, "Colored Freedmen," *Social Hist.* (1969), p. 46; Quoted in Vianna Moog, *Bandeirantes and Pioneers*, trans. L. L. Barrett (New York, 1964), p. 120.

[51] Maria Graham, *Journal of a Voyage to Brazil and Residence There, During Part of the Years 1821, 1822, 1823* (London, 1824), p. 195; Richard Graham, *Britain and the Onset of Modernization in Brazil 1850–1914* (Cambridge, 1968), p. 16; Freyre, *Mansion and the Shanties*, pp. 333f.

and Brazil. Whether this ethic of work in English culture was the result of Protestantism, Calvinism, or simply English history need not be resolved here. The significant point is that in the English colonies, work was a moral value and not something to be associated with the slave. Even in the slave states of the United States it was menial labor, not work in general that was looked down upon. Some United States historians, it is true, differentiate between the South and the North by seeking to measure the degree of commitment to the work ethic in the two regions. It requires little argument, however, to show that, viewed from the distance of Brazil, the mind of the United States South was suffused with the Puritan ethic. Authorities on colonial history, such as Perry Miller, Edmund Morgan, and Babette Levy, for instance, have heavily documented the strong Calvinist infusion into the life of the seventeenth century southern English colonies.[52]

Moreover, in comparing national attitudes toward work, one is reminded of Vianna Moog's provocative comparison between Brazil and the United States. In his book *Pioneers and Bandeirantes* Vianna Moog contrasts the hard-working, plodding pioneer of the United States with the wide-ranging, indefatigable *bandeirante* of Brazil as archetypes of the respective national characters. It is significant that the ambition of the *bandeirante* both in historical fact and in Vianna Moog's symbolism was to gain quick wealth through the discovery of gold, and precious stones, or the capturing of slaves, and not by steady labor.[53]

Social values regarding work, however, are only some of the differentiating elements in the broader cultural patterns of the

[52] David Bertelson, *The Lazy South* (New York, 1967) is careful to notice that southerners worked hard, though he asserts that they lacked the commitment to the virtues of work that distinguished their northern contemporaries. C. Vann Woodward, "Southern Ethic in a Puritan World," *William and Mary Quarterly*, 3rd Series, XXV (July 1968), 343–48 critically appraises the Bertelson book, though he continues to argue for a difference between North and South. Scholarly examinations of Puritan attitudes in the South include Perry Miller, "Religion and Society in the Early Literature of Virginia," *William and Mary Quarterly*, 3rd Series, V (October, 1948), 492–552 and VI (January, 1949), 24–41; Edmund S. Morgan, "The Puritan Ethic and the American Revolution," *William and Mary Quarterly*, 3rd Series, XXIV (January, 1967), 3–43; and Babette M. Levy, "Early Puritanism in the Southern and Island Colonies," in American Antiquarian Society *Proceedings*, LXX (1960), Pt. i, 60–348.

[53] Vianna Moog, *Bandeirantes and Pioneers*, especially pp. 120–24.

two societies. The differences in race relations in Brazil and the United States grew out of the many differences between a dynamic, competitive, Protestant, socially mobile society and one that was stable, traditional, hierarchical, and Catholic. Until well past the middle of the nineteenth century, change in Brazil was slow, social competition muted, and the social structure stable. Thus while the industrial revolution of the early nineteenth century was transforming western Europe and the United States, the old ways of doing things still dominated Brazilian economic life. Brazil, it is true, was a predominantly agricultural country, but even as late as the Civil War, so was the United States. Yet as contemporaries recognized, even in the realm of agriculture, in which it presumably specialized, Brazil was primitive by United States or western European standards. "There is no farm implement aside from the hoe and no machinery aside from the wretched slaves," a report on Maranhão in the early nineteenth century concluded. "Transportation is for the most part by river, and when overland, by oxcarts, even poorer than those of Portugal." Almost half a century later, an essay published in 1865 by a native of the same province pointed out that the hoe was still the principal piece of agricultural equipment in the production of cotton in Maranhão. Planters not only continued to farm in the traditional way, the report went on, but they encouraged their descendants to have an "antipathy for reform ideas." Even after the middle of the century, the writer continued, estates were cultivated as they had been a century before. "The plantations, which in general are poorly built, present more the aspect of an encampment or simple shelter rather than that of a farming establishment." Yet Maranhão had been opened up to staple agriculture in the middle of the previous century and was known for its agricultural riches. The old-fashioned cotton producers of Maranhão could successfully compete in European markets with United States producers—who also used slave labor—only during the American Civil War, when access to Europe was closed to Confederate cotton growers.[54]

[54] Freyre, *Mansions and the Shanties*, p. 184; F. A. Brandão, Jr. *A Escravatura no Brazil precedida d'um artigo sobre agricultura e colonisação no Maranhão* (Bruxelles, 1865), pp. 125–26, 130–33, 151. I am deeply indebted to Robert Toplin of Denison University for procuring a copy of this rare work for me.

The Englishman Henry Koster, living and traveling in Northeast Brazil, was struck by the low estate of sugar cultivation, a species of agriculture in which he himself was actively engaged. Contact between planters was virtually absent, he pointed out, as a result of which, the exchange of ideas or techniques was slight. "They continue year after year the system which was followed by their fathers, without any wish to improve, and indeed without the knowledge that any improvement could be made." Maria Graham, visiting outside of Rio, at a plantation pottery wrote that "all that we use spades and shovels for is done by the bare hands of the Negroes." The varieties of sugar grown at the opening of the nineteenth century, one modern Brazilian historian has noted, were the same varieties used at the start of the industry three centuries earlier. The same slowness to innovate was evident in the use of power to drive the sugar mills, the great majority of which were powered by human beings or animals. Although water sites were available, as late as 1777 only eighteen of the 369 sugar mills in the province of Pernambuco were powered by water. The cotton gin spread like wildfire across the cotton regions of the southern United States after its invention in 1792, but it took decades for the cotton growers of Maranhão to adopt it.[55] An English visitor at a plantation in Rio de Janeiro province in 1812 was astonished at the old-fashioned equipment in the sugar mill and distillery. When he told the owner that the furnace could not be worse, the answer was that there was none better in the neighborhood. As might be expected, the visitor found that Negro slaves operated and cared for the equipment, a fact that was hardly conducive to efficient operation or good care. The slaves told him they thought the equipment first-rate and up-to-date, which may have been their honest opinion, but given their limited knowledge of the outside world, they were hardly in a position to know. The Englishman commented that "this aversion to improvement I have often observed among the inhabitants of Brazil."

Perhaps the epitome of the traditional outlook still evident in Brazilian agriculture at the end of the nineteenth century was expressed best by a certain coffee planter. He was advised in the

[55] Koster, *Travels in Brazil,* II, pp. 122–23; Graham, *Journal of a Voyage,* p. 194; Prado, *História economica,* pp. 89–90.

late 1880's, when it seemed clear that abolition was in the offing, to shift his labor force from slaves to immigrants or free Negroes. "My children who will inherit from me will do as they see fit," he replied, "but as for me I cannot get used to other laborers." [56] Obviously, to him planting was a form of economic activity in which the rationalization of resources and profit-making were not central goals. Something of this attitude could be found among cotton planters in the United States in the antebellum years. But the growth and competitiveness of the southern economy make it clear that even in the slave states of the United States the outlook was modern and progressive when compared with that which dominated the habits of contemporary Brazilian *fazendeiros* [planters]. As one of the authorities on the Brazilian economy has written, "most of the people throughout the colonial period within Brazil lived an everyday life with a pre-capitalistic or even non-capitalistic mentality. The emphasis on personal and family rather than rationalized economic motivation continued to be preferred as a basis for society long after the end of the colonial period." Moreover, most free workers did not own their own land in Brazil, while even in the slave states of the United States the great preponderance of farmers (as many as 80 per cent) owned their own land, thereby giving them an incentive to work, innovate, and accumulate that was lacking in Brazil.[57]

The urban and commercial sector of the Brazilian economy of the nineteenth century was as backward as the agricultural sector.

[56] Quoted in Freyre, *Mansions and the Shanties*, p. 332; Stein, *Vassouras*, pp. 229–30.

[57] Eugene D. Genovese, *The Political Economy of Slavery* (New York, 1965) is the best known proponent of the view that the economy of the antebellum South was precapitalistic and that the planters' attitudes were similarly precapitalistic. Genovese's conception of the antebellum southern economy is implicitly and sometimes explicitly contradicted by the work of the new economic historians of the slave South, much of which is discussed and summarized in Stanley L. Engerman, "The Effects of Slavery Upon the Southern Economy: A Review of the Recent Debate," *Explorations in Entrepreneurial History*, 2nd Series, IV (No. 2, 1967), 71–92. The quotation on the Brazilian colonial economy is from Alexander Marchant, "Colonial Brazil," in H. V. Livermore, ed., *Portugal and Brazil* (Oxford, 1953), p. 299. For statistics on the distribution of land holding in the Old South see Frank Owsley, *Plain Folk of the Old South* (Baton Rouge, 1949) and Herbert Weaver, *Mississippi Farmers, 1850–1860* (Nashville, Tenn., 1945).

When the Portuguese court went to Brazil in 1808, for example, some of the courtiers were amazed that many things they considered commonplace made a great impression upon the Brazilians, who had not seen them before. Virtually all travelers were taken aback, too, by the dearth of wheeled vehicles throughout mid-nineteenth century Brazil. Indeed, as late as 1867 one writer commented that "there did not exist . . . five hundred miles of wagon road over which a coach-and-four could pass throughout the year." Goods and people moved instead on the heads and shoulders of the ubiquitous blacks. The sedan chair and the palanquin, carried by slaves, were still to be seen in the 1850's. On almost any day in mid-nineteenth century Rio one could see gangs of slaves jogging through the streets in rhythm to rattles, carrying on their heads heavy sacks of coffee. In the age of the horse and the railroad, one American visitor commented, "the almost entire absence of horses and mules in the streets did not cease to appear singular." The British visitor Walsh believed that "so many persons have an interest" in work "being performed by slaves alone" that it "prevents the adoption of machinery in abridging manual labor." Although the first railroad was built in the United States in 1828 and by 1860 some thirty-thousand miles of track had been laid—more than in western Europe—the first railroad was not constructed in Brazil until 1852. In 1870, when the age of railroads was in full and productive stride in the United States, there were no more than 450 miles of track in all of Brazil. The principal means of transporting goods long distances overland was still the muletrain and the oxcart. Ocean-going vessels were the chief means for communicating among the larger population centers, which, perforce, tended to hug the coast.[58]

As one might suspect in view of the foregoing, large-scale business enterprise was rare in nineteenth century Brazil. Only four

[58] Marchant, "Colonial Brazil," in Livermore, ed., *Portugal and Brazil*, p. 293; R. A. Humphreys, "Monarchy and Empire," in H. V. Livermore, ed., *Portugal and Brazil* (Oxford, 1953), p. 312; Conrad, "Abolition of Slave Trade," p. 50; Freyre, *Mansions and the Shanties*, pp. 306, 311–12; Prado, *História economica*, p. 196; Rollie E. Poppino, *Brazil. The Land and People* (New York, 1968), p. 206; Graham, *Britain and the Onset of Modernization*, Chapter I.

corporations, for example, were formed between 1838 and 1850 and all of them were small. Even the legal basis for large-scale enterprise was late in coming to Brazil. To form a joint stock company or corporation required the permission of the government, even after European countries like Belgium and France followed the English lead in 1862 in making the granting of corporation charters an administrative rather than a legislative function. Significantly, the so-called free corporation movement got under way in the United States before 1840 and most states permitted the chartering of corporations without legislative consent prior to the Civil War. Brazil did not get around to doing so until 1882.

This failure of Brazilians to innovate in business was a source of despair among some progressive Brazilians. André Rebouças, the famous engineer, complained of "the lack of spirit of association in this country, the ignorance of the capitalists, and the miserable trait of routine." Rebouças' comment was echoed and expatiated upon in the life and work of Baron Mauá. A Brazilian banker and businessman, Mauá significantly enough received his early business training under an Englishman and always looked to England as a model for Brazil. He devoted his public life in the middle years of the nineteenth century to shaking Brazilian businessmen and statesmen out of their stubborn adherence to traditional ways of doing business and running governments.[59]

As one European who published a book on the business activity of Rio in 1856 wrote, "the commerce of Rio de Janeiro is governed by a series of unjust and outmoded usages of customs which the Portuguese, in their state of decadence, have not known how to revise, and which the other foreign merchants in Brazil, less numerous than they, have not yet been able to change." And it was true that even at that date government intervention in a variety of phases of economic activity stifled innovation, impeded progress, and reduced efficiency. Government agencies, for example, set prices for certain staple foods; many kinds of economic activities required government licenses, while transportation was slowed by numerous inspections and production was cut by the

[59] Ibid., pp. 222, 230; for a recent biography of Mauá that stresses his admiration for England and his efforts to modernize Brazil, see Anyda Marchant, *Viscount Mauá and the Empire of Brazil* (Berkeley, 1965).

need for formal concessions before a business could be opened. It was no wonder that Mauá called for greater individual freedom in Brazil in order to encourage economic initiative. Only very late in the nineteenth century, particularly with the establishment of the Republic in 1889, were these legal and traditional restraints eased and Brazil began to move into the mainstream of modern economic and social life.[60]

On this traditional economy rested a rigid and stable social structure, typified by an Imperial court with all its social trappings and an established Roman Catholic church. The hierarchically organized church and the paternalistic, grandfatherly Emperor Dom Pedro II reflected, as they supported, a traditional, class society. Class positions in Brazil were remarkably stable, even in the middle of the nineteenth century. One visiting Frenchman, for example, observed that a person's status in Brazilian society was immediately ascertainable even if one met him in a forest. An Englishman commented that "Brazilians pay great regard to distinction and ranks, and perhaps in no other language are these so precisely determined." Nothing set forth more succinctly and sharply the paternalistic class relationships of the traditional Brazilian society of the nineteenth century than the ritual acted out twice a day on the sugar plantations. Maria Graham tells of a scene she witnessed. Each slave, "as he or she came in, kissed a hand, and bowed [to the superintendent of the estate], saying, either, 'Father, give me blessing,' or 'The names of Jesus and Mary be praised.' This is the custom in old establishments; it is repeated morning and evening, and seems to acknowledge a kind of relationship between master and slave." (Interestingly enough, Professor Richard Graham tells how, while growing up in a remote area of Brazil, in this century, he was asked for blessings from Brazilian children of the lower class, even though some were older than he.) The German traveler Burmeister remarked in 1850 that he was struck with the attention Brazilians paid to niceties of class deference. "One observes a species of devotion on the part of all, even of the whites, for high government officials or for the very rich. He who enters the house of another is considered his equal or he who does not desire to be,

[60] Freyre, *Mansions and the Shanties*, pp. 182, 265; Graham, *Britain and the Onset of Modernization*, p. 216.

remains in his house. One observes a very rigorous etiquette, however, in treating with strange persons." [61]

A traditional society like that of Brazil discouraged social and economic competition, if only because opportunities were limited and social values opposed such behavior. In the United States, on the other hand, society fostered, as well as valued, equality of opportunity, competition, and social mobility. Certainly these were the values and practices that foreign travelers commented upon when they visited the United States of Andrew Jackson and Abraham Lincoln. After his visit to America in the 1830's Alexis de Tocqueville concluded that democratic societies like the United States were "ardent, insatiable, and invincible" in their passion for equality. "They will endure poverty, servitude, barbarism, but they will not endure aristocracy." Even the military academy at West Point came under attack in those years for being, as the Tennessee legislature put it, an "aristocratical institution." Equality of opportunity was stressed by Americans because, as Emerson, wrote, "America is another word for opportunity." One of the consequences as well as one of the causes for the belief in opportunity was the denial of strong class lines. As the German immigrant Francis Lieber wrote home, "In America there is no peasant. . . . He is a farmer, and may be rich or poor! that is all the difference." Another new citizen remarked that "the lines which divide" Americans "are so delicate that they melt into each other; and that . . . there are neither castes nor ranks." [62] Such an accent upon equality and opportunity was an open invitation to competition, for the status of each person in

[61] Ibid., pp. 16, 18n., 197; Freyre, *The Mansions and the Shanties*, p. 608. For recent conclusions on the character of Brazilian society in the nineteenth century see João Camillo de Oliveira Torres, *Estratificação social no Brasil* (São Paulo, 1965), Chapter IX and Emilio Willems, "Social Differentiation in Colonial Brazil," *Comparative Studies in Society and History*, XII (January, 1970), 31–49. In both studies the point is made that there were several rather than only two social levels among free people in Brazil as some earlier writers had contended. Oliveira Torres goes so far as to write that "Brazilian society up to the second quarter of the twentieth century . . . presented a scheme which reminds us, in general terms, of Europe of the middle ages. The large part of the population lived in and from the country —the family constituted the basic unit of society." *Estratificação social*, p. 178.

[62] Quoted in Degler, *Out of Our Past*, pp. 143–45.

such a society depended upon his own achievement; few could count on an established, inherited, or fixed status.

In Brazil, where class lines were difficult to penetrate and economic opportunities limited, whites who were poor had little incentive to seek social advancement by invidiously distinguishing themselves from blacks. Moreover, in Brazil, where miscegenation had been going on for a long time, it was impractical to attempt to draw a clear line between the colors. Thus the white Brazilian who was poor was more likely to consider a Negro or mulatto a member of his class than a threat to his individual status or a rival to be outdistanced or removed. It is not accidental, certainly, that in Brazil the abolitionist movement of the 1880's counted workers' groups among the active participants. In the province of Ceará, for instance, where slavery was abolished four years earlier than in the rest of the nation, one of the groups pressing for abolition was the *jangadeiros*, or boatmen. They invoked the slogan "In Ceará there will be no more loading of slaves" when they refused to participate any longer in the seaborne internal slave trade. Similarly, in São Paulo a little later, on the eve of national emancipation, the railway workers were especially active in helping slaves to run away from the plantations to the cities.[63] In the United States, on the other hand, as is well known, workers' groups were generally cool, when not actually hostile, toward abolition and Negroes. Perhaps the most extreme, but certainly not the only example of such hostility, were the attacks upon Negroes made by Irish and other workers in New York City during the draft riots of 1863.

There were good reasons why workers were conspicuous by their absence in the abolition movement in the United States. There, whites were in the majority, miscegenation limited, and social status (except for blacks, of course) undefined and dependent upon individual effort. In sum, there were economic and

[63] Richard Graham, "Causes for the Abolition of Negro Slavery in Brazil: An Interpretive Essay," *Hispanic–American Historical Review*, XLVI (May, 1966), 123–37 surveys the literature; the reference to help for runaway slaves by railway workers is on p. 133; see also Robert Brent Toplin, "The Movement for the Abolition of Slavery in Brazil: 1880–1888," Ph.D. Thesis, Rutgers University, 1968. Girão, *Abolição no Ceará*, Chapter IX tells the story of the jangadeiros. Many of them, it can be noted, were blacks or mulattoes; some were even former slaves.

social incentives to singling out black as inferiors. The demographic circumstances and social values reinforced the human propensity to make distinctions and to fear differences. The Negro was not only identifiable by his color, but his close historical association with slavery rendered him particularly vulnerable to denigration and exploitation as well. In thus drawing invidious distinctions between black and white, the whites not only removed a possible economic and social rival, but automatically placed a floor under their own slippery status in a loosely structured society in which mobility was at once a value and a threat, and individualism a constant goad.

Democracy's Contribution

The society of the United States as compared with Brazil's was not only competitive and mobile; it was also politically democratic, even in the colonial period. It is the political role of the ordinary citizen in the political processes of government that explains the continuation and even proliferation of discriminatory laws in the United States at the same time that similar laws were being abandoned in Brazil. Simply because the ordinary citizen played a growing part in government in the United States, he was able to have his concerns about status and mobility translated into laws as well as practice.

Sometimes, under special circumstances, the political influence of ordinary white citizens was brought to bear against slavery when it proved to be economically competitive. Or so John Adams thought in 1795. He wrote a friend that emancipation came in Massachusetts because of "the multiplication of labouring white people, who would no longer suffer the rich to employ these sable rivals so much to their injury." [64] In the antebellum South, however, few poor white men argued against slavery as such, though Hinton Rowan Helper's *The Impending Crisis of the South* of 1857 made just that appeal in the name of the poor whites. Generally, however, slavery was not the main competitor in the minds of poor whites; it was blacks, free or slave. A few poor whites like

[64] Quoted in Ulrich B. Phillips, *American Negro Slavery* (New York, 1928), pp. 119–20.

Helper might oppose Negroes by fighting against slavery, but most poor southern whites concentrated upon opposing the competition of blacks, whether they were free or slave. Thus throughout the antebellum years, as members of labor organizations and as citizens with power at the polls, white workers opposed the teaching of skills to slaves and the self-hiring of slave artisans (which would make them economic competitors of whites). White working people succeeded in making self-hiring illegal in most southern states, but the interest of slave masters was not on the same side of the issue, and so hiring and self-hiring were always widely practiced in the Old South as they were in Brazil. When slave labor was introduced in the skilled jobs at the Tredegar Iron Works at Richmond, Virginia, in 1847, for example, the white workers went out on strike, to make clear, as they said, their objections to the management's "wishing to employ and instruct colored people in our stead." In the cities of the South in general, after 1830, Richard Wade has pointed out, whites took away an increasing number of jobs from Negroes.[65]

Wade's reference to the change after 1830 highlights an important point in this consideration of competition between whites and blacks, namely that the rising political power of the mass of whites is related to the development of legal segregation. It is surely not accidental that the removal of Negroes from jobs in southern cities after 1830 coincides with the growing participation in politics by the ordinary white man. The 1830's was the Age of Jackson, a period in which new cognizance was given in both society and politics to the wishes and prejudices of the "common man." It may be ironical, but it is certainly relevant that at the very time poor whites were achieving suffrage free from property qualifications (1820–40), Negroes were being legally denied the vote. Well into the nineteenth century free Negroes legally voted in North Carolina, Tennessee, and Maryland among the slave states, as well as in the five New England states, and in New

[65] Richard B. Morris, "The Measure of Bondage in the Slave States," *Mississippi Valley Historical Review*, XLI (September, 1954), 228, 237; Taylor, *Slavery in Arkansas*, p. 111; Joe Taylor, *Slavery in Louisiana*, pp. 83, 89; Sydnor, *Slavery in Mississippi*, p. 180; Charles B. Dew, *Ironmaker to the Confederacy. Joseph R. Anderson and the Tredegar Iron Works* (New Haven, Conn., 1966), pp. 24–25; Richard C. Wade, *Slavery in the Cities. The South 1820–1860* (New York, 1964), p. 275.

York, Pennsylvania, and New Jersey. During the 1820's and 1830's, however, the three slave states, as well as Pennsylvania, New York, New Jersey, and Connecticut either prohibited Negro suffrage altogether or narrowed it severely as compared with that of white men. Moreover, everyone of the new states of the West, as they entered the union after 1820, resolutely excluded the Negro from the vote even as they proclaimed their democratic proclivities by enacting universal white manhood suffrage.[66]

During these same years of democratic upsurge (for whites), southern states placed new and more stringent limitations on the free Negro population. Between 1829 and 1836, for example, six states in the South enacted laws requiring newly freed Negroes to leave the state. Charles Sydnor, the historian of slavery in Mississippi, emphasizes that after 1830 the sentiment in that state regarding slavery shifted markedly, from tolerating it as a necessary evil to defending it as a positive good. The shift coincided, it is worth adding, with the rise of the white democracy, which in 1832 obtained a new constitution, embodying, among other things, such democratic innovations as the removal of all property qualifications for the suffrage and the popular election of judges. By 1839 the Democratic party in Mississippi, the party of the small farmers, was also the more vehement of the two parties in defense of slavery, although the Whig party was the more closely identified with the large planters in the state. In the early 1830's, during his visit to the United States, Alexis de Tocqueville noticed a significant connection between democracy and discrimination in the law against Negroes. "I do not believe," he wrote in *Democracy in America*, "that the white and black races will ever live in any country upon an equal footing. But I believe the difficulty to be still greater in the United States than elsewhere. An isolated individual may surmount the prejudices of religion, of his country, or of his race; and if this individual is a king, he may effect surprising changes in society; but a whole people cannot rise, as it were, above itself. A despot who should subject the Americans and their former slaves to the same yoke might perhaps succeed in commingling the races; but as long as the American democracy remains at the head of affairs, no one will undertake so difficult a task; and it may be foreseen that the freer [that is,

[66] Leon Litwack, *North of Slavery* (Chicago, 1961), p. 79.

the more democratic] the white population of the United States becomes, the more isolated will it remain." [67]

By 1830 Negroes were excluded by law or by practice from public schools in all northern states; mob violence or popular white protests compelled even private schools at times to end integration, as the famous closing of Prudence Crandall's school in Connecticut in 1833 demonstrated. When white workingmen in the cities of the North obtained a chance to express themselves through trade unions in the 1830's and after, they, too, excluded blacks from their ranks.[68] After slavery was abolished in the South, many Negro skilled workers lost their jobs or customers to whites, who used their political and social power to obtain the Negroes' jobs. As slaves Negroes had enjoyed the protection of their masters— out of self-interest, if nothing else—in their right to work as carpenters, coachmen, barbers, bricklayers, and so forth. As freedmen, however, they had few powerful friends and were often prevented from using the ballot for self-protection. It is relevant, too, that the almost total disfranchisement and legal segregation of the Negro in the South in the 1890's and first decade of the twentieth century took place within the context of increasing political and social awareness on the part of the mass of white people. The Populist upheaval of the 1890's was one of the great movements looking toward the participation of the ordinary citizen in the processes of government and politics. It was accompanied and followed by, if it did not actually cause, the legal disfranchisement of blacks and the rigid separation of the races by law, both of which have since become the hallmark of southern white behavior toward the Negro.[69]

The point is not that the masses of whites had more virulent prejudices against Negroes to start with, but that their economic

[67] Sumner Matison, "Manumission by Purchase," *Journal of Negro History*, XXXIII (April, 1948), 149; Sydnor, *Slavery in Mississippi*, pp. 245–47; Edwin Arthur Miles, *Jacksonian Democracy in Mississippi* (Chapel Hill, N.C., 1960), p. 158; Alexis de Tocqueville, *Democracy in America*, Phillips Bradley, ed. (New York, 1948), I, pp. 373–74.

[68] Litwack, *North of Slavery*, pp. 114–20; 157–60.

[69] On disfranchisement after Reconstruction, see Paul Lewinson, *Race, Class and Party* (New York, 1965), especially pp. 76–79, and C. Vann Woodward, *Strange Career of Jim Crow*, 2nd rev. ed. (New York, 1966), pp. 83–86.

interests and their social status were more threatened by Negroes than were those of the upper classes. In a mobile, individualistic, loosely structured society the poor white man on the make had much to gain in status as well as in material goods if he and his fellows could single out Negroes as inferiors. As they gained political power they used it to enhance their own position by legally and otherwise reducing the status of Negroes. To that extent segregation statutes were popular as well as racist measures. In a fluid, competitive social structure, all devices are called upon to assist in the gaining and maintenance of status and economic advancement.

Such recourse to law was neither necessary nor possible in Brazil. With the mulatto escape hatch working, a line between white and black was extremely difficult to draw. Moreover, lower-class whites were in the minority and most of them lacked the ballot anyway, as they still do today. Politics in Brazil has been traditionally the preserve of the upper and middle classes, the very classes that did not need to use the law to secure their position against the threat of social and economic competition. The class structure and historical tradition assured the upper class of its place; the small middle and upper classes could even permit an individual mulatto or Negro to rise above his class because there was sufficient distinction between people of color and whites to prevent serious rivalry. Besides, in any dubious case, the whites could close off any threat to their position, for in the last analysis it was the upper- and middle-class whites who controlled the avenues of mobility for blacks and mulattoes.

The modern history of race relations in Brazil provides some evidence to support the view that in an open, competitive society hostility toward Negroes rises. It will be recalled from Chapter III that prejudices and discrimination against blacks and mulattoes in Brazil tend to be more severe in the southern part of the country than in the Northeast. It is pertinent to note that southern Brazil is the industrialized and more socially mobile part of the country. Even today the Northeast is a backward, principally agricultural region, whereas São Paulo is the most highly industrialized area in Latin America. Though little more than impressionistic, this comparison is suggestive. For the correlation between a high level of discrimination—measured in Brazilian terms—and social mobility is precisely the association that has been emphasized here in comparing the history of the United States with that of Brazil as a whole.[70]

The Differences As National Ideologies

Until now, in attempting to account for the different racial patterns in the United States and Brazil, the emphasis has been upon the social conditions, institutions, and events that shaped those relationships. The role of ideology as an independent determinant has been passed over, though the general problem that we have been considering is certainly one in the history of ideas as well as in social mores. Indeed, Louis Hartz has sought to account for the differences in the race relations of the two counties in just that way, [71] even though to place so much explanatory weight upon ideology seems to be more than it can bear. However, now that we have examined the social history of the two countries, Hartz's sketchy intellectual analysis can be fleshed out with social fact, thereby providing us, it is hoped, with a new, yet complementary view of the problem. Let us look, for example, at the familiar question of the origin of a biological or genetic definition of a Negro—that is, the failure for the mulatto escape hatch to develop in the United States. This time, however, let us view that question through the sociopolitical ideologies of Brazil and the United States.

The English political ideology that the American colonists

[70] Roger Bastide, *Brasil, Terra de Contrastes*, trans. M. I. Pereira de Queiroz (São Paulo, 1959), pp. 188–92 notes that southern Brazil lacks one of the three elements that Freyre pointed to in accounting for the special character of race relations in the Northeast. The South had experienced slavery and the plantation, but the patriarchalism of the Northeast was missing. Moreover, he goes on, the South was more closely connected with Europe as well as being more commercial, that is, more competitive, than the Northeast. In another place he makes the same point this way: "prejudice appears everywhere when the Negro's vertical mobility threatens the social status of the white man. Whether the mobility is individual as in the Northeast, or collective, as in the South, the effect is the same." Roger Bastide, "Race Relations in Brazil," *International Social Science Bulletin* IX (1957), 511.

[71] Louis Hartz, *The Founding of New Societies* (New York, 1964), Chapter 2.

brought with them was distilled from a long history of conflict between Crown and people. In the course of those years of conflict, particularly during the seventeenth century, individual freedom became an increasingly central concern, the classic expression of which appears in the writings of John Locke. For our purposes the important point is that the political ideology of North Americans in the seventeenth century, as afterward, was built upon this English heritage. The central feature in that heritage was that freedom was defined in absolute rather than in relative terms. A man was either free and equal to all other free men or else he was not a political person. Thomas Jefferson, as he admitted, was following Locke when he wrote in the Declaration of Independence that all men were created equal and that a government derives its just powers from the consent of the governed. In basing the Declaration upon those principles, Jefferson did not mean literally all persons in society; he assumed, for example, the exclusion of women, Indians, and aliens, as well as Negroes. Similarly, because of the English liberal principle that there were no gradations between freedom and slavery, in the antebellum years free Negroes, both North and South, as we have seen, were anomalous. They just did not fit into the ideological structure. Because they suffered under a variety of legal disabilities, they could not be considered free and equal to other free men, yet they were obviously not slaves, for that class possessed even fewer rights. As a result of the tension between the political ideology of the society and its actual practices, it was to be expected that some resolution of the anomaly would be made. One attempt at resolution is to be seen in the fact that most of the states of the Old Northwest prohibited free Negroes from entering their boundaries, whereas the slave states required newly freed Negroes to leave the state. Between them, these two sets of laws left the free Negro literally without a social place. The tension between ideology and social fact was reflected also in the laws in some slave states that threatened to reduce the free Negro to slavery. For that was another way in which the anomaly of a quasi-free man in a liberal society could be removed.

Furthermore, by drawing a sharp line between freedom and slavery, United States social ideology was easily led into an either–or interpretation of man as well as of status. The simple duality was quite conducive to the development of the view that a man was either Negro or white, there being no more room for an intermediate person in the biological schema than there was for an intermediate status in the law. There was no place, in short, for the mulatto; in the liberal ideology there could be no mulatto escape hatch.

Moreover, once this polarization was begun, the stage was set for a racial defense of slavery and for the assertion of the racial inferiority of the Negro, free or slave. According to the liberal creed all men are created equal; the thrust of the ideology is in the direction of freedom and equality. It follows therefore that slaves ought to be either freed or declared to be something less than men—as women were. The choice posed by the ideology was not an easy one for the heirs of the English political tradition in America. For though it was true that the ideology preferred freedom, the considerable weight of a going and profitable system of slavery was against a choice of freedom for blacks. During the eighteenth century, to be sure, some slaveholders, like George Mason of Virginia and Henry Laurens of South Carolina, toyed with the idea that the contradiction between slavery and freedom ought to be resolved in favor of freedom. But by the early nineteenth century it was clear that the weighty economic and social considerations had triumphed. The contradictions were resolved by asserting instead that those who were slaves were intrinsically, that is, racially, inferior. In that way, even though it might appear that some men were being held as slaves, the ideology could still assert the equality of all men. Negro slaves simply were not men in the political sense.

In Brazil there was no ideological compulsion for a neat division between slavery and freedom. Brazilian political ideology lacked the English—or Protestant—emphasis upon the individual and the definition of freedom as absolute. Instead, the Brazilian conception of the good society was hierarchical, traditional, and Catholic; it was pre-Enlightenment in outlook rather than a product of the Age of Reason. No pretense was made that all men were free and equal; each man had his place in the social hierarchy, some high, some low, some in between. In such a scheme there was a place for white, black, or brown; for free, half-free, and slave. Because some men were recognized as socially inferior to others by the explicit terms of the social ideology, there was no need to work out a racial justification of slavery or of social subordination. The kind of racist defense of slavery that flourished in the United States was ideologically unnecessary in Brazil. Similarly, Brazilians never gave to the argument of Negro racial inferiority the degree of respectability that it enjoyed for so long in United States social thought.

Without seeking to determine which came first, social development or ideology, it is evident that the mulatto escape hatch was as compatible with Brazilian social thought as it was incompatible with the thought of North Americans. As one might expect, ideology and social history reinforced each other in both societies.

Although it is true that racial patterns have differed in both origin and character in Brazil and the United States, it does not follow that the future will be merely a continuation of the past. History lies like an Alp upon the brains of men, Karl Marx wrote long ago; yet even as we are aware of the burden of the past, we recognize that its weight is not beyond lightening. The United States today is in the midst of facing up to its history of racism. This act in itself begins to modify the historic sources of United States attitudes and behavior. Therefore, in the next and final chapter an attempt will be made to assess the future of race relations in the United States and Brazil in the light of what we know of their historical roots.

VI

A Contrast in the Future?

If anyone deserves to be indemnified, indemnify
the slaves!

> —Rui Barbossa, when he ordered
> the destruction of slave records
> in Brazil, after abolition.

Why talk about compensating masters? Compensate them for what? What do you owe them? . . .
It is the slave who ought to be compensated. The
property of the South is by right the property of
the slave.

> —Dr. John Rock of Boston,
> Negro dentist, physician,
> and lawyer, 1862.

The Gap Narrows

For many years scholars and journalists interested in race
relations have compared and contrasted the patterns in Brazil
and the United States, usually to the discredit of the latter. Donald Pierson's *Negroes in Brazil* (1942), for example, received a
warm welcome from North Americans wishing to point up the
racist character of race relations in the United States, whereas in
Brazil the same book evoked strong approval from writers who
wanted to emphasize the racial democracy of their country. Indeed, just because comparison has often had this effect, some
recent Brazilian students of race relations have deplored comparisons, contending that the result is to obscure, if not to deny,
the existence of prejudice and discrimination in Brazil. Frank
Tannenbaum's *Slave and Citizen,* for example, has been singled
out for criticism on just those grounds.[1]

---

[1] Roger Bastide, "Race Relations in Brazil," *International Social Science
Bulletin,* 9 (1957), 507, notes that Pierson's book did not make Brazilians
feel uncomfortable when Brazil was compared with the United States. Luis
A. Costa Pinto, *O Negro no Rio de Janeiro* (São Paulo, ca. 1952), p. 171n.
observes that Tannenbaum misjudged the opportunities for social mobility
available to former slaves in Brazil. He further suggests that one source of
Tannenbaum's error was his desire to put the racist practices of North
America into relief. Brazilians, on the other hand, he points out later
(p. 311), make the comparison in order to extol Brazil so that what emerges
"is the conclusion that all goes well because it is not as bad as in the Deep
South."

Perhaps the time has now come to recognize that today comparison of race relations in the two countries is not always favorable to Brazil. For one thing, as we have seen in this book, Brazil is not devoid of color prejudice or discrimination. For another, since World War II, race relations and attitudes in the United States have strikingly altered. This is not the place to elaborate upon the nature of, or causes for the improvement in white attitudes and behavior toward blacks in the United States, though certainly one of the causes has been the recognition that other nations in the past—like Brazil, for example—have done better by the black man than has the United States. Suffice it to say, though, that thanks to the Supreme Court's decisions, the rising self-consciousness of black people themselves, and the enactment of certain laws, particularly the Civil Rights Acts of 1964 and 1965, the old legal structure of segregation and separation has been repudiated and largely dismantled. This is not to say, by any means, that racial prejudice or discrimination have disappeared, for they have not. But it is to say that the legal and ideological support of a century and more of discrimination has been removed. Moreover, Negroes now have access to education, jobs, and social position to a degree not only unknown, but largely unanticipated a mere quarter of a century ago. The assiduity with which universities, business firms, and governments have sought out qualified—and occasionally not so qualified—Negroes is but one measure of the new climate of opinion and action in the United States in the 1960's. Even in the traditionally Negrophobic South, Negroes today hold over five hundred local and state political offices, usually as the result of elections. Blacks serve on police forces in southern cities as they have not since the late nineteenth century. Literally millions of Negroes now vote in the South for the first time in the twentieth century.

When we recognize, then, that color prejudice and discrimination exist in Brazil, as they still do in the United States, but that those practices that once distinguished the United States from Brazil are now largely gone, we begin to see that the patterns of race relations in the two countries are converging. Today neither society accepts the doctrine of Negro inferiority officially or publicly, though in both Brazil and the United States private citizens may and often do perpetuate the idea. Even George Wallace and Lester Maddox cannot permit themselves the luxury of assertions of racial inferiority of blacks such as Senator Theodore Bilbo or Representative John Rankin of Mississippi freely indulged in during the 1930's and 1940's. For, as E. Franklin Frazier predicted in 1944, "As the attempt to maintain a caste system becomes less effectual" in the United States, "it is likely that the racial situation will approximate the situation in Brazil." [2]

Today, in the light of what we know of the situation in the two countries, we might go even further. On one level, at least, the United States has passed beyond Brazil. For not only have discriminatory laws been repealed, but the burdens of the past that have lain heavily upon the Negro's aspirations have recently been recognized as ones that society ought to shoulder, at least in part. The clearest, though not the only statement of the attitude is the famous address of President Lyndon Johnson at Howard University in 1965. Freedom from slavery was not enough, he pointed out. "You do not wipe away the scars of centuries by saying: Now, you are free to go where you want, do as you desire, and choose the leaders you please. You do not take a man, who for years has been hobbled by chains, liberate him, bring him to the starting line of the race, saying 'you are free to compete with all the others,' and still justly believe you have been completely fair. Thus it is not enough to open the gates of opportunity. All our citizens must have the ability to walk through those gates. This is the next and more profound stage of the battle for civil rights." [3]

It is this realistic recognition that lies behind not only the black demands for compensatory action, but also behind the crash programs to accept Negroes into jobs, government offices, and universities. Not all white people in the United States, it is true, wholeheartedly accept this philosophy of positive equality—indeed, there is some evidence that many reject it [4]—but that the

[2] E. Franklin Frazier, "A Comparison of Negro–White Relations in Brazil and in the United States," in G. Franklin Edwards, ed., *E. Franklin Frazier on Race Relations* (Chicago, 1968), p. 102.

[3] The full address is in *Public Papers of the Presidents. Lyndon B. Johnson* (Washington, 1965), II, pp. 635–40.

[4] A survey of opinion reported in *Newsweek*, October 6, 1969, p. 45, found that of middle-income white Americans ($5,000 to $15,000 a year), 44 per cent thought that blacks had a better chance to get well-paying jobs than they; 41 per cent thought blacks had a better chance to get a good education for their children; 65 per cent thought that blacks had a better chance of getting financial help from the government in the event of unemploy-

view is widely held, especially among those who have social, economic, and political power is undeniable. Indeed, the principle is embodied in the antipoverty legislation as well as in other programs for retraining Negroes and for the rapid and thorough integration of schools and universities.

Brazil, however, has yet to recognize that blacks there suffer from a similar disability. Roger Bastide, for example, notes that the passage of the Afonso Arinos law in 1951 did not meet the issue, for the Negro in Brazil is historically in no position to compete economically with immigrants or other whites in an industrial society. Brazilian society must recognize, Bastide contends, "that there is, in fact, a black group which must be helped to advance and become integrated. [Bastide refers to full participation in the urban economy here, not simply the opposite of *segregated*, as North Americans use the term.] Such help might be by the creation of special schools and scholarships so that poor Negroes could go to technical schools, the establishment of workshops for Negroes" and so forth. To North Americans, Bastide's cry of 1965 seems old-fashioned, for it is reminiscent of the technical education advocated for United States Negroes by Booker T. Washington seventy years ago. Yet, despite the similarities, the point is not that Bastide is a latter-day Booker T. Washington, but that even the limited approach of a Washington has been ignored in Brazil. As some Brazilian Negroes point out, Janio Quadros, who was President of Brazil in 1961, was the first high official of the country to admit the Negro's disabilities. Souza Dantas quotes him as saying, "I desire to offer to the Brazilian black those conditions which he never had, those conditions of effective social and economic integration, finally to give him that role which is his by right, having in mind his contribution to the

---

ment. As recently as February 8, 1970, the *New York Times* ran a long, front-page article detailing the extent of, as well as the resistance to equality in the South, which began: "Blacks and whites may now eat together publicly in the South and frequently do. But they are still not permitted to drink together in many places. They go to baseball games, political rallies and carnivals together, but it is still hazardous to go to church together. They go to school together, but not to school dances." For, the report goes on, "resistance to change in the south continues to shape and to confine the lives of its blacks almost as much as change itself."

nationality."[5] Paradoxically, the reason recognition has been so late is that the very benign character of race relations in Brazil has precluded the recognition of the need for compensatory action. For to offer or even suggest such social aid implies that the Negro suffers disabilities no other group does. It requires the admission of color prejudice, which the national myth explicitly denies.

Even those who sing the praises of race relations in Brazil, as contrasted with those in the United States, recognize the limitation on the Negro's opportunities, even though these same persons may not be aware of the causal connection between the two. Thus a white Brazilian, A. de Silva Mello, in 1958 called for the establishment of "The Brazilian Association for the Rehabilitation of the Colored Man." Although Mello asserted that the Negro is better treated in Brazil than anywhere else, the projected organization, in his opinion, is still needed to provide for blacks the opportunities and choices presently lacking. The purpose of the organization would be to provide scholarships to promising young Negroes so that more of them could attain a university education, to help in improving the position of Negroes in the professions, and to publish works about and by Negroes in an effort to raise their self-esteem.[6]

It is true that today in Brazil, as in the past, unlike the situation in the United States, there has been no overt or legal exclusion of Negroes from schools, jobs, or public office. But that is not to say that all jobs are open, either. As we have seen already, the whites have always controlled access to jobs and to education, usually through criteria of class. Moreover, given the Negro's concentration at the bottom of the social and economic scale, class barriers have been very effective racial or color barriers. In

[5] Roger Bastide, "The Development of Race Relations in Brazil," in Guy Hunter, ed., *Industrialization and Race Relations: a Symposium* (London, 1965), pp. 21–22. The quotation from Quadros is in *80 Anos de Abolição. Serie Cadernos Brasilieros* (Rio de Janeiro, 1968), p. 52.

[6] A. de Silva Mello, *Estudos sobre o Negro* (Rio de Janeiro, 1958), pp. 212–13; 222. The organization Mello proposes is needed, he contends, because "in all countries, even in Brazil, the great majority of colored persons have been kept in a socially inferior position, especially materially, which has not permitted them their natural rise nor the development of their potentialities and capacities."

the United States, segregation laws and frankly racial discrimination have been the principal means for excluding Negroes from equality of opportunity. Now, however, the segregation laws are gone and in their place are laws prohibiting discrimination. It is for that reason one speaks of the United States as coming abreast of the Brazilian situation. Insofar as the United States has now moved in the direction of compensatory action, such as special job training programs, and active recruitment of blacks on all levels of jobs and education, it is moving beyond Brazil. Obviously, there is still very much to be done in the United States to overcome the centuries of deprivation inherited from slavery and segregation, but at least in the United States recognition of that need has been given. It is not at all clear that Brazilians recognize that obligation or need as keenly or as practically. Janio Quadros is no longer President and his successors so far have not sought to emulate him.

Negroes See a New Contrast

If Brazilian whites do not recognize the need for compensatory action, Brazilian Negroes are well aware that such action must be taken if the cycle of poverty, prejudice, and low social and self-esteem is to be broken. A manifesto of leading Negroes and Negro organizations in the early 1950's pointed out that abolition "extirpated a horrible cancer of the social organism of our fatherland. However, there was no concern with the organ that was attached, which in this case was the Negro. A complete cure was not carried out. Instead the society preoccupied itself with the extirpation of the malignant tumor and left in place the old situation without the necessary precaution of cauterization. Thus, the Negro element, without a period of transition necessary to its complete accommodation within a society of free men, remained in the most constrained of situations. It was without plans, without objectives, without direction, without anything that would make it possible for a suitable adaptation in entering upon the new conditions."[7] This failure to provide positive assistance to the

[7] Florestan Fernandes, A Integração do negro na sociedade de classes (São Paulo, 1965), I, p. 63.

Negroes emerging from slavery has prompted some blacks to call for a "National Service for the Protection of the Negro" in emulation of the well-known Brazilian governmental agency in behalf of the Indian. One Negro informant pointedly noted that in the United States private philanthropic foundations have long been active in helping Negroes overcome the handicaps of slavery and prejudice, but that in Brazil "the white 'sharks' care only for their own interests"; not surprisingly, therefore, he went on, "there are no Negro millionaires" in Brazil.[8] That informant's remarks might have been more accurate, if less graphic, if he had pointed out that the lack of white philanthropic aid is also related directly to the historically benign character of race relations in Brazil. When there is no recognition of a race problem, when a mulatto escape hatch exists, there does not appear to be any need to help Negroes as a group, either through private or public agencies.

Like the United States, Brazil is a country of immigrants. In neither country, however, are the opportunities open to Negroes emerging from slavery to be equated with those available to immigrants. For the United States, the subject was canvassed most recently in the so-called Kerner Report on Civil Disorders, which was written in response to the urban riots of 1967.[9] The Report pointed to the severe disabilities of race and slavery that weighed upon Negroes seeking jobs and housing and to the quite different situation in the northern urban economy when blacks arrived, as compared with immigrants in the nineteenth and early twentieth centuries. When the great northern migration of Negroes began after World War II, the economy was already shifting to skilled workers and advanced technology, for which undereducated southern black migrants were not well suited. But it was the refusal of whites to accept Negroes as they did accept European and even Asian immigrants that stands out as the great burden upon black advancement and the fundamental reason why the Negro's achievement has lagged behind that of other minorities or immigrant groups. In Brazil a similar differentiation has been made by Brazilian students. "Other national or ethnic

8 Ibid., II, p. 200.
9 See *Report of the National Advisory Commission on Civil Disorders* (Bantam Books, N.Y., 1968), Chapter IX, "Comparing the Immigrant and Negro Experience." See also Karl E. and Alma F. Taeuber, "Is the Negro an Immigrant Group?" *Integrated Education*, I (June, 1963), 25–28.

minorities had an easier road," writes Florestan Fernandes, "thanks to the patterns of sociability, of solidarity, and of institutionalized cooperation, which were a part of their social-cultural heritage." Negro informants also pointed to the lack of such aids to adjustment and organization among blacks reared in slavery and burdened with poverty.[10]

But Negroes in Brazil lacked more than the advantages of immigrants; they lacked even the initial and negative advantages to be derived from overt racial discrimination, which in the United States, at least compelled blacks to recognize their commonality. Numerous Negro informants in Brazil spontaneously pointed to this difference in the racial situations in their country and in the United States. "Although they did not desire it [segregation] and condemned it morally, they saw in it the true cause of the progress of the Negro in the United States." Another black informant complained of the failure of blacks in Brazil to join together to resist prejudice. "I find that the Negroes may not have special· prejudice against them by the whites, but they are discriminated against by the economic situation, which they confront generally." Then he drew the inevitable comparison with the United States. "I know something of the situation in the United States, of the struggles and the prejudice. But I find that the situation there is better than that here, because it stimulates the Negroes to join together and to fight for a better situation." Among Negroes in São Paulo, Fernandes found it widely held that Negroes did not work together against prejudice and discrimination as they did in the United States, where the color line was sharper and more rigid.[11]

The same point was discussed at great length by a number of participants in 1968 at a conference on the state of the Negro in Brazil eighty years after abolition. As Lauro Salles, a lawyer and former superintendent of education in the state of Guanabara (Rio de Janeiro), said, "I think that the problem, from a strictly moral point of view is worse here than in the United States of North America. There no one deludes himself as to discrimination; the sharp line of color clearly traces its way without causing surprise. In Brazil the eye tires trying to follow the sinuous,

[10] Fernandes, Integração do negro, II, pp. 172–73.
[11] Ibid., II, pp. 172–73, 330–31.

lengthy line of the many curves, which confuses the inexperienced and the incautious in a situation in which, with the constitution and the laws in hand, one believes he has a secure guidebook for the mapping of his life." Abdias do Nascimento made the point even more strongly. "It is very easy to fight against manifest usurpation. From such a perspective the North American Negroes, or South Africans, Rhodesians, and Angolans—each with his own peculiarities—enjoy a situation paradoxically more advantageous than us, the Brazilian Negroes. For what are the forces that bar our progress? Are our enemies declared or adversaries rancorous? No. Obviously not. Among us racism has the shape of a chameleon, constantly changing in tactics and strategy. It even takes the form of paternalism, cordiality, benevolence, and good will, as if it stood for miscegenation, acculturation, assimilation. . . ." And he closes by quoting from Martin Luther King to the effect that it is better to have an outright enemy rather than be fooled by someone of ostensible good will.[12]

The significant point is that the mulatto escape hatch, which in the past has done so much to make prejudice and discrimination milder and the opportunities for colored people greater in Brazil than in the United States, has also had the effect of inhibiting the advancement of the Negroes as a group. Thus as the social situation of Negroes and the attitudes of whites toward them in the United States change, the very differences between Brazilian and North American racial patterns have a new and changed effect upon race relations in the two countries. What was once a drawback, under new circumstances, becomes a gain for the Negro in the United States, but just the opposite in Brazil. The historical and deep virulence of North American racism has welded Negroes into an effective social force, whereas the ambiguity of the color–class line in Brazil has left the blacks without cohesion or leaders. Even as economic opportunities open up in an expanding Brazilian economy, the tendency will be for the rising mulattoes and educated Negroes to be drawn off from the mass, for that is the genius of the Brazilian pattern of race relations: individual, rather than group mobility. In that way the mass of Negroes and mulattoes will lose their natural leaders and

[12] "8 Anos de Abolição," *Cadernos Brasileiros*, X (May–June, 1968), 10–11, 4.

thereby the means for extracting from society the measures necessary for the uplifting of the mass.

Even for the mass of blacks, as we have seen already, the existence of the mulatto escape hatch often prevents them from perceiving the presence of prejudice. Souza Dantas, the journalist and diplomat, in 1968 told how, even though he was a Negro, for many years believed that there was no prejudice in Brazil. Only after he had been in Rio de Janeiro for some time—he was born and raised in Sergipe, in the Northeast—did he become aware of the fact that few Negroes occupied high positions in government or society in general. Similarly, the ordinary Brazilian Negro sees some mulattoes rising and thus is led to believe that if he can marry lighter at least his children may be able to rise and improve their lot. Thus the sense of identification with other blacks, which is so essential for effective social agitation and change, is weakened or destroyed. Black organizations, as well as leaders, are discouraged in the face of the easy confusion between class and color prejudice, which is the mulatto escape hatch. The Negro, commented one writer in 1956, "only left physical slavery to enter moral slavery," which is hard to combat, "for it is not recognized and it is susceptible to controversy among the victims." Or as the writer Marcos Santarrita phrased it in 1968, in Brazil, "the Negro is always marginal to white culture, around which he always circles. When he can sometimes manage to penetrate, he forgets entirely his color. The cases of Machado de Assis and Cruz e Sousa [two mulatto writers of the nineteenth century] are, for this point, sufficient illustrations; no one reading their works will say that one is dealing with a mulatto and a Negro." And as Bastide has pointed out, in the United States the very clarity of the caste line permits resentment by blacks to be expressed in clear conscience, thereby reinforcing a sense of unity among them. "In Brazil, on the contrary, it insinuates itself silently, like a gnawing vermin." Even Donald Pierson has noticed this difference between Brazilian and North American Negroes. "It is perhaps also true that individuals of African descent, mixed-bloods as well as blacks, have risen in class more slowly than has the Negro in the United States. Being less under the stigma of racial inferiority, the Brazilian blacks and mixed-bloods have naturally had less incentive to demonstrate to a hostile white world their personal competence and ability to achieve. Hence, it is likely that they have been less ambitious, less aggressive, than their northern brothers, and consequently have risen as a group less rapidly." [13]

One consequence of the lack of solidarity among Negroes in Brazil is that they have not adopted the "aggressively" defensive attitudes that for a long time have characterized blacks in the United States. During the 1920's, for example, North American Negroes mounted a successful campaign to have the word "Negro" capitalized, as a symbol of acceptance, by analogy with "Indian" and other nationality groups. A similar campaign in Brazil got nowhere; moreover, many Brazilian Negroes do not understand the objection to the "mammy," who in Brazil is lauded by both whites and blacks as the "black mother"—an important person in their common history. Negroes in the United States have also carried on a successful campaign to remove from the mass media caricatures and stereotypes of the Negro. In Brazil, caricatures of the Negro with exaggeratedly thick lips, flat nose, and large whites of the eyes are "frequently seen . . . during Carnival, even in the clubs of the non-whites," reports one Brazilian sociologist.[14] In a sense, of course, the less defensive attitudes of Brazilian Negroes is but another manifestation of their unsureness of white attitudes. They simply cannot tell whether they are being discriminated against or simply being joshed in a friendly way.

From what has been said already, it is evident that the movement toward black nationalism that has flourished in the United States in the last decade or so has little basis for development in

[13] Fernandes, *Integração do negro*, I, p. 64. *80 Anos de Abolição* (Rio de Janeiro, 1968), pp. 47–51; 171. Bastide is quoted in Richard M. Morse, *From Community to Metropolis. A Biography of São Paulo, Brazil* (Gainesville, Fla., 1958), p. 256n. For the statement from Pierson see Donald Pierson, *Negroes in Brazil* (Chicago, 1942), p. 176.

[14] Oracy Nogueira, "Preconceito de marca e preconceito racial de origem," *Anais do XXXI Congresso Internacional de Americanistas* (São Paulo, 1954), pp. 428n.–29n., 427n. See also João Baptiste Borges, *Côr, profissão e mobilidade. O Negro e o Rádio de São Paulo* (São Paulo, 1967), pp. 181–89, in which the derogatory stereotypes of Negroes that appear on radio and television in São Paulo are discussed. A TV program is quoted at length in which Negroes speak of other Negroes as looking like monkeys, being unacquainted with marriage, prone to stealing chickens, and addicted to dancing and extravagant clothes.

Brazil. Certainly, there are no organizations like the Black Muslims or the Black Panthers in Brazil. In fact, as we have noticed already, any organization that speaks of restricting membership to blacks or that seeks to act in behalf of blacks in denounced as racist. As the Negro leader Abdias do Nascimento recently pointed out, even newspapers designed for Negroes are suspect among many whites. "Always the fear of anti-white racism," he exploded. Do not such people, he inquired, know "that the hypothesis of anti-whites attitudes stemming from the Negroes is much less dangerous than the effective, concrete, immediate anti-Negro behavior of our society? Who is advocating segregation? We, the segregated? Or our segregators?" [15]

The fact that the protest against discrimination that resulted in the passage of the Afonso Arinos law in 1951 came from a North American Negro is significant. It was Katherine Dunham, while on a visit to São Paulo, who protested her exclusion from a first-class hotel. Miss Dunham, familiar with the racial prejudice of the United States, had no illusions as to what was happening to her when she was excluded from the Hotel Esplanada, nor did she have any doubts as to what she ought to do. A similar incident had occurred four years earlier in Rio de Janeiro to Irene Diggs, a Negro sociologist from the United States. In a later interview, Miss Diggs put her finger upon the difference between the reactions of North American and Brazilian Negroes in such situations. "I am now convinced that in Brazil there is more prejudice than in any other country in America, with the exception of the United States," she began, with some exaggeration. "In my country that prejudice tends to disappear, while here the tendency is for it to grow. And I'll explain why; American Negroes are today the most advanced Negroid group in the world. They have achieved such a degree of cultural and economic well being that they cannot be treated like pariahs. . . . They still do not love us, but they do respect us in the United States. I will reveal then what everyone ignores in my country, which is that this great country, where the Negro race has already produced geniuses and heroes like Henrique Dias, Aleijadinho and others, hides its racial prejudice like a hot coal in the ashes. There is racism in Brazil and with a

[15] Abdias do Nascimento, *O Negro revoltado* (Rio de Janeiro, 1968), pp. 18–19.

tendency to grow. I say further; it is the one Latin American country where such a hateful prejudice is cultivated. I am disenchanted." [16] In her anger and disenchantment, Miss Diggs forgot that in the United States in 1947 there were hundreds of hotels, restaurants, and theaters which did not permit Negroes to set a foot inside. The important conclusion to be drawn from her outburst is not that her comparison of opportunities for blacks in Brazil and the United States was accurate, but that in Brazil it is often left to the North American Negro to protest what overt discrimination there is.

Today some Brazilians recognize that the conditions of the Negro in their country justifies even the kind of violent protest that has marked United States race relations in the late 1960's. Thus after detailing examples of color discrimination in Brazil at a conference on the Negro eighty years after abolition, held at Rio de Janeiro in 1968, one participant asked, "Then, one will ask, why does not our Negro revolt, like the North American Negro? For a very simple reason; despite the persecutions, and lynchings, the North American is privileged in comparison to ours —he takes part in an economic and social structure that allows him to have an awareness of his problem to a degree of which ours does not dream. In the United States, contrary to what occurs here, there is a complete Negro society, with rich and powerful groups who can finance journals, reviews, movies, etc. only for the race, and thus to have at their disposal a going machine to provide each day more reasons for protest to citizens of color without counting, even, the fact that the Government itself gives the indispensable minimum for this: literacy." [17]

As the speaker implied, Negroes lack solidarity and the incentive to protest, not only because the mulatto escape hatch makes upward mobility seem possible, but also because the stronger class lines inhibit solidarity and protest. Cardoso found that in Porto Allegre, for example, the middle-class blacks do not mingle with poor blacks and therefore they withdraw within their individual families, for they lack the numbers of the North American black bourgeoisie to enable them to create their own middle-class black institutions. Moreover, the very correspon-

[16] Ibid., p. 26.
[17] "80 Anos de Abolição" *Cadernos Brasileiros*, X (May–June, 1968), 171.

dence between class and race, which leaves most blacks in the lowest class, confuses the issue. Again and again surveys show that blacks do not know whether they are being discriminated against because they are black or because they are uneducated or poor. And, even when a Negro or mulatto suspects racial prejudice rather than class prejudice, he is inhibited from voicing his suspicion by the argument that to raise such a cry is a "threat to the 'social peace.'"[18] Always whites assure him that there is no prejudice in Brazil. Moreover, since most Negroes are in the lowest classes, they do not test the racial barriers, for they know they lack the money and the proper etiquette for entering an upper-class restaurant or hotel. Indeed, as one sociologist familiar with the Brazilian scene has written, "Colored persons are so afraid of rejection that they spontaneously avoid contact with individuals, institutions, and groups when attitudes of discrimination might be expected."[19]

Finally, in Brazil, whites, as we have noted, are much less open and aggressive in supporting discrimination than whites in the United States, so that Negroes do not feel threatened by rigorous actions such as obtain in the United States. White Brazilians dissimulate prejudice rather than discriminate openly.

As a citizen, in short, the Negro is impelled to identify with the going order, to ignore the fact that he is a black, but in his daily life he knows that he is Negro. Yet even when he becomes conscious of discrimination, there is little that can be done about it, even if he joins with his fellow blacks. The overwhelming majority of the blacks are at the bottom of the political as well as the economic scale. Negroes generally cannot vote in Brazil, not because they are Negroes but because they are poor and uneducated. Literacy is a requirement for the suffrage in Brazil even though less than half of the population can read or write. Thus even if the Brazilian black should organize to seek laws and benefits for his improvement, he lacks the degree of power at the ballot box that the Negro in the United States today possesses.

[18] Fernando Henrique Cardoso, "Le Préjugé de couleur au Brésil," *Presence africaine* (1st trimestre, 1965), 127; Fernandes, *Integração*, II, pp. 292, 311, 313–14; Roger Bastide, ed., *Relações raciais entre negroes e brancos em São Paulo* (São Paulo, 1955), p. 123.

[19] Emilio Willems, "Race Attitudes in Brazil," *American Journal of Sociology*, LIV (March, 1949), 406.

It is for this reason that Florestan Fernandes has recently called upon the black man to assert himself. "The Negro himself must launch the initial challenge provoked by the Brazilian racial problem. He must achieve one immediate objective—a more equitable share in the benefits of the competitive economy. He must strive for a long-term objective, the building of real racial democracy in the community. If he strives toward this goal, he will lead the white people of the various social classes to defend his cause, on which a balanced operation and development of the competitive economy largely depend." [20]

As we have noted in a previous chapter, the tendency of the mulatto escape hatch is to siphon off the potential leadership of blacks, that is, the mulattoes. This pattern will continue in Brazil so far as one can tell. But given the changed nature of white attitudes toward blacks in the United States, the inclusion of the mulattoes among the Negroes will give increased impetus to further change. As opportunities open up for blacks in education, government, and the economy in general, those mulattoes or blacks who profit therefrom will remain as "Negroes," to act as examples and leaders, for further advancement of the position of the black man in United States society. This leadership potential, however, has not been and probably will not be available in Brazil.

A Brazilian Dilemma

Yet as Brazil continues to industrialize and the competitive society of classes spreads, the likelihood of increasing discrimination grows, too. Racial tension and color prejudice, as we have seen, already exist in Brazil, but if the experience of Negroes in São Paulo tells us anything, it is that a competitive society encourages discrimination and tension. In part at least, therefore, the history of race relations in the United States may well be in the future of Brazil. For as the social system of Brazil approaches the competitive model of the United States, as the example of São Paulo in this century suggests it is, then antagonisms between

[20] Florestan Fernandes, "The Weight of the Past," in John Hope Franklin, ed., *Color and Race* (Boston, 1968), pp. 300–301.

black and white can be expected to rise. Florestan Fernandes points out that in 1950 Negroes and mulattoes made up 70 per cent of the population in Bahia and that about 11 per cent of the nation's diplomas from secondary schools were accounted for by them. In São Paulo state, where blacks and mulattoes constitute only 11 per cent of the population, they provided 7 per cent of the country's total number of secondary school graduates. The difference Fernandes rightly attributes to the growth of and therefore the opportunities provided by the *paulista* economy as compared with the Bahian. An expanding economy encourages Negroes and mulattoes "to fight for equality of opportunities and for equality of treatment." A similar experience can be expected, he predicts, as other regions of Brazil develop economically. In 1960 the London *Times* was quoted on the subject of discrimination in Brazil. The Brazilians, the newspaper observed, explain particular examples of discrimination by reference to the low level of Negro education. But the *Times* writer did not wholly accept that nonracial explanation. "A Negro waiter is a rare thing in a high class hotel or restaurant and the big shops never have them as salespeople," the paper accurately noted. "What concerns a great number of Latin Americans, primarily Brazilians, is that, with industrialization and the gradual raising of the level of incomes and consequent educational facilities, the occasion will soon come in which the Negroes will want to go beyond these limited positions. They ask—what will be the attitude of the whites who have to face that fact?" [21]

More recently, an article on race relations in Brazil carried in the prestigious *Jornal do Brasil* commented that although some Brazilians expect to see race antagonisms decline in the future, others foresee social and racial tensions rising as Negroes compete more and more with whites. Then, the writer pointed out, the antagonism "which today is directed at social class" will be directed against color. Even a student of Brazilian race relations like

[21] Florestan Fernandes, "Mobilidade e relações raciais," *Cadernos Brasileiros*, X (May–June, 1968), 56; Nascimento, *O Negro revoltado*, pp. 28–29. A North American student of race relations has written recently that "during the twentieth century Brazil has moved away from its old fraternalistic type of race relations toward the competitive model," Pierre L. van den Berghe, *Race and Racism. A Comparative Perspective* (New York, 1967), p. 70.

Edison Carneiro, who deplores appeals to "negritude," or even the formation of Negro organizations, recognizes that the trend in his country is toward greater prejudice against color. At the conference on the Negro since abolition, held in 1968 and already referred to, Carneiro said, "I have the impression that we are entering a bad future, that is, a growing increase in prejudice in Brazil. The facts told here [examples of discrimination] are naturally a little old, but we are a type of society which promotes prejudice; we are in a period of Brazilian life also in which economic development itself, the development of the country, and social development can be as much ahead as behind; the fact is the country is growing, is experimenting with its powers in various fields and all of this will create much more prejudice than we have today. To the extent that the Negro educates himself, that the Negro gains money and notoriety, becomes more visible, there will be more prejudice than before. Only recently has the Negro competed with the white, it has been what Abdias [do Nascimento] remembers: he [the Negro] knew his place. Today the Negro knows more and in a manner that begins to compete with the white. To the extent that such occurs, which is inevitable, in view of Brazilian development, to that extent prejudice will increase." [22]

Someone as understanding of and sympathetic to Brazil in its history of race relations as Charles Wagley, the North American anthropologist, also has some doubts that the future will be as smooth as the past in this regard. "There are indications both in the present studies and in reports from the great metropolitan centers of the country," he writes at the end of his *Race and Class in Rural Brazil*, "that discrimination, tensions, and prejudices based on race are appearing." As more and more Negroes rise socially, challenging those above, he goes on, race will become increasingly important. [23]

Insofar as young Negroes become increasingly conscious of their position in Brazilian society, the antagonism between the colors will be accentuated. Some Brazilian sociologists like Flore-

[22] Eduardo Pinto, "Preconceito de class atinge negros 80 anos após Abolição," *Jornal do Brasil* (May 12, 1968); *80 Anos de Abolição* (Rio de Janeiro, 1968), pp. 83–84.

[23] Charles Wagley, ed., *Race and Class in Rural Brazil*, 2nd ed. (New York, 1963), p. 155.

stan Fernandes and Oracy Nogueira point to evidence of young blacks and mulattoes breaking out of the old traditional patterns, but there is not much evidence that the kind of uprising that erupted among young Negroes in the United States in the early 1960's is in the offing in Brazil. Roger Bastide, however, asserts that Brazilian Negroes will be less timid as time goes on.[24] And Abdias do Nascimento pays tribute to the example of the North American Negroes "whose brave struggle is a most important lesson not only there, but here, in our country." He also suggests that the example of the new African states will not be lost on the Brazilian Negroes. "The very presence of their diplomatic representatives functions as an implicit supervision and criticism of white and black relations in our racial democracy." L. A. Costa Pinto, too, notes that the stage is set for rapid change. He observes that most Negroes are barred from educational opportunities in Brazil; "it is that more profound and structural matter that is at issue. On that day in which the masses of color become conscious of that, then will commence the most acute and decisive problem in the race relations of this country." Finally, it is worth quoting a recent conclusion of a long time student of race relations in Brazil. "The social ascension of the Negroes in a class society," writes F. H. Cardoso, "contrary to what one supposed in the past, far from signifying the end to prejudice, can indicate, in fact, the beginning in Brazil of a 'Negro problem' in the same terms as it exists, for example, in the United States."[25]

The implication or outright prediction that Brazil may be going

[24] Oracy Nogueira, "Relações raciais no município de Itapetininga," in Roger Bastide, ed., *Relações raciais* (São Paulo, 1955), pp. 547–50. Bastide himself, in the same volume, p. 176 comes to a similar conclusion.

[25] Nascimento, *O Negro revoltado*, p. 54; Costa Pinto, *O Negro no Rio de Janeiro*, p. 165; Fernando Henrique Cardoso, "Le Préjugé de couleur au Brésil," *Présence africaine*, 128. Not all Brazilian students of race relations, however, see a value in comparing race relations in Brazil with those in North America. Edison Carneiro, for example, condemns all those organizations of blacks and mulattoes in Brazil that "attempted to give voice to racist manifestations, to the emotional supremacy of the Negro, to the end of dressing up the problem in accord with the North American inspiration, formula, and solution. What else could one expect of almost 20 years of sentimentality in the search for Africa, of the 'cultural personality' of the Negro, of the 'why-I-am-proud-of-myself-because-of-the-contribution-of-the-slave?' " *80 Anos de Abolição* (Rio de Janeiro, 1968), p. 116.

the way of the United States ought not to be misunderstood. It is certainly not meant that Brazilians will move to the kind of racial situation from which the United States has just emerged— that is, to one in which segregation is legal and a racial defense of Negro inferiority is commonplace and the basis of the laws. History does not run backwards; moreover, the existence of the mulatto escape hatch would certainly prevent it from happening. Nor is lynching, often recognized as a peculiarly American practice, likely to come to Brazil. What does seem in the offing is that Brazil will see more, rather than less, racial friction, but that the friction will be on a low level of violence and that Negroes will remain at the bottom of the social and economic pyramid.

If the United States continues to follow a policy of compensatory assistance to Negroes, the material lot of blacks will probably continue to be better in the United States than in Brazil. For one lesson seems inescapable from the Brazilian and United States experiences: in the absence of positive aid to Negroes newly emerged from slavery, full social and economic integration into society is difficult, if not impossible to achieve. In fact, over a century after emancipation in the United States and eighty years after abolition in Brazil, Negroes in both societies are still at the bottom of the economic and social pyramids. "In the next year 1968," writes Abdias do Nascimento, "we will complete 80 years of legal abolition. Analyzing today's reality we could almost say that the Golden Law was signed yesterday. The situation of the free Negro is changed little in the 80 years since abolition: low social, educational, economic, political, and sanitary status, and the list of frustrations transformed into a strong potentiality of just resentments by the race." Nascimento goes on to observe that John F. Kennedy, in his famous speech in behalf of the Civil Rights bill in 1963, noted that the average Negro's opportunities lagged far behind those of the average white. But, Nascimento goes on, if in the United States a Negro had only half the chance of a white child to finish secondary school, in Brazil a Negro had only one-third the chance of a white; if a Negro child in the United States enjoys only a third of a white child's chance to complete college, a black in Brazil has less than a tenth of a white child's.[26] And it seems likely that the opportunities for

[26] Nascimento, *O Negro revoltado*, pp. 21, 57.

blacks in Brazil will not improve appreciably unless positive efforts are made to draw them into the mainstream of economic and social life. The positive efforts recently made in the United States to expand opportunities for blacks have certainly not yet met the need, but they have undoubtedly been in the right direction. Unless Brazil recognizes a similar need for positive help for blacks, the pattern of race relations there will not improve and probably will worsen as competition spreads throughout the economy and society.

Indeed, in this development it might be said lies the Brazilian dilemma to place beside the American dilemma about which Gunnar Myrdal wrote twenty-five years ago. The alternatives for Brazilians are not as sharp or obvious as they were then for Americans; Brazilians have not brazenly denied equality through legal segregation and outright public assertions of Negro inferiority. Nevertheless, there is a contradiction between their professed racial democracy and the social facts of life as we have reviewed them and Brazilian Negroes perceive them. Brazilians have the choice of continuing to insist upon their racial democracy in the face of the social facts or else they must admit that the society does not live up to its ideals. Either choice, as in any dilemma, is unpalatable for many whites. But in Brazil, as in the United States, the question is one for the whites to decide. It is they who have created the present situation. As one Negro in São Paulo rightly said, "If the problem of the Negro comes to assume in Brazil the proportions that it has acquired in the United States there will be only one group to blame: the whites."[27] Besides, as Fernandes has pointed out, there is no social group with power in Brazilian society which also has a stake in making the ideal of a racial democracy work. The blacks who are poor and without the vote therefore lack the necessary economic and political means for effecting change, whereas the colored elite "either does not feel the necessity of this defense or does not consider it advantageous to compromise themselves for such objectives, which concern the future of the community rather than their own personal situation."[28] Hence he calls for a conscious

[27] Fernandes, *Integração de negro*, II, p. 326.

[28] Roger Bastide and Pierre van den Berghe, "Stereotypes, Norms, and Interracial Behavior in São Paulo, Brazil," *American Sociological Review*, XXII (December, 1957), 692; Fernandes, "The Weight of the Past," in Franklin, ed., *Color and Race*, p. 299.

policy of racial integration by the Brazilian government because no longer can Brazil "continue to maintain, without grave injustice, the Negro on the margin of the development of a civilization that he helped to build. As Nabuco wrote, 'We have to reconstruct Brazil under free labor and the union of the races in liberty.' As long as we have not reached that objective, we do not have a *racial democracy,* nor a *democracy.* By a paradox of history, the Negro has become, in our era, the touchstone of our capacity to forge in the tropics this foundation of modern civilization." [29]

Always That Indelible Color

Although the foregoing comparison of the contemporary situation in Brazil and the United States would seem to forecast a somewhat brighter future for race relations in this country than in Brazil, the facts do not justify complacency or even optimism. The so-called race question has not been "solved." The Brazilian experience should make it clear that even in a society without legal segregation or publicly accepted anti-Negro attitudes, prejudice and discrimination do not automatically disappear, even three generations after the end of slavery. Physical differences between groups are always noticed. It is my conviction that blacks will be recognized as different and discriminated against whenever nonblacks have the power and an incentive to do so. So long as men perceive identifying physical differences that can be used to discriminate against another group, they will do so. The tendency is especially likely to manifest itself if there are strong historical reasons for singling out a particular group, like Negroes, who are not only identifiable, but who have also been held in the degrading position of slaves for a long time. Physical differences and degraded status reinforce each other, even if the sense of difference came first.

This tendency to discriminate, to be sure, is not irresistible or uncontrollable, but it seems to be universal. In the last chapter, we referred to other historical and contemporary examples of discrimination by color to demonstrate the universality of prejudice where there are visible differences among peoples. Now is an appropriate time to look at another analogy that not only

[29] Fernandes, *Integração do negro,* II, pp. 393–94.

illustrates further the role of visible differences in the growth of prejudice, but may also throw some light on the future of race relations in Brazil and the United States.

In his book on the Negro in Rio de Janeiro, Costa Pinto compared the position of the Negro in Brazil to that of the Jew in the United States.[30] With that analogy he hoped to bring home to his readers something of the different—milder—quality in the impact of prejudice on the Negro in Brazil as compared with it in the United States. From the standpoint of the subtlety of prejudice the analogy is helpful, but in another sense it misses a major point. Jews, unlike Negroes, are not instantly identifiable. It is possible for a Jew to escape detection by even the most observant anti-Semite, at least for a time. During that interval the Jew may be able to establish himself in a job or in a neighborhood and thus break down prejudices against him and even forestall discrimination. As the black psychiatrist Frantz Fanon has poignantly commented, "All the same the Jew can be unknown in his Jewishness. He is not wholly what he is. One hopes, one waits. His action, his behavior are the final determinant. He is a white man, and apart from some debatable characteristics, he can sometimes go unnoticed. . . . The Jew is disliked from the moment he is tracked down. But in my case everything takes on a *new* guise. I am given no chance. I am overdetermined from without. I am the slave not of the 'idea' that others have of me but of my own appearance. . . . When people like me, they tell me it is in spite of my color. When they dislike me, they point out that it is not because of my color. Either way, I am locked into the infernal circle." [31]

Actually, the social group that bears the closest resemblance to Negroes is not Jews, but women, as Gunnar Myrdal noted a quarter of a century ago. Neither the great force of sexual attraction nor the needs of the family have caused men to ignore the fact that women *look* different and, therefore, as a social group can be and ought to be treated differently from men. The whole long history of discrimination against women attests to the fact with which we began Chapter V, that observable physical dif-

[30] Costa Pinto, *O Negro no Rio de Janeiro*, 326.
[31] Frantz Fanon, *Black Skin, White Masks*, trans. C. L. Markmann (New York, 1967), pp. 115–16.

ferences easily translate themselves into intellectual and moral distinctions. This is not the place to develop the argument that women have been treated in a manner remarkably analogous to that accorded Negroes, but it is worth a little space to suggest some of the comparisons.[32] Like Negroes, women have been excluded from certain jobs, denied education on the grounds that they either did not require it or could not profit from it, barred from political office, denied the suffrage, and assigned a special social place in which they, like Negroes, were appreciated—so long as they did not step out of it. But above all, like Negroes, women are ever visible and so cannot escape prejudice; their very arrival on the scene at a forbidden job or activity arouses hostility among those who are prejudiced against them. Unlike other minorities—Catholics, children, Jews, immigrants—women never lose their visible identity. It is in part accidental that the Civil Rights Act of 1964, which invoked the power of the federal government in support of Negro equality, also invoked it in behalf of equality of opportunity for women. The fact is, nevertheless, that these two minorities are most in need of such support, for they are susceptible to discrimination by virtue of visible differences.

On the other side, however, it ought to be said that discrimination against women is not reinforced by class prejudice, as it is for Negroes. For, as we have already noticed, most Negroes in both the United States and Brazil are poor and so class prejudice reinforces racial or color prejudice (or becomes confused with it, as in Brazil). But the discrimination against women has been and is without reference to class; a middle-class woman rarely has a better chance at a job denied to a lower-class woman. It is their sex, not their class, that is held against them. The point is that even in the case of women, where class is not operative at all, discrimination still occurs, because appearance differentiates and identifies them.

All of this is not to say that discrimination—whether against

---

[32] The analogy between Negroes and women has been drawn by a number of writers. See Gunnar Myrdal, *The American Dilemma* (New York, 1944), Appendix 5, "A Parallel to the Negro Problem"; Lillian Hacker, "Women as a Minority Group," *Social Forces*, XXX (October, 1951), 60–69; Caroline Bird, *Born Female* (New York, 1968), Chapter 6, "The Negro Parallel."

blacks or women—cannot or ought not to be mitigated, controlled, or even prohibited. Equality of opportunity is no longer a debatable social goal in the modern world. The real question is, how does a society achieve it, even if only imperfectly, since it does not happen by itself? In fact, only society's enforcement of the ideal of equality prevents discrimination from occurring when individuals or groups have the power to impose it. To use an old-fashioned terminology that expresses the point: it is human nature to have prejudice against those who are different but it is the obligation of a civilized society to control or check the behavior that may result from that tendency, however natural it may be.

As this book has tried to demonstrate, mere association between blacks and whites over time, of itself, will not ensure equality of treatment or of opportunity so long as differences in appearance are observable. Changes in laws, such as have taken place in the United States, it is true, will make some difference. For if the Brazilian experience has relevance for the United States, it suggests that racial discrimination in the future will be much less overt and outspoken in this country than it has been in the past. From now on there will be legal and even social penalties visited upon those who discriminate racially. Probably discrimination in the United States will be more dissimulated, as it has been in Brazil, and practiced under different rubrics. Signs of such a change are already evident in the use of a phrase like *law and order* as a covert way of signalling a concern about urban Negroes. The change is also evident in the growing reference to class differences as a justification for prejudice against Negroes, a device, as we have seen, widely used in Brazil.

It is important to recognize, too, in thinking about the future of race relations in the United States in the light of the Brazilian experience that miscegenation offers no "solution." Over the very long run, as we have seen, Brazilians may bleach themselves to the point where all are of the same color, thereby eliminating one important basis for discrimination. But such a denouement is not possible in the United States, given the North American definition of a Negro. All offspring of whites and Negroes are Negroes; therefore, if intermarriage did become widespread the result would be a Negro majority—or a change in the definition of a Negro. It follows, then that only acceptance of blacks on a basis of equality in a pluralistic society is a realistic racial policy for the United States in the foreseeable future.

At one time in the struggle for Negro equality in the United States, the hope and expectation were that the society would become color blind, that differences in appearance would be able to be ignored or go unnoticed. Color, it was said, was and ought to be irrelevant. Ideally, of course, color or appearance *are* irrelevant. Practically, however, they are not, as the Brazilian experience once again makes evident. There, laws of segregation and distinction have all fallen into disuse or been repealed, yet consciousness of color remains. On a more scientific level, a recent authority on color symbolism has arrived at a similar conclusion. "Although hardly conclusive," Kenneth J. Gergen cautiously summarizes, "the . . . evidence suggests that whenever there are distinctively different color lines within a society, there will be a pronounced tendency toward strife between the light and the dark. Further, alterations in laws or social structure, loosening of economic biases, and reduction of prejudice within any period of time will not serve as a trans-historical panacea. Rather, each new generation may have to learn anew the irrational basis of their antipathy. While race prejudice may be to some extent learned, persons may also have to be taught *not* to be prejudiced. The often noted tendency for the dark-skinned to feel inferior may have an initial basis in color symbolism. Such feelings may serve to reinforce exploitation by the lighter skinned, and thus diminish further the self-esteem of the dark. Again, an extended period of relearning may be entailed." [33] Or as a less scientific observer put it, "Racism exists," one Bahian black of the professional class

---

[33] Kenneth J. Gergen, "The Significance of Skin Color in Human Relations," in Franklin, ed., *Color and Race*, p. 122. A Dutch sociologist who has worked extensively in the Caribbean countries as well as in Brazil sums up his conclusion on the importance of color differences in this fashion: "[It] may be deduced that these prejudices [between people of different colors] can be regarded genetically as instruments of the human desire to make distinctions. There is so far no psychological evidence that group prejudices stemming from this desire will ever disappear as the result of the spread of rational explanations of their function. I therefore suggest that if within one society groups occur with clearly different physical characteristics, the existence of racial prejudice cannot be denied." H. Hoetink, *The Two Variants in Caribbean Race Relations* (New York, 1967), p. 89.

told an investigator, "but I do not believe it will ever completely cease to exist; it will always exist, though secret and hidden." [34]

To make believe color is not noticed in social situations is to end up permitting discrimination by default. To recognize that discrimination is an ever-present tendency in any society in which there is a physically identifiable group is to take the first step in guarding against prejudice. In the future both the United States and Brazil blacks will not pass unseen by the majority, as some have hoped would be the case, but the laws and mores of the society can prevent prejudice from escalating into discrimination. Furthermore, the irrationalities and injustices of racism can be countered in schools, in the press, and over television, and through laws that penalize those who discriminate on grounds of color or other irrelevant indicia. Positive, continuous action, however, seems necessary for the foreseeable future. Mere good will, propinquity, and the passage of time are not enough. We have to recognize that the price of equality in pluralism, like the price of liberty, is eternal vigilance.

[34] Thales Azevedo, *Cultura e Situação racial no Brasil* (Rio de Janeiro, 1966), p. 96.

Index

Brazil (*Cont.*)
aspirations of white and colored children in, 165
bandeirantes in, 247
class positions in, stability of, 243–54, 254 *n*.
color gradations in, 102–103
discrimination in. *See* Discrimination in Brazil
discriminatory laws in:
neither necessary nor possible, 260
overturned by practice of integration, 218
fidalgo tradition of, 246
future of race relations in, 282–87
individual exception to general dislike of blacks by whites, 198–99
intermarriage in. *See* Intermarriage in Brazil; Miscegenation in Brazil
literature of:
appearance of Negro in, 9–13
derogatory representations of the black in, 113
miscegenation in, 5–6, 18, 185–95. *See also* Intermarriage in Brazil; Miscegenation in Brazil
mulatos in, 102, 103. *See also* Mulattoes in Brazil
Negro families in. *See* Negro families
Negro history in, 7–9
Negro rights organizations in. *See* Negro rights organizations
Negro writers in, 15
Negroes in. *See* Negroes; Negroes in Brazil
as percent of total population in, 3–5, 193–94
place of Negro and mulatto in culture of, 14–16
prejudice in. *See* Color prejudice in Brazil; Prejudice in Brazil
"progressive Aryanization of," 191
proportion of free Negroes in, during slavery, 43 *ff*.
proportions of whites, Negroes and mulattoes in total population of, 193–94
restraints by Negroes in, upon their own ambitions, 164–67
"saving the appearance" in, 201
slave trade of. *See* Slave trade
slavery in, 25–92. *See also* Slave(s); Slavery
capitães de mato, 84
continuation of slave trade between Africa and Brazil, 52–61, 74–75
decline of, after closing of slave trade, 67
defense of, 86–88
definition of slave, 26–27

during booms and busts of the economy, 44–45
free Negro and mulatto as props in, 84
high infant mortality among slaves, 65–66, 70
iron or tin masks worn by slaves, 70, 73–74
lack of interest in slave breeding, 64–67
lack of protection for slave family, 37–39, 71–72, 75
manumission, 40–47. *See also* Manumission
negros dos ganhos, 44
public whipping posts to control slaves, 68 *n*.
rebellions, 47–51. *See also* Quilombos; Rebellions
return of former slaves to Africa, 60
role of African-born slaves, 53–58
Roman Catholic church and, 33–37
sale of children into, 38, 231
slave as "hands and feet" of his master, 245–46
slave's peculium, 42
slave's position in court, 30–32
slave's right to hold property, 41–42
suicides of slaves, 72
use of females as prostitutes, 70
social structure in, rigid and stable, 253–54, 254 *n.*, 255
suffrage in, 280
use of term *preto* rather than "Negro" in, 201
white men in, low social value placed upon work and manual labor by, 245–46
Brazilian Negro Front, 177, 180, 183
Britain, role of, in compelling Brazil to stop slave trade, 91–92, 92 *n*.
British colonies. *See* English colonies
British West Indies. *See also* English colonies
miscegenation widely practiced in, 229, 239
mulatto escape hatch in Jamaica, 239–40
mulattoes barred from voting or testifying against whites in Barbados, 240

Cabo verde, 103
Caboclos, 114, 167, 213
Cabra, 103, 114
Capitães de mato, 84
Carneiro, Edison, 109–110

Education in Brazil (*Cont.*)
the schools and universities, 143–144
Elkins, Stanley M.
on comparative analysis of treatment of slaves, 73
on differences in slavery systems of U.S. and Latin America, 20–21, 26, 33
critique by Eugene D. Genovese of, 33 *n.*
English colonies
immigration of free mulattoes encouraged by Georgia legislature, 240–41
miscegenation in, 217, 228–29
position of white women in, 235–37
Equality of opportunity, competition, and social mobility in the United States, 254
Escuro, 103

Families, Negro. *See* Negro families
Favelas, 136, 147
Fear and hatred of Negroes by North Americans, 89–90, 200–201
Fidalgo tradition of Brazil, 246
First Brazilian Congress of the Negro, 158, 183
Free Negroes. *See also* Manumission
Abraham Lincoln's plan for founding of settlement in Central America for, 89
competition between whites and, in the United States, 257, 259
during busts of economy in Brazil, 44–45
fear of, by southern states, 83–84
nonsupport of abolition in Brazil by, 84 *n.*
as a prop in Brazilian slavery, 84
proportion of, during slavery, 43 *ff.*
vs. number of free mulattoes, 231
Freedom and slavery, sociopolitical ideologies of Brazil and the United States on, 261–64
Frente Negra Brasileiro, 177, 180, 183

"Henriques," 8

Illegitimacy in Brazil, 175
highest rates of, in states with large numbers of Negroes and mulattoes, 176 *n.*
Incomplete families in Bahia and São Paulo, 172–73, 175, 176
Indentured servitude, 25, 45

Indians in Brazil, 213. *See also* Caboclos
Insurrections, slave, fear of, 82–84
Intermarriage. *See also* Miscegenation
attitudes of college students in the United States and Brazil toward, 131–32
Intermarriage(s) in Brazil
astonishment and resentment to, if contrast in colors is great, 186, 187
attitudes of secondary school children toward, 133, 134–35
number of, in selected areas, 186–87
resistance to, according to class, 187–88
ways in which Brazilians justify refusal to marry Negroes, 186
with blacks or mulattoes not acceptable to majority of whites, 185, 187

Jamaica, mulatto escape hatch in, written into law, 239–40
Johnson, Lyndon B., 1965 address of, at Howard University, 269

Kerner Report on Civil Disorders, 273

Limpeza de sangue, 214
Lincoln, Abraham, plan of, for founding of settlement in Central America for free blacks, 89
Lisboa, Antonio "Aleijadinho," 15–16
Literature
appearance of Negro in, Brazil and United States compared, 9–14
denigrating portrayal of Negro in, Brazil and United States compared, 12–13
derogatory representations of the Brazilian Negro in, 113
hatred for Brazilian Negro in, 11
Negro writers in Brazil and the United States, 14–15
sympathy towards Brazilian slaves in, 9–11
Lynching in the United States, 95–96

Machado de Assis, Joaquim, 15, 107, 276
Manumission
in Brazil, 40–47, 89
different attitudes toward, in North America and Latin America, 19–20, 39–47
greater ease of, in Brazil than in the

harshness about relations between whites and, 200
Negroes in Brazil on position of, 184 *n.*
opposition of white workingmen of the North to employment of, 259
position of, in the 1960's, 268, 269
positive equality of, 269, 270 *n.*
segregation and discrimination against, despite Fourteenth Amendment and passage of civil rights acts, 218
suffrage of, 257–58
Negros dos ganhos, 44
Nordeste, relations between races easiest in, 98–99
Nordestinos, 131

Octoroon, 102, 190
Opportunity, equality of, in U.S., 254
Overseas Council, 80, 216

Palmares, 9, 12, 48, 49
slave hideaway (*quilombo*) in, 8, 48, 53, 53 *n. See also* Quilombos
Pardo, 102, 103, 105
Paulistas, 77, 130, 131
Peculium, 42
Pernambuco, 48, 49
Pessoa de sangue infecta, 214
Pierson, Donald
on concentration of Negroes and mulattoes at bottom of economic and social pyramids, 140
on race relations in Brazil, 98–99, 113–14
Pombal's decrees, 217 *n.*
Prejudice, 18
Bogardus scale of social distance for measuring prejudice, 130–32
distinction between discrimination and, 112
Prejudice in Brazil, 96–138. *See also* Color prejudice in Brazil; Discrimination in Brazil
of color, rather than racial, 111
"covered up" by mulatto escape hatch, 276
denial of, 96–97, 111
existence of class prejudice rather than color or racial prejudice, 98, 107, 111, 141
revaluation of idea of, 111–12
failure of educated mulattoes to identify with blacks, 109–110
hostility toward mulattoes, 108–109

"money whitens," 105–107. *See also* "Whitening"
Negro children's experiences and attitudes concerning their blackness, 159–61, 162–66
unawareness of, by many Negroes, 276
variety of interpretations of race relations, 100
varying from region to region, 98–101, 202
Prejudice in the United States, 100–101, 111
Preto, 103
use of, in Brazil, rather than *Negro,* 201
Preto retinto, 103
Professionals in Brazil, Negroes as percent of total number of, 140

Quadroon, 102, 238
Quadros, Janio, admission of Negro's disabilities by, 270
Quilombo(s), 48–49. *See also* Maroons
confusing "revolts" with, 49
great number of, in Brazil, related to continuation of slave trade, 52–53
of Palmares, 8, 12, 48, 53, 53 *n.*
role of African-born slaves in, 53, 53 *n.*

Race awareness in young children, 209, 209 *n. See also* Color awareness
Race relations, future of
in Brazil, 282–87
in the United States, 290–91
Rebellions. *See also* Slave insurrections
in Bahia, 51, 55–56, 59
difficulty in planning of, 50
in the United States, 54
related to continuation of slave trade in Brazil, 54–59
runaway slaves and, 47–52. *See also* Maroons; Quilombo(s)
Recife
attitudes about intermarriage in, 135
color prejudice in, 136
prejudicial attitudes of college students in, 131–32
Rio Grande do Sul, 49
high degree of color prejudice in, 99–100
Rio de Janeiro
absence of segregation among the poor, 136
attitudes of secondary school children in, toward intermarriage, 133

White men
in Brazil, low social value placed
upon work and manual labor by,
245–46
in English colonies, belief in virtue
of work by, 246–47
White women. *See also* Women
position of, in Brazilian families, 232–
234
position of, in English colonies and
in later slave states of the United
States, 235–39
seclusion of, in Brazil, 233–34, 234 *n*.
"Whitening" in Brazil
by money, 105–107, 191
by racial mixture, 191–95. *See also*
Miscegenation in Brazil; Mulattoes in Brazil

as factor in improving children's
status, 192–93, 195
"progressive Aryanization of Brazil," 191
slow progress in, 193–94
Women
discrimination against, 288–90
negro, burdens of, 172–73
white. *See* White women
Work
belief in virtue of, by English colonists, 246–47
low social value placed upon, by
white men in Brazil, 245–46

Zumbi, 8, 9, 48